D0072145

Essential Islam

A Comprehensive Guide to Belief and Practice

DIANE MORGAN

PRAEGER
An Imprint of ABC-CLIO, LLC

A B C ☰ C L I O

Santa Barbara, California • Denver, Colorado • Oxford, England

Clinton College Library

Copyright 2010 by Diane Morgan

All rights reserved. No part of this publication may be reproduced, stored
in a retrieval system, or transmitted, in any form or by any means, electronic,
mechanical, photocopying, recording, or otherwise, except for the inclusion
of brief quotations in a review, without prior permission in writing from the
publisher.

Library of Congress Cataloging-in-Publication Data

Morgan, Diane.
   Essential Islam : a comprehensive guide to belief
and practice / Diane Morgan.
      p. cm.
   Includes bibliographical references and index.
   ISBN 978-0-313-36025-1 (alk. paper) — ISBN 978-0-313-36026-8
(ebook) 1. Islam. 2. Islam—Doctrines. 3. Islam—Customs
and practices. I. Title.
   BP174.M67   2010
   297—dc22   2009030397

14   13   12   11   10   1   2   3   4   5

This book is also available on the World Wide Web as an eBook.
Visit www.abc-clio.com for details.

ABC-CLIO, LLC
130 Cremona Drive, P.O. Box 1911
Santa Barbara, California 93116-1911

This book is printed on acid-free paper ∞
Manufactured in the United States of America

Contents

Notes on Language and Orthography

- The words "God" and "Allah" are exact synonyms. Allah is simply the Arabic word for God. Some English-speaking Muslims prefer "God," and some prefer "Allah." Because "Allah" is mutually understandable to Muslims all around the world even if their native language is not Arabic, I have chosen to retain it in these pages.

- This book employs standard Western dates rather than Islamic ones. The Islamic calendar begins in 621, the year of the Muslim immigration to Medina. Because the Muslim calendar is lunar-based, it is about 11 days shorter than the solar one more commonly in use around the world.

- In Arab culture, a person may go by various names. *Ibn*, sometimes shortened to *b.*, means "son of." When a man's first son was born, he might also take an honorary title called the *kunya*, which is created by adding the word *abu* ("father of") after his name. For women, the corollary titles are *bint* ("daughter of") and *umm* ("mother of").

- Arabic terms are in italics, and their definitions are given in the glossary, as well as in the text when the term is first explained. Quotations from the Quran, Islam's holy book, are printed in italics; those from the hadith, or reports about Muhammad's words and deeds, are enclosed in quotation marks. All quotations from the Prophet come from various authenticated hadith, most of which have multiple attestations. Unless otherwise stated, the hadith quoted are categorized as good or authentic.

- Arabic can be transliterated in a number of ways. "Amin," for instance, a name that means "trusted one," can also appear as

"Ameen." Many words and names such as "surah" or "Khadijah" may be spelled with or without an "h" at the end. I have used my own judgment in these matters, in general using the most familiar form, sometimes, perhaps, at the cost of consistency.

- In this text I have chosen to omit diacritical marks (writing Quran, for instance, rather than Qur'an) because they represent sounds not readily conveyed in the Roman alphabet (such as those employed to render the glottal stop *hamzah* and the gutteral character *ayn*) and are not helpful in pronunciation for the average English-speaking reader. I have likewise omitted the macron (a bar over a vowel), which serves to lengthen a vowel sound, and the underdot used to make certain consonants emphatic.

- Although "Islam" is sometimes translated "peace" and does derive from the same Semitic root as its Hebrew cognate *shalom*, the correct meaning of the word Islam is "surrender," interpreted to mean surrender or submission to Allah. The word "Muslim" refers to one who has "submitted" to the will of Allah. (In Arabic, adding the prefix *mu* to a root indicates one is referring to a person, someone who performs the action indicated.) Some Muslims also distinguish between a mere "muslim," that is one who submits to the laws of Allah (even if he does not understand them or possibly not even believe in them) and the deeper belief of a believer (*mumin*), that is, one who not only acts on Allah's word, but also has a deep and abiding faith in it.

- The older term "Mohammadan" is incorrect and offensive to Muslims, for it implies that Muslims worship Muhammad, which they do not. Muslims believe that the name "Islam" was given to Muslims by Allah himself. Muhammad was only a prophet in a long line of prophets, not a divine figure.

- The word "Muslim" generally applies to people; when speaking of countries or cultures, it is more proper to use "Islamic."

- In the Quran and in this book, Allah is referred as "He," the traditional pronoun. Muslims maintain, however, that Allah has no gender. (In Arabic, however, all words are assigned a masculine or feminine gender; there is no neuter.) In this text the pronouns referring to various deities are not capitalized unless they begin a sentence.

- It is the author's opinion that the Quran, like the Bible, is a human work, not a divine revelation, an assumption that is clearly evident throughout these pages.

Author's Note

This book is written from a purely secular viewpoint. I am not a Muslim, Christian, Jew, Hindu, Buddhist, or member of any other religion. Although I believe all religions impart important values to their believers, I also believe none of them is literally true.

This book is intended to be neither an attack upon nor a defense of Islam; its only goal is to shed a clearer light on the foundations of this faith. Some readers may end up with a renewed respect for this worldwide tradition; others may decide that they like it less than before. I hope that both groups will understand it a little better.

Introduction
and Background

Islam is a worldwide religion. About one out of every five people on earth is a Muslim. In other words, there are about as many Muslims as there are people living in China. Islam is the second-largest and fastest-growing religion on earth. (This fact alone explains why understanding Islam is critical for everyone.)

Estimations of the total number of Muslims range from 0.8 to 1.3 billion worldwide and from 1.1 to 7 million in the United States. About 70 percent of Muslims live in Asia, and most of the rest live in Africa. Only 10 percent of Muslims are Arabic, and only a quarter of them live in the Middle East. Muslims represent the majority in 56 countries around the world, including Indonesia, Bangladesh, Pakistan, Egypt, Iran, Iraq, and Nigeria. There are about 44 Islamic nations, and Muslims constitute a substantial minority in countries such as France, the United States, and India. It is already the second-largest faith in Canada and Europe; it will soon be the second-largest in the United States as well. In fact, since 1971, the Muslim population of the United States has increased sixfold. Its growth rate in the United States has been estimated at 6 percent a year—compared to the national average of 0.9 percent. And it's a young religion: about two-thirds of Muslims in the United States are under 40 years old, whereas in the rest of the population, two-thirds are over 40 years old.

In the wake of World War II, many European and American Muslims came to the West in search of economic opportunities. Europe, especially, was short on labor. (Muslims were already established in the Balkans.)

Islam, Judaism, and Christianity are Sister Religions. Judaism, Christianity, and Islam share many beliefs and claim a common sacred history. All claim to be monotheistic religions that worship the same God. All claim physical or spiritual descent from Abraham. All believe in prophets and share the same ethical system. All maintain belief in angels, the Day of Judgment, and the Afterlife. All believe God works through history to achieve his ends. But they have important differences as well. Jews and Muslims do not accept the divinity of Jesus. Jews and Christians do not accept Muhammad as a prophet. Muslims and Christians believe their scriptures fulfill or override the Hebrew Bible. Whether, in the end, the commonalities between these faiths will conquer their differences remains to be seen. Perhaps because of sibling rivalry or perhaps because of simple propinquity, Jews, Christians, and Muslims seem to have fought more among themselves than with the vastly different faiths of Hinduism, Buddhism, or Taoism.

Throughout its history, Islam has been the source or conduit for many cultural, artistic, scientific, and technological advances. Islamic scholars were instrumental in transmitting lost classical, particularly Hellenistic, philosophical and literary works to Europe, especially via Islamic Spain and, to a lesser extent, Islamic Sicily. The most notable flowering of Islamic culture took place from the 11th through the 13th centuries, in which Muslim scholars contributed to fields such as astronomy, geography, medicine, and optics, as well as pseudo-sciences such as alchemy and astrology (although these latter practices were rejected by the more discerning Islamic scholars). Most famously, Islam introduced Arabic numbers (including zero) to the West, a tremendous improvement over the Hebrew or Greek method of using letters for numbers and light-years ahead of Roman numerals.

Islam was also important in the transmittal of material goods and the technology to manufacture them: carpets, glassmaking, bookbinding, and metalwork were all highly advanced in Islamic cultures. And Muslim traders brought silk and paper to Europe as well as the knowledge of how to cultivate cotton, citrus, and sugar.

It is not always easy to define the term "Muslim." The conversation about Islam has grown increasingly prickly since September 11, 2001. It gets no easier when we realize that not only does Islam have many faces, but in the final analysis, "Islam" does not even exist. There are only people who call themselves Muslims. The same is true for Christians and Jews. Each person interprets faith in his or her own way. For some this means becoming a model citizen and a servant of humanity. Such people build hospitals and give to charity. For others it means becoming a terrorist or snake-handler. Some Christians, for example, are strict pacifists. Others are gun-toting militiamen. Which is the true Christianity? In the same way, Muslims have drawn on their religious beliefs to justify war and peace, mercy and vengeance. Who are the "real Muslims"?

And how religious does one need to be to be Muslim? Some Muslims are basically secular people who seldom pray, go to a mosque, read the Quran, or make a conscious effort to follow Muhammad's example. Others strive to fulfill Islamic teachings with their every breath. Most people float somewhere in between these two extremes, believing in Allah, praying sometimes, and following some, but not all, Islamic customs. All of them, however, may label themselves Muslims if asked.

It is commonly said that "bad actors" or "extremists," whether Muslim or Hindu or Christian, are perverting the noble essence of their tradition. Less sympathetic observers may say, "See, that's what those people are *really* like!" It is equally common for people to condemn objectionable behavior of their co-religionists as being "not really Islam" or "not true Christianity." However, these views are simplistic; they assume there is some monolithic entity called Christianity or Judaism or Islam to be perverted. There is not; there are only believers. (Despite the claims of the faithful that Islam never changes, it does, just as every other faith does, if not in its "essence," whatever that may be, then in the way human beings understand it and act upon its tenets.)

It would be a mistake to say that any one person, even a religious leader, truly "represents" any religion or its attitude toward other faiths. For example, some Muslims regard Christians as "people of the book," fellow monotheists who believe in the same God as themselves; others see Christians as unbelievers who deserve ill-treatment in this life and hellfire in the next. Precisely the same thing can be said of Christians in regard to Muslims. Both can find justification for their views in interpretation of their scriptures. And because we are dealing with human beings and ever-shifting situations, these interpretations are themselves constantly changing. Faith is, and always has been, a dynamic event, not a static entity.

Because there is no such thing as "real" Islam or "real" Christianity, it is impossible to get a "real picture" of either tradition. (There's no "there" there.) At most, we are compelled to take a series of snapshots, each one limited in time, space, and subject matter. Each is one view, perhaps badly focused, of one event. Together, they form only a provisional glimpse of a shifting reality.

Islam owes much of its success to the very demands it places upon its adherents. Unlike Western cultures that encourage people to work out their own fate (and provide the necessary freedoms to accomplish that goal), Islam demands sacrifice and a collective consciousness that is centered not on the individual but on Allah and other Muslims. Individualism, in fact, is frowned upon and often coupled with the term *bidah*, or dangerous innovation. Islamic values do not revolve around consumerism, political or religious liberty, or economic prosperity. In that respect, Islamic cultures have proven resistant to Westernization, although they have seized upon Western technology to further their own ends.

HOW ISLAM AND THE WEST SEE EACH OTHER

Relations between Islam and the Christian West have been complex and often, although by no means always, hostile. During some periods, the relationships between the three monotheistic religions have been quiescent, even friendly. At other times, open war has broken out. Many suggest that the misunderstandings between the faiths are comparatively recent. This is not true. They go back go back a long way—to the time of Muhammad himself.

Christianity and Islam are by definition exclusivist, each regarding itself as the possessor of ultimate truth; each often views "the other side" as a spiritual, economic, political, or military threat. Sometimes these fears are well-founded, sometimes not. All parties have traditionally misunderstood and often mistreated the other when in power. There is nothing new about this; the animosity among the different traditions is almost as old as the traditions themselves, and there is plenty of blame to go around. Even when motives appear noble (usually having something to do with obeying God's will), they can result in crusades, jihads, and holy wars that cause the suffering and death of millions. From time to time, members of each group have labeled the others as infidels, usurpers, persecutors, hypocrites, traitors, and sinners. And they have all, on occasion, been quite right in these assessments. They have also done much worse things, all in the name of religion, although their real motives may have been quite secular. Intentionally and unintentionally distorted portrayals of "the other side" have only exacerbated what may ultimately be fundamental differences in outlook. It would be puerile to deny these differences; it would be irresponsible to exaggerate them.

Especially after the terror attacks of September 11, 2001, interest in Islam has never been higher or more important. Despite this interest, however, many Americans remain ignorant about or hostile to this important religion. A Gallup poll of American households, conducted in 2005, listed "Nothing" as the most frequent response to the question, "What do you most admire about Islam?" The second most frequent response was "I don't know." These two responses together represented 57 percent of the answers. (One can expect the same statistics if these questions were reversed and asked of Muslims about Christianity.) Things are not made easier by the fact that Christianity and Islam each regard itself as a "true religion" with competing claims, both of which cannot be logically true (although both can logically be false).

In some ways, Muslims are more familiar with Christianity and Judaism than vice versa, given that Islam inherited many narratives and articles of belief from its sister faiths. Christians however have remained largely unaware of Muhammad's life story and basic Islamic beliefs—unsure whether to consider "Allah" as the same God they worship. And Muslims, while acknowledging the importance of Jesus as a prophet, have a radically different understanding of his status than do Christians. Judaism is closer to Islamic beliefs, but because of the very early problems Muhammad faced with the Jews of Medina, relations have never been easy between Muslims and Jews.

The rift between the Abrahamic faiths is ancient. Although many Christians and Muslims call for tolerance and even pluralism, a portion of both groups see the other as competitors vying for the souls of the rest of us. These same people also believe followers of the rival tradition are not only theologically wrong but also doomed in the eyes of their God. Unfortunately, some of these extremists hold a great deal of influence within their separate traditions.

Misunderstandings can be socially reinforced. In non-Islamic countries, Muslims may be separated from members of the majority religion not only by mutual prejudices but also by isolating elements within Islamic culture itself, some enjoined by Islam, and some of which are culturally based. These elements include religious laws and traditions, dietary practices, dress, language, and beliefs and may serve to enhance internal cohesion within the Islamic community, much as these same features helped to mold the European Jewish community in early modern times.

On the other hand, more liberal Christian and Jewish attitudes toward Islam are often softened by the Western ideals of fairness, tolerance, and sensitivity toward the religions of others. Most Westerners have gone to amazing lengths to treat Islam with respect, recognizing the incontrovertible fact that, after all, most Muslims are not terrorists. And many highly placed Muslims, such as King Abdullah II of Jordan, are important peacemakers.

Curiously, it has been difficult for Western scholars to find objective narratives of the beginning of Islam, and they have had to rely almost entirely on Muslim sources. However, in recent years, Robert Hoyland (*Seeing Islam as Others See It*), Alfred-Louis de Prémare (*Les fondations de L'islam*), and especially Michael Cook and Patricia Crone (*Hagarism: The Making of the Islamic World*), building on earlier works by Goldziher, Schacht, Wansbrough, and Noth, have attempted, by using non-Islamic as well as Islamic sources, to develop a demythologized Islamic history. Wansbrough's *Quranic Studies: Sources and Methods of Scriptural Interpretation* (1977) and *The Sectarian Milieu: Content and Composition of Islamic Salvation History* (1978) have been particularly important. Although this has been good for history, it has produced tensions between Muslim and non-Muslim scholars.

MUSLIMS, CHRISTIANS, AND JEWS

Most Muslims recognize a kinship between Judaism and Christianity. All three faiths are based on revelation, in the case of Islam, the word of Allah to humankind. Muslims believe that they, Jews, and Christians are all "children of Abraham," worshipping the same god. The "word" refers to the revealed scriptures of each faith. However, Muslims believe that Christians and Jews distorted the divine message given to Moses and Jesus and that today's Hebrew Scriptures and Christian Bible are flawed documents, unlike the Quran. *They distort the meaning of the revealed words, taking them out of their context, and they have forgotten much of what they have been told to bear in mind.* The Quran also warns Muslims against the perfidy of the People of the Book: *from all but a few of them you will always experience treachery.* However, it concludes charitably: *But pardon them and forebear: verily Allah loves the doers of good* (5:13). Christians and Jews do not believe the Quran was divinely inspired.

Despite the fact that they are said to worship the same god as Muslims, Christians and Jews are classified as "unbelievers" (*kafir*) although they are several steps above Hindus (perceived as polytheists) and Buddhists (perceived as atheists). However, at certain times and places, Hindus, Buddhists, and Sikhs have also been accorded "People of the Book" status.

The Quran lays certain charges against Jews and Christians that betray an inadequate understanding of their beliefs. For example: *The Jews say Ezra is the son of God* (9:30). This statement is clearly in error—Jews have never made such a claim—and the Quranic misstatement did nothing to smooth relations between the two groups. The same passage mentions that Christians hold Jesus to be the Son of God, which *is* true, but it adds that such sayings are like the sayings of infidels, which also soured relationships. (For a long time, there was no proper word in Arabic for "Christian." The Arabs called Christians Nasrani, from "Nazareth". More recently, the term *Masihi* has been introduced; it is the Arabic equivalent of "Messiah.")

Perhaps Muhammad foresaw all this. He knew that Jews and Christians regarded themselves as in some sense "chosen people," and so the Quran declares: *Never will the Jews be pleased with you [Muhammad], nor yet the Christians, unless you follow their own creeds* (2:120).

Relations between Christians and Muslims sank to their lowest level during the Crusades (1095–1453), where blood was spilled on both sides. However, it is a mistake to think that the entire period of the Crusades was a holy war or that all or even most crusaders were fired by a religious zeal. Of the thousands of Christians who participated in the Crusades, only some were driven by a compulsion to kill the "heretics" or reclaim the Holy Land. Some went as a penance ordered by the Inquisition, some went to sightsee, and some went for gold. Some were on a personal pilgrimage, and some were simply anxious to get out of a bad situation at home. The same can be said for Muslims who took their faith with them as they went to North Africa, Spain, and Indonesia. Some were driven by religious motives, some by economic ones. Some were stricken with plain old-fashioned wanderlust, a simple curiosity to see how the other half lived.

Until the Middle Ages, Islam's main point of contact with the Christian world was Byzantium, not Rome, Paris, or London. These early contacts were military or commercial; no substantial *theological* dialogue occurred between the two faiths until the 12th century. The earliest Muslims showed little interest in traveling to Europe or in learning its languages; indeed, later Muslims felt that European civilization was debased, inferior, and not worth bothering with. They took particular exception to European lack of hygiene, with one medieval traveler remarking that Europeans bathed only twice a year and wore clothes until they rotted and fell off. Others were scandalized by the fact that European women were allowed to walk about with their faces unveiled. This attitude, a combination of resentment, condescension, and fear, has permeated down through the ages. In modern times, it is exemplified in the writings of Ali Shariati (1933–1977), one of the founders of the Iranian Revolution, who wrote, "Come, friends, let us cease this nauseating, apish imitation of Europe."

By the 16th century, Muslims became increasingly fascinated by European architecture, technology, and especially weaponry. Admiration turned quickly to resentment, however, as the West used its superior armaments to establish hegemonies in Islamic countries. Napoleon's "visit" to Egypt sparked Muslim interest, but the French fiscal policy was so destructive to the Egyptian economy that the Muslims revolted (unsuccessfully) for four and a half months after the invasion. In 1952 the Egyptians mounted a more successful revolt, this time against the British, who had taken over from the French. The rebel leader, Jamal Abd al-Nasir (Nasser), took office and nationalized the Suez Canal Company in 1956, an action that propelled him to leadership status all across the Arab world. In the same year, Morocco and Tunisia received full independence. After much bloodshed (1954–1962), Algeria negotiated independence with the French and embarked on a socialist, non-Islamic government.

Similar actions were taking place in other Middle East countries. In 1956 Jordan's King Husayn dismissed the British officer in charge of Jordan's army; in 1958 an army revolt ended British interference in Iraq. Pakistan was formed almost single-handedly in 1947 by Muhammad Ali Jinnah (1876–1948) as a home for Muslims of the Indian subcontinent.

National autonomy, however, did nothing to help resolve the knotty problem of the relationship between Islam and the various governments it found itself in. The desired degree of secularism within a Muslim country is still a hotly contested issue. Riza Shah (1878–1942) and Ataturk (1881–1938) chose to follow secular paths in Shia Iran and Sunni Turkey, although Islam has made a strong comeback in both countries.

Today there is considerable disagreement about what a Muslim state is. Most Muslims believe that it means that Islamic governments should follow Islamic law. The idea is to make Islam easier for its adherents to practice; most Islamic governments, for example, forbid the manufacture or sale of alcohol, drug trafficking, creating or distributing pornography, and the like. The head of a Muslim state should by definition be a Muslim, but others within the society are supposed to be granted equal access to the courts, the right to engage in business, and so forth. Some Islamic states, such as Saudi Arabia, strictly forbid the open practice of any faith other than Islam within its borders, even though many of Saudi's immigrant workers are non-Muslims. Muhammad himself permitted Jews and Christians to worship in their own way, so this intolerance seems definitely non-Islamic. In Pakistan "blasphemous statements" against the Quran or Muhammad can be punished by life in prison—or death. Other Muslim countries, such as Lebanon, were established on the basis of proportional representation for their citizens, who include Sunni Muslims, Maronite Christians, Shia Muslims, and Druze.

The issue of pluralism is a challenging one for Islam. Yet for Muslims, Islam is the one true faith. *The true religion with Allah is Islam* (3:19), and further, *if anyone seeks a religion other than Islam, it will not be accepted from him* (3:85). Yet the Quran explains that diversity is the nature of the universe. *Among his signs is the creation of the heavens and the earth, and diversity of your languages and colors. Surely these are signs for those who reflect* (30:22). The Quran then proceeds to establish a reason for this diversity: Allah is testing us. *If Allah had so willed, he could surely have made you all one single community, but he willed it otherwise in order to test you by means of what he has given you. Race one another then in doing good works* (5:48; see also 10:99). Another passage, however, suggests a more benign reason. *O humankind, We created you male and female, and gathered you into nations and tribes for you to get to know one another* (49:13). On a darker note, the Quran declares, *Muhammad is Allah's apostle. Those who follow him are ruthless to the infidels, but tender to one another* (48:29). In many places the Quran urges quiet attempts at conversion of Jews and Christians:

> *Do not argue with the followers of earlier revelation otherwise than in a most kindly manner—unless it be such of them as are bent on evil-doing—and say "We believe in that which has been bestowed from on high upon us, as well as that which has been bestowed upon you, for our God and your God is one and the same, and it is under him that we all surrender ourselves."* (29:46)

The Western concept of separation between church and state does not exist in many Islamic societies, nor is religious tolerance always considered a virtue. This has not always been true, however; Muslims provided a haven for Spanish Jews when the Christians expelled them from Spain, and for Christians during the Inquisition. Still, most claims for Islamic tolerance are based on the case in Turkey, which once was the most liberal Islamic regime. Even here, however, the situation for non-Muslims could be grim. In 1662 the English ambassador at Constantinople complained that the current vizier presided over the razing of churches and consigned the Christian clergy to prison. Another British ambassador reported in 1758 that the Sultan had a Jew and an Armenian executed for little more than being in the wrong place at the wrong time. Later a law was passed that ordered execution for any Greek, Armenian, or Jew spotted outside their homes after nightfall. It is also likely that the Turkish government insisted the inhabitants of Macedonia and Bulgaria convert to Islam or be killed (sometimes by burning alive).

The attitude of Christians and other non-Muslims to Islam has been equally complex. In the Middle Ages some Christians regarded the rise of Islam as a sign of the advent of the Antichrist, believing that the Muslim religion was the "great apostasy" referred to in the Second Epistle to the Thessalonians. The fact that the old Jewish Temple Mount was now the site of an Islamic monument (Muslims conquered Jerusalem in 638) was also regarded as a very bad sign.

Until the middle of the 20th century, the official position of most Christian churches, especially fundamentalist Protestantism, Eastern Orthodoxy, and Roman Catholic, was that there was no salvation outside Christianity. This is the same position that Islam holds about itself and it makes for sticky dialogue.

The traditional Catholic position was stated in 1442 at the Council of Florence: "The Holy Roman Church firmly believes, confesses, and proclaims that no one outside the Catholic Church, whether pagan or Jew or unbeliever or one separated from the church, will participate in eternal life; rather he will fall into the eternal fire prepared for the devil and all his angels." The Second Vatican Council of 1964 softened this stand: "Those who through no fault of their own, do not know the Gospel of Christ of his church, but who nevertheless seek God with a sincere heart, try in their actions to do his will as they know it through the dictates of their conscience—those too may achieve eternal salvation." However, this weakly stated position, which seems condescending, has done little to ease relations.

Social relations have been little better than theological ones. For Christians, Islam became known as the "religion of the sword" during the period of the Crusades, even though the penchant for swordplay was equally divided between the competing faiths.

On a less bloody but no less combative note, medieval Christian writers were anxious to introduce Islam to the Christian world—not usually in a favorable light. One of the earliest Christian writers on the topic, the Syrian monk John of Damascus (676–749), was actually a secretary in the Umayyad Caliphate. However, he lost his job when Caliph Umar II (r. 717–720) accused him of plotting treason, possibly because he wrote a book aimed at strengthening faith among resident Christians (as well as answering some questions about Islam). The Caliph ordered John's right hand cut off, although later pious biographies declared that it was magically restored and the Caliph begged him to come back to work. John was probably quite angry about his dismissal, to say nothing of the mutilation. In his *Source of Knowledge* he attacked both Islam and Muhammad, writing that Islam was not a genuine religion and that Muhammad was no prophet; he charged him with fabricating his entire revelation. He also referred to Islam as "Christianity gone wrong," in other words, a Christian heresy. Muslim scholars such as Al-Jahiz (d. 869) countered by saying that Christian doctrines were so murky that no one could possibly understand what they were, claiming for proof that different Christian sects could not even agree on what divinity was. One Christian-turned-Muslim, named Ali ibn Sahl ibn Rabban al-Tabari (d. 855), accused Jesus of contradicting himself, by simultaneously claiming that God sent him and that he was God himself.

Writing for the other side, Nicetas (d. 912) of Constantinople complained that the Quran was a "coarse booklet," expounding a "mythical and barbarous belief." Nicetas further labeled Muhammad as someone who was "by nature perverse and talkative, or rather stupid and bestial, a coward too, quick to anger, distrustful and arrogant."

In the mid-12th century, Peter the Venerable, Abbot of Cluny (1092–1156), commissioned a group of scholars in a Cluniac monastery in Toledo to produce the first Latin translation of the Quran, a collection of Islamic legends, a "Muslim" history of the world, and a discussion of Islamic beliefs. These documents were among the first to make a somewhat objective study of Islam available to Western scholars. Even though he claimed to approach the Muslim "in love," one of Peter's own efforts was titled *Summary of the Whole Heresy of the Diabolic Sect of the Saracens*. Titles such as this did nothing to assuage animosities.

Anti-Islamic feelings were given added fire by the preaching of churchmen such as Bernard, the Abbot of Clairvaux (1090–1153), who was partly responsible for firing up the Second Crusade. When that Crusade failed, he tried to start a third, but by then no one was listening to him. According to the Lateran Councils of 1179 and 1215, Christians were forbidden to work for or dine with Muslims or Jews. Later, Pope Gregory IX (r. 1227–1241) decreed that Muslims and Jews must wear distinctive clothing and forbade them from holding office or even appearing on the streets during Christian holidays.

Most medieval Christians regarded Islam with a mixture of fear and disdain, although Islamic achievements in science and philosophy were honored and imitated. Saladin, the Sultan of Egypt (1137–1193), was respected as a model of chivalry. William of Malmesbury (1096–1143) recognized that Islam was not "paganism," writing accurately, "The Saracens and the Turks both worship God the Creator and venerate Muhammad not as God but as their prophet."

Some of the Christians who tried to break through the cultural and religious barriers had an ulterior motive, namely conversion. Saint Francis of Assisi (c. 1181–1226) appeared before Egyptian Sultan al-Kamil and respectfully attempted to make him see the light. The Sultan listened politely and even asked the kindly saint to pray for him, but there is no evidence he surrendered his own faith. Some of Francis's friars were less tactful. They went into Spain to attempt to convert Muslims, but they were so abusive that they were executed, a procedure the friars apparently regarded as martyrdom. In fact, they did everything possible to make sure it happened.

When religious matters were left out of the equation, however, Christians, Jews, and Muslims were often able to get on like a house afire, with Christian academics studying alongside renowned Islamic scholars and scientists, such as Avicenna (980–1037) and Averroes (1126–1198). The Jewish sage Maimonides (1134–1204) was the court physician to Saladin.

During the Protestant Reformation, some compared Islam to Protestantism, with its doctrine of "justification by faith." Martin Luther (1483–1546) objected to this comparison, and he feared Islam would eventually overwhelm Christianity. More sympathetic was John of Segovia (d. 1458), who planned a conference of Islamic and Christian scholars for their mutual understanding, but he died before he could bring it about.

In 1652 the Scotsman Alexander Ross (1590–1654) published *Pansebia, or View of All the Religions in the World, with the Lives of Certain Notorious Hereticks*, an important work with a generally objective view of Islam, despite the title. The year 1697 saw the publication of Barthélmy d'Herbelot's (1625–1695) *Bibliothèque orientale*, a compendium of reference sources. In 1705 *De Religione Mohammedica* was published by the Dutch Orientalist Adrian Reland (1676–1718); it was promptly put on the Index of Forbidden Books, as being too friendly to Islam. Reland died of smallpox, but this event probably had nothing to do with Rome's disapproval.

In modern times, Napoleon (1769–1821) stands out as a moderate in Islamic–Christian relations, although he was more interested in managing public perception than discussing theology. Upon his arrival in Egypt, he reportedly said, "I respect God, the Quran, and Muhammad," although there is little evidence that Napoleon respected anyone but Napoleon. He did, however, invite some scholars from the university mosque of Al-Azhar to his quarters for chitchat and supposedly made a good impression on them. When Napoleon was defeated by British and Turkish troops, he went back home, and the colloquy was at an end. Napoleon's exact contemporary and countryman, the politician and diplomat Chateaubriand (1768–1848), did not share Napoleon's generous view. He considered Islam a "cult" and an enemy to civilization; indeed, he complained that the Muslims he saw and detailed in his *Journey from Paris to Jerusalem and from Jerusalem to Paris* were in a "savage" condition.

The fascination of Westerners with Islam has largely not been reciprocated. There are thousands more books attempting to clarify Islam for non-Muslims than works explaining Christianity and Judaism to people of the Islamic faith. Despite the gap, however, good work has been done on all sides by scholars and interested laypeople seeking to increase tolerance and come to a fruitful understanding of one another's beliefs.

However, this understanding must be based in fact, not based on what we might like to believe, for good or evil. Like Christianity and Judaism, Islam is a faith that has engendered peace and war, tolerance and brutality, enlightenment and abysmal ignorance. Like other religions, it makes claims to a divine origin and promotes itself as a guide to correct and holy living. Like other religions, it promises salvation to its believers. Like other religions, its members belong to the large, complex, squabbling, glorious, and puzzling race we call human. Its practitioners are doctors, housewives, mystics, terrorists, businesspeople, scientists, writers, college students, criminals, philanthropists, soldiers, diplomats, policemen, teachers, scholars, actors, and veterinarians: people who love, pray, work, worship, write, and raise families. To non-Muslims, some of their beliefs and practices may seem odd or outlandish; others may seem comfortably familiar. One thing is certain, however: Islam is an important religion that deserves to be understood. That is the aim of this book.

BEFORE ISLAM

Islam did not spring into the world fully formed, like Athena from Zeus's skull. Although its appearance on the world stage seems sudden, it is the product of long tradition, which it adopted and then transformed. To understand where Islam is today, it is important to know where it came from.

Islam has its roots in pre-Arabic culture. For Westerners wishing to comprehend this vast and complex faith, we have to start at the beginning—before Muhammad. The roots of Islam lie in the land that gave it birth: harsh, beautiful, and unforgiving Arabia. It was a land that made its people tough and resourceful, enduring and passionate. The Arabian Peninsula is about a million square miles in area, but much of it is barren, the Arabia Deserta, or "desert Arabia." (The middle of the country is a true wasteland deservedly known as the *al-Rub al-Khali*—the Empty Quarter.) The most climatically blessed part of the peninsula, the so-called Arabia Felix, or "fortunate" Arabia, was in the south, the area we know today as Yemen. Arabia Felix was noted for producing incense and other highly desirable items; it controlled the trade in spices such as cinnamon, which came ultimately from India. This ancient "incense road," powered by camel trains, led up to Jerusalem and the Byzantine Empire and passed from Arabia Felix directly through the caravan town of Mecca.

Islam was born in a matrix that nourished ancient values as well as the constant flow of new ideas that poured in along the trade routes. The original inhabitants of the area, the Arabs, belong to a larger group of people collectively known as Semites, who speak a variety of related languages such as Arabic, Hebrew, Aramaic, Ethiopic, and Syriac. The word "Semite" derives from the biblical Shem, one of Noah's sons. All Arabs, both Bedouin nomads and town-dwellers, were organized into tribes.

Mecca is located in the western sector, the so-called Hejaz (or Hijaz), most of which is an arid, rocky desert, with neither lakes nor rivers—just a few precious oases. The Hejaz contained both nomadic (Bedouin) and sedentary peoples, but there was considerable interaction between the two groups. This is the area where Muhammad was born and has thus been called the "cradle of Islam." Mecca was an important caravan stopping point. It was located near a well, a resource rare and highly prized. It was also the site of the Kaaba, the ancient "house of the gods" and thus a pilgrimage destination. The Kaaba made Mecca holy long before the advent of Islam. Pilgrims assembled there annually, making a solemn circumambulation (*tawaf*) of the shrines, a practice still seen today among contemporary Muslims during the annual pilgrimage to Mecca, where violence was prohibited during four months of the pilgrimage season. This was more than a concession to peace; it also assured the commercial success of the shrine. When people are assured of safety, they are more like to come and spend their money.

All religious traditions have roots in a particular time and a local culture. Islam is no exception, although it transformed many of those traditions to a different, more universal level. Muslims call the pre-Islamic period in their history the Age of Ignorance, or *Jahiliyyah*. It was the mission of Muhammad to lead people out of this ignorance (or darkness) into the light. Unfortunately, we are pretty ignorant ourselves about pre-Islamic culture, as the present Saudi government has been suspicious of most archaeological investigations in the area. However, it can be assumed that just as life on the desert has changed little over the years, the values supported by that life have not altered much either. The Bedouins lived a harsh existence, and food was never plentiful, the staple diet being camel's milk and dates; meat was a comparative luxury.

A hard life breeds hard virtues. For the Bedouin, the most important virtue was (and to some extent remains) the desert-bred attribute of manly courage (*muruwwah*), with its attendant qualities of loyalty, oath-keeping, fierceness in battle, retaliation for an insult, perseverance in hardship, patience (*sabr*) in suffering, and hospitality, all critical virtues in the hard world of arid Arabia. *Muruwwah* was believed to be inherited by blood; each tribe was assumed to have its own special brand of it, which was to be cultivated if the tribe itself were to survive.

The most highly regarded act of *muruwwah* was *najdah*, or deliverance, in which one performed a heroic or lifesaving act without any thought for oneself. Usually such a deed was a reflection of *asabiyyah*, the internal cohesion of one's clan, tribe, or other group. There was no aristocracy, and men advanced by virtue of their manliness and merit. This essential egalitarianism (at least for males) would become part of Muslim worldview as well.

The Bedouins' dignity or nobility (*karamah*) was also a point of pride. If that were destroyed, life was no longer worth living. Arabs then and now are unafraid to risk their lives in defense of their dignity. The Quran itself declares, *We have given dignity to the children of Adam* (17:70), thus making dignity an inherent right of every human being, every child of Adam. One endowed with visible *karamah* was a person of immense esteem and influence, who had great responsibilities as well as honor. He was expected, for example, to help others by being generous. Indeed, generosity (*jud*) remains a hallmark of the Arabic peoples, and the Quran constantly exhorts its readers to be generous and "spend in the way of Allah." Loyalty to one's tribe or clan (a sub-tribal unit) was also a powerful force; it was said that clan loyalty was sufficient to make a husband give up his wife. Under Muhammad's guidance, Islam itself became the "new tribe," superseding old loyalties. Muslims were expected to show loyalty to one another and succor *each other*, regardless of what tribe or clan they belonged to.

However, more modern virtues such as tenderness and sensitivity were not much in evidence among the old desert tribes. It is recorded in the biographical material about Muhammad that a Bedouin was surprised to learn that the Prophet kissed his children. Muhammad responded, "Can I help it if Allah has stripped your heart of mercy?"

Another important Bedouin trait was a propensity for revenge. A pre-Islamic poet boasted, "We slew in requital for our slain an equal number of them and carried away an uncountable number of prisoners!" Feuds could erupt suddenly and continue for generations. Male tribal members were expected to defend themselves and their tribe and to wreak vengeance upon their attackers. Typical forms of retaliation included killing the opposing males, raping and enslaving their women, slitting the noses of their slaves, and stealing their camels. Women, who were considered dependents, were not expected to undertake retaliation themselves.

Honor, or *ird*, was equally prized, at least among men. The concept of *ird* was essential to the operation of a tribal unit. In this culture, blood was repaid with blood to uphold the honor of the individual or his family. Not everyone was (or is) considered to have *ird*. Prostitutes, for example, and people guilty of sexual sins such as adultery are considered to be without honor. Although this virtue was not attributed to females, men could be *dis*honored through the actions of their women, who were expected to behave modestly. Child marriage and infanticide were both common, and women were considered more as property than as independent individuals. Women who committed adultery, or even who were raped, brought "dishonor" upon their families. Other social practices that Islam inherited from its Arabic roots included polygamy, slavery, divorce, modest dress, circumcision, and ceremonial cleanliness.

The pre-Islamic Arabs had a fatalistic worldview. There appears to have been no idea of heavenly reward before Islam, for the simple reason that Arabians had no real concept of life after death. The Afterlife was likened to a dark pit where one was imprisoned, although not actually tortured. The individual retained only a shadowy existence. In place of Heaven, the ancient Arabian poets spoke of Time (*dahr*), an implacable and impersonal force that had the final word in human life, including its ultimate happiness or misery. This concept produced a definite note of fatalism in the Arabic outlook that remains to this day.

Before the time of Muhammad, Arabians were polytheists, worshipping, it is said, more than 360 deities of both sexes, located in the holy shrine, the Kaaba. The number 360 may be symbolic, representing the number of days in a lunar calendar, or it could be that these gods, or totems, were merely markers of the days. In any case, the Arabs regarded Allah as the High God, above the others, and father of them, too.

Allah created the universe, so honor was due to him. In the pre-Islamic world, Allah had two important functions, one physical and one ethical. First, he was a rainmaker and so provided for the physical well-being of the area. Second, he was a guarantor of oaths and promises and so supported the social structure of the tribe. In preliterate cultures, the spoken oath was a solid commitment, to be broken only at one's peril. This ideal passed on to Islamic times: *And keep your commitments: truly, concerning commitments you will be questioned. Fill the measure when you measure, and weigh with a right balance: that is good and right in the end* (17:34–35). And there was something else unique about Allah. Of all the gods honored in the Kaaba, he was the only one *not* represented by an idol. (Christian and Jewish influences may have been at play here.) Muhammad came to believe that Allah was in fact the sole Lord of the cosmos and that other gods did not exist.

The images of all the gods were stored in or around Mecca's central shrine, the granite cube-like structure called the Kaaba. It was not only the building itself that was sacred; the entire surrounding 20 miles was holy ground, safe from violence of all sorts. The whole area was so holy that no tree-cutting or hunting could occur there. The Kaaba remains sacred in Islam, although it is now dedicated to the worship of Allah only. (Indeed the Quran calls it the first house ever established to worship Allah, or even the first building erected for any purpose.)

The original builder of the Kaaba is a matter of some confusion in Islamic circles. Some authorities maintain that Abraham and his son Ismail (Ishmael) built the first Kaaba, although a later legend claims they rebuilt it on an old foundation originally raised by Adam.

However, no matter who built it, in pre-Islamic days, Allah had to share it with the other gods, including his three "daughters": al-Lat, al-Uzzah, and al-Manat. Al-Lat, whose name means simply "goddess," was possibly a solar deity. Al-Uzzah (the "Strong One") was Venus, the Morning Star. She was the most important deity of the Quraysh tribe;

human sacrifices were offered up to her. Al-Manat, the goddess of destiny, was worshipped in the form of a rock located between Mecca and Yathrib (later Medina). At one time the Kaaba was even said to have contained icons of Mary, Jesus, and Abraham, all of whom had shrines within the Kaaba.

Another important deity was the moon god Hubal, possibly an import from Mesopotamia or Nabataea, now Jordan. His image was made of red agate or cornelian; at some point his right hand had been severed and replaced by one of gold. The name Hubal means "mist" or "spirit," and next to his image were stored the famous "divining arrows" that people used to discern their future. Hubal was once a prominent feature of the Kaaba; indeed the structure was probably dedicated to him. Besides the gods inhabiting the Kaaba, there were portable deities who traveled with the Bedouin and sedentary gods who resided in (or were actually made up of) natural features such as mountains, water sources, or rocks. Each tribe and community had its own deity or deities as well.

Interestingly, there seems to be no mythology associated with any of these deities, no stories of war or love, no tales of greed or pride or intrigue. From the beginning, these gods carved in stone represented abstract concepts.

The Kaaba idols kept getting stolen, so it became necessary to enlist custodians to protect the sacred shrine. These guardians were members of the powerful tribe of Quraysh, Muhammad's own tribe, who were not desert Bedouins, but city-dwellers. They were said to have originally brought the three goddesses and Hubal to the shrine at Mecca and to have charged themselves with caring for the deities, a job bestowing honor and status. By keeping the Kaaba in good repair, they also extracted tribute from the pilgrims who visited it.

However, it was not easy to keep things shipshape. The Kaaba was situated in the very lowest part of the valley and subject to flashfloods. At one point it became so dilapidated that the worshippers pulled down the whole thing and started from scratch, although somewhat nervously. They were afraid the gods might attack them for the demolition work. Nothing happened, of course. During the rebuilding, each of the four major Quraysh clans took one wall and rebuilt it. According to one story, the young Muhammad (in his pre-Prophet days) himself had the sacred Black Stone secured in place. He placed it on his mantle, and a member of each of the four clans lifted it into place together. Then he inserted the stone into the niche where it remains to this day. His tact in handling the feuding tribes and getting them to work together was a hallmark of his later leadership.

However, not all ancient Arabians were idol-worshippers; indeed, monotheism was a familiar mode of belief, at least in some parts. These early monotheists were labeled *hanifs* in the Quran, meaning those who did not believe in the old idols, even during the Jahiliyyah or "age of ignorance." The entire concept of *hunafa* (plural of *hanif*) has been challenged by some revisionist critics, but there is not enough information to know definitively, one way or another. The Arabian Peninsula contained many Jewish communities in Yathrib (Medina), Khaibar, Yemen, Fadak, and Taima, all north of Mecca, as well as Christians in the south and east, near Yemen. There were also Gnostic, Monophysite, and Nestorian Christians in various parts of the peninsula. Mecca itself had some Christian inhabitants, mostly slaves.

Although western Arabia was largely but not entirely polytheistic, the rest of the Middle East was mostly populated by Christians, Jews, or Zoroastrians. The most important, but rapidly fading, powers of the day were the Sasanian (Persian) Empire, headquartered in modern-day Iran, and the Byzantine Empire, which included much of the old Greco-Roman Empire. The Byzantine Empire was largely Christian; in the Sasanian Empire, most people were Zoroastrian, although there was a smattering of Christians, Manicheans, and even Buddhists. Christian Copts lived in Egypt, Syria had its Orthodox Jacobites, and Iraq was home to Nestorian Christians. The difference in outlook between the Greek-influenced culture of the Byzantine Empire and the Persian influence of the Sasanian Empire was political as well as religious; the two empires were pretty much constantly at war between the fourth and sixth centuries.

It is possible that the over-intellectualized, highly creedal Hellenized Christianity available to the Arabs at the time was uncongenial to the Bedouin cast of mind. Judaism would perhaps have been more conducive, but the Jews were not ardent proselytizers, although Medina had three sedentary tribes of Arab Jews living there. Neither the Judaism nor the Christianity available to the nomadic Bedouins would be considered "orthodox," and the Bedouins rejected them. Neither religion gained a powerful foothold in the interior, but Muhammad had early contact with both faiths. He appears to have assimilated many ideas from them, and Islam holds basically the same worldview and the same ethical structures as Judaism and Christianity.

CHAPTER 1

What Muslims Believe: Essential Articles of Faith

Muslims consider Islam to be, as the "Short Islamic Catechism" of Turkey states, the "last religion, the religion of understanding and science, the religion of morality, and the religion of peace and order." They believe their religion is simple, reasonable, and obvious, based on certain basic beliefs promulgated in the Quran. These beliefs are considered just as important as outward actions in the matter of salvation. Generally, these *Iman al Muffasil* (beliefs in detail) are counted as five:

- Belief in the oneness of Allah
- Belief in angels and other supernatural beings
- Belief in books of revelation, especially the Quran
- Belief in prophets, especially Muhammad
- Belief in the Day of Judgment and the Afterlife (*akhirah*) of Heaven and Hell

The Quran itself declares this core complex of beliefs: *O believers, believe in Allah and his Messenger and the book he has sent down on his Messenger. Whoever disbelieves in Allah and his angels and his Books and his Messengers, and the Last Day, has surely gone astray into far error* (4:136). They are listed in different orders in different sources, both in the Quran and in various hadith (reports about the Prophet's life). The order in which these beliefs are listed is *not* important; they are all essential to the faith.

Another key belief is sometimes added to the ones listed. Muhammad was questioned once by a traveler (later revealed to be the angel

Gabriel): "Tell me about *iman* (faith)." And Muhammad replied, "It is to believe in Allah, his angels, his books, his messengers, and the Last Day, and to believe in divine destiny." Here the idea of destiny or divine decree is added as a sixth core belief; however, these concepts can be subsumed under the idea of Allah, the omnipotent and all-knowing God.

All Muslims are obligated to believe these five (or six) things, and those who deny one or more of them are deemed *kafir*, or non-Muslim, unless that person is a recent convert or raised without knowledge of them. In that case, the correct doctrine is explained, and if the person continues in his disbelief, *then* he is deemed a *kafir*. The word comes from the Arabic *kafara*, which means to cover up or hide something. It is also sometimes applied to Muslims who knowingly disobey Islamic law and do such forbidden acts as committing adultery, drinking wine, or committing murder.

ALLAH, THE ONE GOD

The central core of Islam is that Allah exists, and all morally responsible Muslims (*mukallaf*) are required to believe in him. A morally responsible Muslim is identified as someone of sound mind who has reached puberty (*bulugh*). Even good deeds are insufficient for salvation unless they are accompanied by a saving faith. Muhammad himself said the best deed is "belief in Allah."

Allah, a word that appears about 2,700 times in the Quran, is not a personal name like Zeus or Yahweh. Literally, the word means "the deity" (*il-ilah*) in Arabic and is related to *Elohim*, the Hebrew word for God. *Allah* does take the plural form *aliha*, but such usage is reserved for pagan gods. Although orthodox Jews will not mention the name of the deity out loud, it is meritorious for devout Muslims to pronounce the name of Allah. His adoration is a critical element in Islam, and various acts of worship are referred to as *ibadat*. This word comes from the same word as *abd*, meaning "slave" or "servant," so that *ibadat* are services to Allah.

Allah's Oneness

The most important concept about Allah is that he is a unity (*tawhid*). Islam is a strictly monotheistic faith. Allah is the only, absolutely unique god; no one and no thing can share his divinity. It is blasphemy to believe otherwise. Denying the oneness of God (*tawhid*) by associating anything else with the divine is considered *shirk*, the worst possible sin in Islam, worse than murder or adultery and the only one for which there is no forgiveness (4:48). One who commits this sin is a *mushrik*, or idolater, and is doomed to hell-fire forever. A similar concept to *shirk*, and sometimes considered a synonym, is that of *dalal*—going astray or becoming lost. When we remember that Islam developed in a desert country where getting lost amounted to death, we can readily appreciate what a calamity "going astray" would be.

Allah has no consort, no children, no parent, and no partner. It is true that in the Quran, Allah refers to himself as "We"; however, this should be taken as the "royal we," not as a sign that there is more than one god or that Allah was speaking of himself and his angels. *Say, "He is God, the One. God, to Whom the creatures turn for their needs. He begets not, nor was he begotten, and there is none like him"* (112:1–4). The last sentence is a rather pointed dig at Christians, whose doctrine includes that of an "only begotten" son.

Since Allah is One, he cannot be divided into "parts," and so cannot be a trinity as Christians believe. *Believe therefore in Allah and his apostles, and say not "Three"* (4:169). In fact, the Quran specifically singles out Christians for admonition: *People of the Book, do not go to excess in your religion, and do not say anything about Allah except the truth: the Messiah, Jesus, son of Mary, was nothing more than a messenger of Allah, his word, directed to Mary, a spirit from him. So believe in Allah and his messengers and do not speak of a "trinity." Stop this; that is better for you. Allah is only one God, he is far above having a son, everything in the heavens and earth belong to him and he is the best one to trust* (4:171). (Interestingly, although the concept of *tawhid* is central in Islam, this word does not actually appear in the Quran.)

Depicting Allah in any way is a form of idolatry and is forbidden. The first clause of the Islamic creed, the Shahadah, clearly states, "There is no God but Allah." This is a nonnegotiable commandment and the closest thing Islam has to a formal "creed." The insistence on the absolute singularity of Allah was a major factor in Islam's prohibition not only of idols but also of the artistic representation of Muhammad or indeed any inanimate object, for fear it might lead to idolatry. "If you must paint," said Muhammad, "then paint trees and objects that have not a spirit in them." In many cases this proscription is interpreted to refer only to mosques, tombs, and the Quran, although it may also have a wider application. On the other hand, the absolute proscription on producing representations of living beings is sometimes ignored, especially by Shia Muslims, who often have paintings of Husayn, their favorite saint, in their homes and elsewhere. In mainstream Islam, however, artistic energy has been largely channeled into calligraphy and architecture.

ALLAH'S TRANSCENDENCE

Allah is utterly transcendent, beyond all: *No vision can grasp him, but his grasp is over all vision. He is above all comprehension, but he comprehends all things* (6:103). He does have personal qualities, but he himself is not referred to as "personal." The transcendence of Allah is clearly expressed in this *hadith qudsi* (a tradition that records a message Muhammad heard from Allah, although not necessarily in Allah's own words and which is not part of Quran):

> O my servants, you will not attain harming me so as to harm me and you will not attain benefitting me so as to benefit me. O my servants, were the first of you and the last of you, the human of you and the jinn of you to be as pious as the most pious heart of any one man of you, that would not increase my kingdom in anything. O my servants, were the first of you and last of you, the human of you and the jinn of you to be as wicked as the wicked heart of any one man of you, that would not decrease my kingdom in anything.

In the Quran, Allah is compared to light, the most glorious element in creation: *Allah is the Light of the heavens and the earth. The similitude of His Light is like a niche in which there is a lamp. The lamp is in a glass; the glass is like a shining star, kindled from a blessed tree, an olive neither of the East nor of the West, whose oil is almost luminous although no fire has touched it. Light upon Light! Allah guides to his Light whom he wills* (24:35). This passage became a centerpiece for mystical Islam because it offers a deeply contemplative vision of the deity.

Allah is Lord as well as God. Although the words "Allah," "Lord," and "God" are coterminous in the Quran, they have different connotations. The term "God" or "Allah" may conjure up a distant, aloof figure, with no interest or concern for humankind. "Lord," however, implies a closer connection between the master of the universe and his creatures, a covenantal relationship. Muslims see the deity in both lights. Allah is completely, utterly transcendent yet at the same time *nearer to man than his own jugular vein* (50:16). Allah not only creates life, but also sustains it continually. *All that is in the heavens and all that is within the earth glorifies Allah* (64:1).

Allah's Power

Allah is all-powerful, all-knowing, and eternal. *Allah the Supreme, the One, Allah is eternal and absolute. There is none born of him. He is unborn. There is none like unto him* (Surah 112). He is "uncaused." He contains all possibilities within himself and requires no sustenance or support from outside. He does not require food or sleep. He has no need to procreate. He controls everything from the movement of the stars to the flickering of a photon.

Allah exists outside space (2:115). The ultimate reality in which he dwells is called *al-ghaib*, the unseen or hidden world. Ordinary existence, the world revealed to the human senses, is termed *al-shahada*, the witnessed world. But it is the unseen world that is of ultimate importance, that we must take on faith. *This is the Book, wherein is no doubt, a guidance to the god-fearing who believe in the Unseen* (2:2).

Allah is in control of all events and can do anything that is logically possible. (Logic is a restriction Allah places upon himself to make the universe coherent.) Therefore he could not make a square circle or create a rock that he could not lift. No other limitations can be placed upon him.

The notion of Allah's being all-powerful, all-controlling, and all-good sparks questions about the nature of human freedom, a knotty issue faced by all monotheistic traditions. Many people have labeled Islam a "fatalistic" religion, and it is true that it has deterministic aspects, many deriving from the pessimistic view of the Bedouin peoples. Most Muslims believe in *al-Qadar*, or divine predestination, a belief rooted in ancient Arabian tradition. In Arabic, this is called *qada wa qadr*, the measure of Allah's plan. The same idea is frequently expressed in Islamic thinking as: "It is written" (*maktub*), meaning that all events are pre-programmed.

If Allah is all-powerful, he must also be all-knowing or omniscient (*al-alim*) because "knowing" is a power. Allah knows and sees everything, past, present, and future. He is present everywhere and aware of all that happens (6:59). "Even if you do not see him," said Muhammad, "he sees you."

The Quran calls Allah the Mighty, the Great One, the Most Great, the Most Strong, the Powerful, and so on. One of the most majestic expressions of his power is found in the "Throne Verse" (2:255) of the Quran, considered by some the greatest single verse in the Quran. It is so beloved it is frequently engraved on a pendant and hung about the neck of believers:

Allah, there is no god save him, the Living, the Eternal
Slumber overtakes him not, nor does sleep weary him.
Unto him belong all things in the Heavens and on Earth.
Who shall intercede with him unless by his will?
He knows what is before humankind and what comes after.
And no man can comprehend whatsoever save by his will.
His throne is as vast as the Heavens and the earth.
And the keeping of them wearies him not.
He is the Exalted, the Tremendous.

Human life also falls under the guardianship of Allah, a concept
meant to comfort the afflicted and humble the successful. *No misfor-
tune can befall on earth or in yourselves but is recorded in a Book of Allah's
decrees before Allah brings it into existence* (57:22). Whatever Allah wills
to occur will happen, and whatever he wills not to occur does not.

Despite the power of Allah in all things, Muslims believe humans
have important choices to make. Although Allah retains control, we
have free will. We can decide whether or not to eat strawberry ice
cream for dessert and, more significantly, whether or not to obey
Allah. Muhammad said, "Every day anew, one is the vendor of his own
soul, either freeing it or bringing about its ruin."

There is a wonderful hadith in which Muhammad found a camel
wandering in the street. When he asked whose it was, the owner
came forth. The Prophet then asked him why he had not tied it up.
"Oh," replied the man, "Should I tie my camel first and then depend
on Allah, or should I set my camel free and then depend on Allah?"
Apparently the nonsensical fellow thought Allah had nothing better
to do all day long than watch out for his camel. The Prophet, however, cleared matters up , explaining it was his responsibility to look
after his own camel, not Allah's.

Still, human power has its limitations; whatever power we have has
been granted by Allah: *It is he who created for you ears and eyes and hearts*
(23:78). There is no such thing as "chance" in the universe—all is governed by the wisdom of Allah. Critical aspects of life are decided by
Allah alone, such as how long one will live, where one will die, and
how much wealth one will accumulate. *No soul can die except by Allah's
leave* (3:145). Muhammad said,

Know that if the Nations were to gather together to benefit you
with anything, it would benefit you only with something that
Allah had already prescribed for you, and that if they gather

together to harm you with anything, they would harm you only with something Allah had already prescribed for you. The pens have been lifted and the pages have dried.

So if Allah controls everything, how can it be said that humans have free will and thus responsibility for their actions? The Muslim philosopher al-Ashari (d. 935) tried to get around the problem by maintaining that although Allah wills everything that happens, the instant before a human being performs an action, the responsibility for how it is performed is switched to the person, so that he or she will be held accountable for it on Judgment Day. Other Muslims make a distinction between what Allah wills and what is pleasing to him. An analogy on the human plane might be a parent who wills his child to get a painful medical treatment, although it is not pleasing to see a child suffer. The analogy appears to break down, however, in that it seems as if Allah could, if he chose, devise a way to make a medical treatment not painful—or prevent the sickness in the first place. The point is not to condemn Islam for an inconsistency (which it shares with its sister religions) but to bring up a point debated even among Muslims.

At any rate, humans do not know their ultimate fate until they have made every possible effort to live a good life. Making such an effort enables them to see the rewards that come in the midst of sorrow and the peace that comes from knowing they are doing Allah's will. This attitude does not resolve the inherent logical problems of trying to combine responsibility and divine predestination, but it does have solid psychological benefits.

Allah, of course, is the Creator of the Universe in general and our earth in particular. The Quran concurs with the Bible that the world was created in six days. It is traditionally agreed that the six days refer to six 24-hour periods, although some scholars point out the Arabic word for day, *youm*, can refer to any period of time. In any case, the Quran pointedly does not concur with the biblical account in which Allah rested on the seventh day as Allah requires no rest.

Although Allah did not need to create the universe, he did so of his own free will and by a word of command. *To Him is due the origin of space and the earth* (6:101). Because Allah is perfect, everything he created is also perfect, within the necessary boundaries of space and time. This world is inherently good but needs to be developed to its full potential.

Although he is transcendent, Allah cares about the world; he sustains and guides the universe and all its creatures. (It is because Allah sustains us that we are called upon to reciprocate the best we can by sustaining the poor and unfortunate.) Here is a passage from a *hadith qudsi*, in which Muhammad reports the words of Allah himself:

> O my servants, all of you are astray except for those I have guided, so seek my guidance and I shall guide you. O my servants, all of you are hungry except for those I have fed, so seek food of me and I shall feed you. O my servants, all of you are naked except for those I have clothed, so seek clothing of me and I shall clothe you. O My servants, you sin by night and by day, and I forgive all sins, so seek forgiveness of me and I shall forgive you.

The similarity here to words in the Christian Gospel is striking. Allah intervenes in history and uses events to display his sovereignty, caring, and power (30:2–9). Surah 7 lists specific instances of Allah's interventions, including some tales familiar to Christians and Jews: Noah and the Flood, Sodom and Gomorrah, and Moses and the Jewish captivity in Egypt. (It is most likely that these vivid stories were the ones most easily remembered, even by non-Jews.) Muslims believe that each human being is created by Allah, who is elevated above the rest of creation by virtue of the spirit of Allah breathed into them.

> *O humanity! Have awareness of your Lord who created you from a single person and created for him a wife of a like nature. From the two, He scattered countless men and women. Be aware of Allah, by whom you demand your rights. Revere the womb of mothers, for Allah watches over you. (4:1)*

Adam and his wife were the first humans, but unlike the book of Genesis, the Quran says nothing about humans being made in the image of Allah. Nor does it adopt the biblical tale that Eve was created from Adam's rib. They were created together as a pair, an important Quranic concept. *And of all things we have created pairs, perhaps you will all reflect on this fact* (51:49).

The Quran states that humankind was created from *alaq*, a word usually interpreted to mean a "clot of blood," although other readings are possible, given that *alaq* can refer to anything that is of sticky consistency and hangs together. One Quranic passage even claims man was created "from the water" (25:54). In a more detailed description, the Quran says,

Now indeed we create humankind out of the essence of clay, and then we cause it remains as drop of sperm in the womb's firm keeping, and then we create out of the drop of sperm a germ-cell, and then we create out of germ-cell and embryonic lump, and then we create within the embryonic lump bones, and then We clothe the bones with flesh—and then We bring all this into being a new creation: hallowed therefore is Allah, the best of artisans. (23:12–14)

According to the Quran, Allah decided to create a new form of free-willed life after he had made the angels and the jinn. We are *the best of forms* (95:4) with a naturally good instinct or *fitrah* that always urges us closer to Allah, not further away from him. Still, humans are weak, *unjust and senseless* (33:72). The angels were not happy about the proposed new class of beings. *And when your Lord said to the angels, "I am going to appoint a caliph on earth," they said, "Will you appoint on it one who will work havoc in it and shed blood, when, already, we glorify you, praising you, and proclaim your holiness?"* The angels knew what was going to happen and were clearly disappointed that Allah was not satisfied with their praising and proclaiming His holiness. Allah's answer was simply, *I know what you do not know* (2:30).

Although Allah has showered us with blessings, we easily forget and are led astray. Only Allah is completely self-sufficient. Those who fail to acknowledge their dependence on Allah are slated for trouble: *Surely man becomes grossly overweening whenever he believes himself to be self-sufficient: for behold, to your Lord all must return* (96:6–8). All creatures, not just humans, depend on Allah. *And there is no creature in the earth but on Allah is the sustenance of it, and He knows its resting place and its depository.* (11:6).

ALLAH'S NAMES AND ATTRIBUTES

Some Muslims believe Allah has physical attributes although he is a spiritual being. Whether Allah has physical attributes is a complex topic. Many Muslim theologians maintain that Allah wills, hears, sees, and speaks. It is sometimes stated that Allah possesses two real eyes because He said: *And build the ark under Our eyes as We reveal* (11:37). Muhammad is also quoted as saying the Dajjal (literally the "Charlatan," corresponding to the Christian Anti-Christ) "is one-eyed and your Lord is not one-eyed." There is similar discussion about Allah "sitting" on His throne. Other Muslims consider Allah to be utterly incorporeal, and such phrases merely figurative.

Although the Quran states, *Sight cannot catch him* (6:103), there is an argument among Muslims as to whether Allah can be "caught" in the Hereafter.

Traditionally, Allah has 99 names or attributes, a number supplied by a hadith. *Allah's names are the attributes of perfection. Invoke him by these* (7:180).

The mystic Sufi philosopher Ibn Arabi (1165–1240) wrote that these names were outward signs of the inner mysteries of the universe. Ibn Arabi also thought it likely that Allah had 300 names, not just 99. Different sources give different lists of the 99 names, and the hadith most commonly used as a source for them is regarded as weak. However, in an authentic hadith, Muhammad said, "Allah has 99 names, one hundred less one," although he did not actually list them. Muslim scholars say that even allowing that Allah has 99 names is not to say that this list is all inclusive, for Muhammad declaims, "O Allah, I ask you of you by every name that you have named yourself or that you have revealed in your book or that you have taught any of your creation or that you have kept hidden, in the unseen knowledge, with yourself." Muhammad said that anyone who learned to live by the names of Allah would certainly go to Paradise. To aid in the memorization of the 99 names, some Muslims use a string of 99 beads, or alternately one of 33 beads to be told 3 times. Sufi Muslims may meditate on one of these names all day or recite the "rosary" 1,000 times to develop the virtue of patience.

The names themselves come partly from the Quran (especially the end of Surah 59) and partly from the hadith. These "most beautiful names" (*asma ul husna*) stress both the gentle and the terrific aspects of the deity, and Muslim babies are often given names from the list, such as Abd-al-Rahman ("slave of the merciful one"). Some of these names are Creator, Fashioner, Life-Giver, Provider, Living, Opener, Bestower, Prevailer, Reckoner, Creator of Death, Powerful, Light, Patient, Unique, Appreciative, Recorder, Noble, King of Kingship, and Lord of the Worlds. It is common for a surah to end with a rhyming pair of these names, such as *al-alim, al-hakim,* "the Knowing, the Wise." One of Allah's most commonly attested attributes is *akbar,* or "great." *Allahu Akbar* ("Allah is most great!") is uttered during the call to prayer, during prayers, during happy times, before the slaughter of an animal, as a call to battle, and in praise of a speaker. They were infamously on the lips of the 9/11 terrorists near the moment of impact.

One name that is *not* attached to Allah in the Islamic tradition is "Father." This word not only suggests the Christian concept of the first person of the Trinity, but also, in the Muslim view, is altogether too a biological a term to associate with the Supreme Lord of the Universe.

Although the matter is not quite settled, most Muslims maintain that Allah is the source of both good and evil. Some of the early surahs of the Quran suggest this: *Say, I betake me for refuge to the Lord of the Daybreak against the mischiefs of his creation.* Some of the "mischiefs" mentioned include *the mischief of the night when it overtakes me, and against the mischief of weird women [i.e., witches who "blow on knots"]; and against the mischief of the envier when he envies [i.e., the Evil Eye]* (113). And further, *If Allah desires to lead you astray, he is your Lord* (11:34). However, some Muslim theologians state that no evil can be attributed to Allah and cite another verse: *Whatever good happens to you, it is from Allah. But whatever wickedness you perform is from your own self* (4:79).

Allah's Justice and Compassion

Allah is both just and merciful. Like the Jewish and Christian versions of the deity, the Quran depicts Allah as both a just judge and a compassionate lord. The Quran is filled with descriptions of Allah's justice; it commands humans to be just likewise. *Allah commands justice* (4:58). Full justice, however, may not arrive until the Day of Judgment, since everyone is aware that evildoers may not get their comeuppance in this life. Muhammad said, "All rights will be restored to their owners on the Judgment Day. Even a hornless goat that is butted by a ram will have justice." (In pre-Islamic times, it was the tribe rather than the gods who ensured that justice was carried out.) The idea is that we will be called to account for our actions.

Allah's mercy is important too. If human beings were to get our just deserts and *only* that, we would all be doomed to hellfire. *If Allah punished us according to what we deserve, He would leave on earth not one living thing* (35:45). However, Allah is merciful and we have hope of Paradise despite our sins. To emphasize this aspect of Allah, every surah of the Quran except the ninth (which contains the alarming and very late "verse of the sword") begins: *In the name of Allah, the Merciful and Compassionate.* This phrase is called the *bismillah.* Muhammad remembered Allah as saying, "O son of Adam, so long as you call upon me and ask of me, I shall forgive you for what you have done, and I shall not mind. O son of Adam, were your sins to reach the clouds of the sky and were you then to ask forgiveness of me, I would forgive you."

(The philosophical problem appears to be that if Allah is merciful to some but not to others, it reflects badly on his *justice*.)

Despite his great mercy, Allah is not above trying his creatures, and earthly life is a pass-fail test. *Every soul must taste death; and We test you by evil and by good by way of trial* (21:35). A failing grade plunges us into the depths of Hell; a passing one exalts us to Heaven. *Do people think that they will be left alone on saying, "We believe and that they will not be tested?" And assuredly we tested those before them. Thus Allah knows those who are sincere and those who are hypocrites* (29:2–3). And further: *And We shall undoubtedly test you with something of fear and hunger, some loss of wealth and lives and fruits. But give glad tidings to the patient, who says, when afflicted with calamity, "To Allah we belong and to him we return." They are those upon whom is Allah's blessing and mercy and they are the ones who are guided* (2:155–157).

Testing, however, is not always interpreted as suffering. The rich are tested by their riches, the powerful by their power, and so on. These apparent benefits can be obstacles on the path to salvation, since they may encourage sinful behavior. Through good times and bad, Muslims are enjoined to be patient and humble. Death itself has no terrors for believers, for it is the gate to Paradise.

KNOWING ALLAH

The Arabic word *alim*, or knowledge, is the most frequently used word in the Quran next to Allah, and its most important context is the knowledge about Allah. We can arrive at this knowledge of from three sources: revelation, reason, and nature.

All nature is the signature of Allah, and its order and beauty are proofs of his power and goodness. In the same way, reason is considered a divine gift, not the enemy of faith. Because both science and creation come from Allah, there can be no conflict between them. Apparent disagreements can be resolved by further scientific inquiry or better understanding of revelation.

Revelation is not limited to human beings; the Quran also speaks of revelation to Heaven and earth (41:11–12; 99:5) and to animals such as bees (16:68–69). However, only human beings have received revelation in the form of holy books, particularly the Quran. Allah may also reveal himself by imparting an idea into the mind, usually as a sudden suggestion, or *wahy*, from "behind a veil" as through a dream (*ruya*) or vision (*kashf*), or when voices are heard or spoken in a trance (*ilham* or inspiration). Muhammad's wife Aishah said that before the great revelation of the Quran, the Prophet received messages from Allah in "true dreams" in which truth "shone forth like the dawn." These experiences made solitude precious to him, and he withdrew to a cave on Mount Hira to meditate, where he received the highest form of revelation: Allah Himself spoke through the medium of an angel. That revelation was the Holy Quran.

ALLAH AND HUMAN BEINGS

Human beings are both the servants of Allah and his vice-regents on earth. We are the most blessed of all Allah's creation because we alone have knowledge of the infinite perfection of Allah. We have two important roles: (1) to worship Allah and (2) to establish a just society on earth.

The Quran places strong emphasis on our role as worshippers of the Divine. *I have created jinns and men, only that they may serve Me* (51:56). To that end, all people on earth should become a single worshipping *ummah*—community. This concept is related to the ancient Arabian concept of *asabiyyah*, or group solidarity. The jinn, too—those elemental spirits of fire, created before humankind—are assigned the task of worshipping their creator. However, they often fail.

Our second role is that of Allah's *khalifa* (regent or viceroy) over the rest of creation. This role is really subservient to the first because it is something Allah calls upon us to do. Every single person is called to be the regent of Allah, and everyone will answer directly to God. Just like a viceroy, we "stand in" for Allah over the rest of his creation and are also utterly subservient to his will.

Although Islam does not recognize "Original Sin," it maintains that human beings are prone to sinful behavior. Although we are naturally created good, we are easily distracted by Satan, as Adam and Eve were, and thus fall into sin. *O children of Adam! Let not Satan seduce you as he caused your first parents to go forth from the Garden* (7:27). Muhammad said, "The major sins are associating other objects of worship with Allah, disobedience to parents, murder, and deliberate perjury." He also said, "Avoid the seven noxious things: (1) Associating anything with Allah; (2) magic; (3) killing one whom Allah has declared inviolate without a just cause; (4) practicing usury; (5) consuming the property of an orphan; (6) retreating from the battlefield; and (7) slandering chaste women who are believers but indiscreet."

All believers are equal in the eyes of Allah. *As for those who believe in Allah and His messengers, and make no distinction among them, He will grant them their recompense* (4:152). The new commitment was to super-sede affiliation to the tribe. In Muhammad's view, once one became a Muslim, all previous misdeeds were wiped out, and the person began with a clean slate. This dedication to Allah is an interior affair—one does not need to "join a mosque" but needs simply to say the Shaha-dah, or declaration of faith, with sincerity and understanding. That alone makes one a Muslim. Muhammad said, "Allah does not con-sider your looks or your wealth. He considers your god-consciousness and your actions."

Believers are all part of the Islamic *ummah*, or community, a com-munity that is to be a witness of the truth of Islam to the world. As Islam developed, the *ummah* was seen as having a spiritual as well as physical dimension, replacing the old tribal loyalties with a community of believers.

ANGELS, DEVILS, AND *JINN*

ANGELS

Muslims believe in the existence of angels, who are "honored ser-vants" of Allah. *But verily, over you are protectors (angels), kind and honor-able, writing down your deeds* (82:10–11). Allah created these angels, and they in turn worship and obey him, although according to tradition, curtains of fire, light, and shadow separate them from Allah's throne. They are the link between Allah and the human world. They are made of light, and each has a different purpose: some carry Allah's messages, some distribute his punishments, and others protect humankind. No precise number of angels is listed, but every person has two of them sitting on our right and left shoulders. They record our actions and write them down in a book, said to open at puberty. One angel records good deeds, the other the bad (6:61, 50:17–18). They are also said to protect children. Important angels include Gabriel, who appeared often to Muhammad; Michael, the provider of food for the body and knowledge to the mind and the guardian of holy places; and Israfil, who will sound the trumpet at the Day of Judgment.

Even though they are composed of light, angels are generally in-visible to people. However, when the occasion calls, they can make themselves known. According to the Quran, the Virgin Mary saw Gabriel as a handsome man. A band of angels, although mostly unseen, was said to help the Muslims beat the unbelievers at the Battle of Badr in 624.

However, the power of angels is limited. *The future and the present are in the hand of Allah, and as many as are the angels in the heavens, their intercession shall be of no avail until Allah has permitted it* (53:26). They do not speak before he does, and they act only by his command (21:27). They do not eat, drink, or reproduce (19:64–65, 35:1); in fact, they have no sex at all. And unlike human beings and jinn, angels have no free will. So as glorious as they are, they rank below humankind, precisely because they are robots without the possibility of choice.

Of the angels, Gabriel (*Jibril*), is the most notable and he is mentioned frequently in Islamic literature. He can overturn a mountain with a single feather and fly from Heaven to earth in an hour's time. He is sometimes referred to as the "spirit of truth" or "holy spirit," but the latter term has a different meaning from the Christian one, where it is a member of the trinity.

This highest among the angels is the one who revealed the Quran to Muhammad—first appearing to Muhammad on the famous Night of Power, when he demanded that Muhammad "recite" the Quran—but at other times as well. On one occasion he assumed the form of a traveler, described as a "man whose clothes were exceedingly white and whose hair was exceedingly black." He spoke to Muhammad in an ordinary human voice and questioned him about Islam; no one but the Prophet recognized him as Gabriel. Another time Muhammad saw Gabriel in his "true shape" with 600 wings. The Quran described him (although he is not mentioned by name in this passage) as *terrible in power, very strong* [literally the meaning of the name "Gabriel"]; *he stood poised, being on the higher horizon, then drew near and suspended hung, two bows'-length away, or nearer, then revealed to his servant that which he revealed* (53:5–10).

Gabriel appeared to other prophets too. In Islamic tradition, he visited Adam 12 times, Noah 50 times, Moses 400 times, and Jesus 10 times. But Muhammad holds the record with 23,000 (or 24,000 or 27,000, depending on the source) visits from the angel.

Jinn

Muslims also believe in the existence of fiery demons called *jinn*. The Quran devotes an entire surah (72) to these rather troublesome spirits, but information about them is scattered throughout the rest of the book and in Muslim tradition as well. (*Jinni, the singular form*, is the source of the English word "genie.") *Jinn* are made of fire, but they live here on earth, usually in desolate and unclean places, or in a parallel universe of sorts. Their fiery temper makes them irascible, and most Muslims consider *jinn* as rather low in the brains department. Unlike angels, jinn are born, procreate, and die. They have some free will and can be saved or damned (mostly damned). Like us, they will be judged on the Last Day.

Normally invisible like the angels, *jinn* can also assume the shapes of humans, snakes, scorpions, and lizards. Most *jinn* are nuisances who plague humans, but the better class tends to leave us alone, so that we are not aware of them. Although we cannot see them most of the time, we can feel their presence. This is not a pleasant experience, and they have been blamed for sterility, mental illness, and epilepsy. On occasion, they can possess a human body and must be exorcized. Those who are so infested are sometimes called *bejinned*, another term for "insane." Most try to corrupt human minds and morals in a more insidious way, however, strengthening the urge to do evil. Sometimes they appear in a more benign light; the Quran intimates that it is *jinn* who possess poets and give them their almost divine powers of speech. Still, *jinn* are not generally trustworthy. They are capable of spying on angels and getting useful information from them to the detriment of humans. Muslims believe that fortunetellers, astrologers, Tarot card readers, and the like are in unknowing touch with the *jinn*. Even if they get some things correct, most of their insight is really a pack of lies. Muhammad said, "For every truth a fortuneteller utters, there are 99 lies mixed in." Muslims who encounter *jinn* are counseled to recite surahs 113 or 114 of the Quran for protection.

SATAN

Besides angels and *jinn*, Islam professes a belief in the Devil or Satan. This being has two names in the Quran: Shaytan (Satan) and Iblis, used pretty much interchangeably, although Shaytan literally means "the adversary." The story of his downfall is reported seven times; it occurred when he refused to bow down before Allah's creation, Adam (2:34 and elsewhere). On the surface, Iblis's reasoning for his refusal seems fairly sound: *"It beseems not me to bow in worship to man whom you have created of clay, of molded loam"* (7:12). He pointed out that he himself was made of fire, a presumably finer substance, however, the important point is that he was acting in direct defiance of a divine command. There is some discussion as to whether Satan is a "fallen angel," given that he was with the angels when they were ordered to bow down, but it seems clear that as a fire-being, he was a *jinni*, as the Quran says elsewhere (18:50). In any case, he was able to persuade other jinn to join his cause. As a result of his disobedience, Allah banished Shaytan and his followers from Paradise (7:13). Thus, his fall came *after* the creation of humankind, not before, as is the prevailing Christian notion (poetically, albeit lengthily, described in Milton's *Paradise Lost*). Muslims believe that Satan will be judged on the Last Day and consigned to Hell; apparently, he is not there now. Satan has the company of other beings, such as Harut and Marut, both of whom, like Satan, are sometimes described as "fallen angels."

Satan asked Allah for permission to tempt humans to lead them astray. Allah agreed but said that those who kept faith would never be misled. *Satan had no authority over them, other than what We allowed him to have to test them to distinguish the one who believes in the next life from the one who doubts it. Your Lord watches over all things* (34:21). It appears that Allah gives Iblis a good deal of free rein: *Entice such of them as you can by your voice; assault them with your horsemen and footmen; be their partner in their riches and in their children, and make them promises: but Shaytan shall make them only deceitful promises* (17:64).

Although Iblis is portrayed as the tempter of Adam and Eve, the Islamic Shaytan has little of the terrifying power of the Christian devil. He tries to lure humankind from "the straight path," often with alcohol and gambling, but he has no power to compel people to commit evil deeds. "The Devil made me do it" is not an acceptable excuse. Shaytan says, *I had no authority over you except that I called you and you obeyed me. Therefore do not blame me but blame yourselves* (14:22). The following passage, intended to comfort Muhammad, makes plain that although Shaytan is a tempter, Allah is infinitely stronger:

> *Never sent We a messenger or a prophet before you but when he recited the message Satan proposed opposition to it. But Allah abolishes what Satan proposes. Then Allah establishes his revelations. Allah is the Knower, Wise; That he may make what the devil proposes a temptation for those in whose hearts is a disease, and those whose hearts are hardened–Lo! the evil-doers are in open schism.* (22:52–53)

THE QURAN

The Living Word of Allah

The Quran is considered to be the living word of Allah and reveals his will for humankind. The Quran is the heart of Islam, more central even than the Bible is to Christians. It is considered Islam's only real miracle. In fact, the place the Quran occupies in Islam is similar to the one Jesus holds in Christianity. Those who do not accept its truth will suffer a terrible doom: *Those who deny the Scripture and that wherewith we send our Messengers will come to know, when shackles are about their necks and chains. They are dragged through boiling waters: then they are thrust unto the fire* (40: 70–72). The Quran is not merely a compendium of religious truth, but is also an integral guide for daily living. Muhammad said, "The best among you are those who learn the Quran and teach it to others." It should be emphasized, however, that simply because Muslims believe the Quran to be inerrant does not mean that the work cannot be reinterpreted over the course of time. There is, in fact, a long tradition of such exegesis, even though it starts from a somewhat different place than biblical scholarship. Bible scholars recognize the human hand in the composition of the Bible; Quranic scholars begin from the assumption that the Quran is the direct, unaltered word of Allah. They do believe, however, that the word had to be understood in a variety of human contexts.

Every word of it is believed to reproduce the words of Allah exactly, unlike the Bible, which contains psalms ostensibly by King David and reports about Jesus by his apostles. For Muslims, it is not a matter of someone, inspired or otherwise, writing *about* God. It is quite literally the words of Allah, revealed to Muhammad by the angel. For Muslims this literalist construction of the Quran is normative, as opposed to Christians and Jews, who have mostly moved away from literal inter-pretations of the Bible. The tone of the Quran is frequently polemical, as if in response to unstated attacks on its truth. *And this Quran cannot be produced by anyone other than Allah* (10:37). Muslims do not believe a literal reading of the Quran conflicts with science. Instead, they main-tain that the findings of modern science corroborate the truths of the Holy Book. They maintain that nothing in the Quran is opposed to human reason or objective fact. Muslims have never objected to sci-ence and the scientific truth about the origins of the universe, so long as room is made for the initial action of Allah.

Although the Quran is not intended to be a textbook on physics, many Muslim commentators search through it for passages that seem to parallel findings made by modern science, in an effort to show the timeless wisdom of the book. Some of these parallels are said to include references to the Big Bang, antimatter, rotating stars, radioactive fu-sion, tectonic plates, and the ozone layer. In some cases, it may appear that a great deal of imagination has been applied to these "parallels."

The reading of this sacred book is important to all Muslims. Muhammad said,

A believer who reads the Quran is like a citrus fruit with a sweet fragrance and delightful taste. A believer who does not read the Quran is like a fresh date which has no scent but whose taste is still sweet. A hypocrite who does not read the Quran is like a basil leaf, with a sweet smell and a bitter flavor. A hypocrite who reads the Quran is like a sweet-smelling flower with a terrible taste.

The Revelation of the Quran

Muhammad is said to have received the Quran from the Gabriel. The Quran declares that this one night is better than a thousand months (97:3). The event memorialized in Islam as the "Night of Power" (Surah 97) occurred in 610 when Muhammad was about 40. The awesome event occurred toward the end of the month of Ramadan, Muhammad's favorite time for meditation. The exact night is not known, but it is believed to have occurred on an odd-numbered night when there was almost no moonlight.

Nowadays, many Muslims commemorate the event on the 27th of the month of Ramadan with nightlong devotions, recitation of the Quran, and acts of charity. Others celebrate during the entire last five days of the month.

Muhammade was meditating in a cave on Mount Hira, as was his custom, when a voice roared out of the dark. An angel of light later identified as Gabriel twice commanded him to "Recite!" (*iqra*) or "Read!"

And then, *though he had never been able to read,* he immediately began to read or recite the revelation: *Recite in the name of your Lord who created, / Who created man out of a clot of blood. / Recite! Your Lord is the most beneficent, / Who taught by the pen / Taught Man what he knew not* (96:1–5). Interestingly, this foundational revelation does not open the Quran, but is located closer toward end of the text. Perhaps the placement is meant to signify the eternal significance of the Quran, and that its revelation, while important, does not mark its beginning.

The Quran was revealed to Muhammad over a period of 23 years (as opposed to 1,500 years for the Bible) in bits of two to five verses at time, presumably for easier memorization. *We have divided the recitations and you may recite it to humankind at intervals, and we have sent it down by successive revelations* (17:106). Muhammad knew that a chapter was finished when he was ordered to say *bismillah al-rahman al-rahim* (In the name of Allah, the Merciful, the Compassionate). As soon as a new revelation was received, Muhammad hurried to the mosque and pronounced it before the people, who then tried to commit it to memory.

The Quran is often called "the Book of Light," but it gives itself about 50 other appellations, such as the "Book of Guidance" (2:2), the "Proof" (4:174), the "Criterion" (25:1), the "Reminder" (6:90), and the "Healing" (17:82).

Muslims take exception to the idea that Muhammad had any hand in composing it, and the work itself declares,

> *So I swear by all that you see and all that you do not see that this verily is the speech of an honored messenger (Gabriel). It is not the speech of a poet; little is it that you believe. Not is it the speech of a soothsayer; little is it that you remember. This is a revelation from the Lord of the Worlds. And if he were to invent any saying concerning us, we would assuredly seize him by his right hand and cut off his life artery, and not one of you could keep us from him. And verily this is a reminder for the God-fearing.* (69:38–48)

His revelations did not always come when he was meditating in a cave, as on the first night. They could arrive at any time, even when he was doing chores. "And sometimes the angel comes to me in the likeness of a man and speaks to me and I retain what he says." Actual visions were quite rare, even when they came the angel did not always appear in the same form. Most of the time, he did not materialize at all, and Muhammad's inspiration was auditory (*wahy*) only. Sometimes, Muhammad reported the message was as clear as someone standing next to him. At other times, it sounded like a muffled bell. That, Muhammad reported, "is hardest on me, then he departs from me and I retain what he says." It was often a painful experience. "Never," he said, "did I receive a revelation without thinking that my soul had been torn away from me."

His wife Aishah also remembered that even on bitterly cold days, his forehead would "drip with sweat" when the revelation came down on him. Others report that his face became extremely red or even that he snored during these moments. Sometimes he just put his head between his knees while listening to the voice from Allah. At other times he looked sad. And according to a rather puzzling hadith reported by

Muhammad's young scribe, once the revelation came when "his thigh was upon my thigh and it began to make its weight felt to me so much that I feared my thigh might be crushed." Especially in the beginning, people accused him of being a madman or thought he was having seizures. At first Muhammad seemed to strain while receiving the divine word, moving his lips as the revelation came to him. However, Allah revealed to him the correct way to receive the words: *Move not your tongue to hasten it. It is for Us to collect it in your heart and enable you to recite it* (75:16–19). After this revelation, Muhammad would simply listen attentively. His job was not to "help" the revelation, but simply to be open to it, so that it would be engraved upon his heart. In an important sense, Muhammad was merely a channel for the divine words, and it is difficult if not impossible to separate the message from the messenger.

From its inception, the Quran has been regarded as the pinnacle of Arabic literature in its breathtaking beauty and purity of language, even apart from its religious significance. Quranic Arabic is in a class by itself. It is generally agreed that no interpretation or translation can do justice to the power and striking beauty of the original. This is true, of course, of the masterworks in any language. Shakespeare, Dante, and Aeschylus shine brightest in the language in which their ideas were originally garbed; translated versions are like borrowed rags.

THE ARABICITY OF THE QURAN

The "Arabicity" of the Quran remains a doctrine in Islam. Translations of the Quran are tolerated, but just barely, and no authorized translations of the Quran exist. It has been only recently that translations were even allowed in Muslim countries. Arabic Muslims find all translations of their beloved Quran profoundly unsatisfying. Arabic is truly a sacred language to Muslims, just as Sanskrit is to Hindus, and Hebrew is to Jews. Christianity alone of "revealed" religions has no sacred language. Attempts to render the Quran into another language are generally called "interpretations"; to change the text in any way would be to corrupt it, which is why only the Arabic Quran is "official," and it is frequently printed alongside the translation.

Arabic is a rich language that builds entire families of words on roots of three letters—the so-called radicals. For instance, *salaam, Islam,* and *Muslim* as well as the proper name Sulayman all derive from the simple radical *slm*. The written language is also unusual, being like Hebrew written right to left, although Arabic numerals are written left to right.

Arabic script has no capital letters and no punctuation. Generally, only the long vowels are recorded; short vowels must be determined from the context.

However, it is important to remember that most Muslims are not native speakers of Arabic, and those who are do not speak the same kind of Arabic used in the Quran. This can make it difficult for non-experts to decide what the Quran actually says.

The Quran is designed to be recited or read aloud—in Arabic. Muhammad said, "Beautify the Quran with our voices, for the beautiful voice increases the beauty of the Quran." Unlike the Bible, the Quran is primarily oral as opposed to literary in character. Reciting or chanting Quranic verses replaces hymn-singing in Christian culture. The chanting or recitation of it is wildly popular in Islamic countries and has no real parallel in Christian or Jewish communities; one very rarely hears of people standing around listening to someone recite Leviticus or Obadiah. Even the word Quran means "recitation"; in fact, reciting it is considered an art form, which has several different styles of recitation, just as there are different styles of Arabic calligraphy. There are public competitions in which the contestants present their own chanted versions of Quranic chapters. Islamic history and legend are full of stories of people who faint, fall into a trance, or even die while hearing the words of the glorious Quran.

READING THE QURAN

It is considered extremely laudatory to memorize the entire Quran in Arabic. A person who learns the Quran by heart is known as a *hafiz* (fem. *hafizah*), one who "carries the Quran in his heart"; such a person is honored by his or her community and awarded various privileges. One hadith tells the story of man who wished to marry a woman, but who had nothing to offer as a dowry, not even an iron ring, but when Muhammad asked him if he could recite any part of the Quran, the man did so. Muhammad decided that was in itself a sufficient dowry, and he allowed the marriage.

The best time to read or recite the Quran is in the early morning while facing Mecca, but there is no bad time. (It is recited nightly in the mosques during Ramadan.) Many Muslims, both men and women, cover their heads when reading or reciting from this book. Before reading, the believer says, "*Auzu billahi minashaitanir rajim,*" which means, "I seek refuge of Allah from the outcast Satan." The same sentence should also be uttered before undertaking other important activity. Immediately after, one is expected to say *"Bismillahir rahmanir rahim,"* which means "In the name of Allah, the Most Beneficent, the Most Merciful." After the reading, the worshipper says, *"Sadaqallahul authzeem,"* which means, "Allah, the exalted, has spoken the truth."

It is also recommended to perform *wudu* (ceremonial washing) before reading it. People in a state of impurity may not touch the Quran until a ritual bath (*ghusl*) is taken. According to some authorities, this includes women who are menstruating.

When the Quran is being read, one is not allowed to smoke, talk, or drink. Humility when reading the Quran is the first requirement. The reader should be in a respectful posture, not sprawled all over the place. Even one's reactions to certain passages are dictated by convention. For example, one should feel afraid when reading the descriptions of Judgment Day and hellfire.

Most Muslims take the texts of the Quran literally and maintain that it contains no contradictions. However, many scholars believe that some Quranic injunctions nullify others, a prime example being 24:2, which abrogates the punishment of adultery, as stated in 4:15–16. It appears that the original penalty was to shut the offending woman into her house, and the later was to flog the offender with 100 stripes. Most scholars say that abrogation (*naskh*) pertains only to jurisprudence or practical matters that can change over time, not essential principles of faith or doctrine. The Quran simply says, *None of our revelations do we abrogate or cause to be forgotten, but We substitute something better or similar: know you that Allah has power over all things* (2:106).

CARING FOR THE QURAN

The physical treatment of the written Quran is a matter of high importance. *When the Quran is recited, you shall listen to it and take heed, that you may attain mercy* (7:204). No other book may be placed on top of the Quran, and it is often kept on a shelf in a special box above all other shelves in the home. However, the Quran is meant to be read and not just looked at—it should not become a mere part of the décor, which might discourage people from actually reading it. Still, a hadith records that Muhammad forbade people to take the Quran on a journey, lest it fall into enemy hands. However, since the Quran was supposedly not written down in Muhammad's lifetime, the story is suspect. Many devout Muslims never leave their homes without taking along a copy of the Quran. When it becomes worn, it is buried carefully in the earth or at sea. Some schools recommend the old copy be burned. (Technically, this applies only to the Arabic versions, given that they are the only "official" ones, but most Muslims recommend treating translations the same way.)

The Quran also has a long history of talismanic use. The final surahs, 113 and 114, are frequently cited to ward off evil. Some scholars say that in times of fear or confusion, the last three surahs should be recited three times in succession. The "Throne Verse" (2:255) is recited at bedtime so that an angel will descend to guard the sleeper during the night.

THE STYLE AND THEMES OF THE QURAN

Much of the Quran, especially the shorter surahs, is written in un-metered rhymed prose called *saj*, a style used by Arabian poets from time immemorial. The Quran itself states firmly that it is not poetry, although it makes undeniable use not only of rhyme but poetic devices such as simile and metaphor. Some parts are so soaringly poetic that its passages are attributed (by skeptics) to the pre-Islamic poet al-Qays. Others believe the writings of al-Qays were altered *after* the coming of the Quran.

The Fatihah, or opening surah of the Quran, is said to contain all the Islamic principles in condensed form:

> *In the name of Allah, the Most Gracious, the Dispenser of Grace: All praise is due to Allah alone, the Sustainer of all the worlds, the most Gracious, the dispenser of Grace, Lord of the Day of Judgment, thee alone do we worship, and unto you also do we turn for aid. Guide us on the straight path, the way of those upon whom you have bestowed the blessings, not of those who have been condemned by You, not of those who go astray.* (1:1–7)

These very early Meccan verses are sometimes called the "Quran in miniature," as they touch on the main themes of the book: monotheism, pious conduct, the Afterlife, the "straight path" of Islam, and prophecy. The Fatihah is whispered into a newborn baby's ears and read into the ears of a dying person. A believing Muslim utters these words about 20 times a day because they are incorporated into the obligatory prayers.

Muslims say that the divine character of the book is easily revealed when one compares its moving, heightened language to the plain words of Muhammad recorded in the hadith. There he speaks like an ordinary person; the language of the Quran is on a different order altogether.

However, the Quran is honored not because of its beauty, but because it is divine—the expressed will of God. The Quran says self-referentially, *And this Quran is not something that could be manufactured without Allah* (10:37). It goes on to challenge others to produce anything so fine: *Do they say that he has forged it? Say, let them bring a chapter like it* (10:38). Indeed, the Quran was used to develop Arabic grammar and linguistics, and its language is known as *fusha*, or "correct" Arabic. However, some scholars point out that the Quran contains incomplete utterances not fully explicable without commentary, unfamiliar Arabic, foreign words, bad grammar, and other linguistic snarls that suggest a more human origin. Arthur Jeffrey's famous study, *Foreign Vocabulary of the Quran*, lists many words of Jewish, Christian, and Persian derivation, including such Quranic staples as *surah* (chapter), *abd* (servant), and *al-rahman* (the merciful). Yet, if the Quran sets the standard for what is correct, it cannot, by definition, be faulty in any particular. In addition, many Muslim scholars argue that any foreign words were thoroughly arabicized by the time of Muhammad. Others claim that Arabic and related languages have many identical words simply by coincidence.

The only authorized version of the Quran is in Arabic, and there is only one such version, recreating the exact words Allah spoke to Muhammad in clear (*mubin*) Arabic. The words cannot be changed without changing their meaning. Therefore, the Quran cannot be modernized or reformed because it is already perfect. Non-Muslim textual studies, however, suggest that in the past, parts of the Quran did undergo revision, a claim not accepted by Muslims. In any case, tradition says that Gabriel reviewed the Quran with Muhammad every Ramadan and checked the received text twice shortly before the Prophet died to make sure it was correct.

Muslims debate whether every mark and letter is the word of Allah, but that the Quran is true *as a whole* is not in doubt. Muslims believe that reading and meditating on the Quran as a whole and in the original Arabic is the surest way to know God, for it is in the Quran that God has revealed himself. *This is the scripture in which there is no doubt* (2:2). On the other hand, reading only individual verses (which may seem contradictory) or reading a paraphrase or translation may produce incorrect knowledge.

Despite the honor the Quran enjoys among Muslims, non-Muslims have always found it a challenge. One difficulty is the organization. The

Quran is organized according to the length of its 114 surahs (chapters), not topically, thematically, or chronologically. With the exception of the first, they are arranged roughly by length, with the longer ones at the beginning. This is true even though the shorter chapters at the end were mostly revealed earlier. Who is responsible for its ordering? According to one hadith, "Muhammad would say, 'Put this verse (*ayah*) in the surah in which such and such is mentioned.'" Muhammad supposedly had the advice of Gabriel, so perhaps the angel is accountable. For Muslims, the apparently disordered chapters of the Quran present no problem, and it has been hypothesized that the disorganization and fragmentary quality of the earlier surahs especially represent the inadequacy of any language to fully express the glory of Allah's words.

Carlyle famously considered the Quran "a wearisome, confused jumble, crude, incondite; endless iterations, long-windedness, entanglement; most crude incondite—insupportable stupidity, in short!" (Perhaps Carlyle was trying to make a joke here—little could be more long-winded than the sentence just quoted.) The whole book is about four-fifths the length of the New Testament. It is traditionally said to have 114 surahs, 6,616 verses, 77,439 words, and 323,015 letters. Only recently, have Muslims taken to quoting "chapter and verse." Previously, it was the custom merely to say, "The Quran says," and quote the appropriate passage without identifying it further. However, following Western biblical scholarship, more exact notation is becoming commonplace.

While most Muslims are not troubled by the Quran's apparent lack of organization, some Muslim scholars such as Hamid al-Din al-Farahi (d. 1930) and his student Amin Ahsan Islahi (d. 1997) have attempted to find a rationale for the arrangement of the chapters. They contend that each surah has a dominant idea around which all the verses revolve and that the surahs themselves come in complementary pairs, falling into seven groups, consisting of one Meccan and one or more Medinan surahs. Most scholars dismiss this attempt to categorize the Quran as arbitrary.

It is not only the lack of identifiable organization that causes problems of interpretation. The style of the Quran is aphoristic, compact, and poetic, difficult even for a native speaker of modern Arabic to get the sense of. It is filled with missing phrases that have since been supplied by translators and commentators. These missing phrases often appear in brackets, but because their content is generally agreed on, I have omitted them here for ease of reading. The contexts in which the different verses were revealed, or "occasions of revelation" (*asbab an-nazul*), are considered important and are included in academic discussions (*tafsir*) of the passage in question. It should be noted, however, that these occurrences are not supposed to change the meaning of the Quran, which is immutable.

The titles of the individual surahs sometimes bear little apparent relation to the main topic. For example, the longest surah, or second chapter, is called "The Cow" (*Al-Baqarah*). But of the 286 verses in this surah, only these 7, which are rather mysterious, mention cows:

> *When Moses said to his people: Surely Allah commands you that you should sacrifice a cow, they said" "Do you ridicule us?" He said, "I seek the protection of Allah from being one of the ignorant." They said, "Call on your Lord for our sake to make it plain to us what she is." Moses said: "He says, 'Surely she is a cow neither advanced in age nor too young, of middle age between that and this; do therefore what you are commanded.'" They said, "Call on your Lord for our sake to make it plain to us what her color is." Moses said, "He says, Surely she is a yellow cow; her color is intensely yellow, giving delight to the beholders." They said, "Call on your Lord for our sake to make it plain to us what she is, for surely to us the cows are all alike, and if Allah please we shall surely be guided aright." Moses said, "He says, Surely she is a cow not made submissive that she should plow the land, nor does she irrigate the tilth; sound, without a blemish in her." They said, "Now you have brought the truth." So they sacrificed her, though they had not the mind to do so. And when you killed a man, then you disagreed with respect to that, and Allah was to bring forth that which you were going to hide. So We said, "Strike the dead body with part of the sacrificed cow, thus Allah brings the dead to life, and He shows you His signs so that you may understand." (2:67–73)*

It is not clear if the chapter titles are part of the Quran proper or were added later on; some surahs are known by more than one title because they address different issues. Twenty-nine of them are headed by cryptic "disjointed letters" that have no apparent meaning. One of them, the Taha (Surah 20), is concerned primarily with Moses' encounter with the Pharaoh. Many Muslims scholars believe these letters have deep spiritual significance; some outside scholars think they were added later, perhaps denoting names of scribes. It may also be that the mysterious letters were meant in some way to point to a special revelation.

The earlier surahs, the so-called Meccan (622–632) verses, mostly deal with Allah's nature, the relationship between Allah and human-kind, and the Last Judgment. The later, or Medinan, verses concern administration of the *ummah* or Islamic community, political affairs, lending agreements, legal codes, and pointed references to "hypo-crites" and "People of the Book." These later verses include many stories from the Bible, with a particular emphasis on Abraham, called "the friend of Allah" (*al-Khalil*). In some cases, Medinan verses are inserted into Meccan surahs and vice versa. Some scholars have main-tained that the Medinan verses are an accommodation to a particular time in Islamic history, which, at least to some extent, limits the uni-versal message of the Quran. For that more universal message, one needs to return to the earlier Meccan verses.

Chronologically, the surahs can be divided into four major groups, any of which may appear anywhere in the Quran:

- Early Meccan (610–615)
- Middle Meccan (615–620)
- Late Meccan (620–622)
- Medinan (622–632)

But if clear organization is not a feature of the Quran, it does not seem to matter. The Quran does not have to be read front to back; it is even suggested that the reader read the shorter, earlier surahs, which often contain the most beautiful and powerful language, first. Some Mus-lims recommend that the reader open the Quran to any surah at all and begin reading.

It is important to understand that the expectations that Western-ers bring to a sacred text are formed by their own culture and literary experiences. These are not shared by many Muslim readers, who have their own set of expectations—which are fully satisfied in the Quran.

THE QURAN AND THE BIBLE

The Quran is dependent on the Bible for some of its content. Both books recount many of the same tales: Adam and his wife, Noah's Ark and the Flood, Abraham and Ishmael, Joseph, the Ten Command-ments, the Ark of the Covenant, the appointment of Saul (Talut in the Quran), David and Goliath, Solomon, Jonah and the Fish, and Jesus and Mary.

However, there are often differences between the stories they tell. Quranic narratives are often abbreviated and (in the view of critics) distorted versions of the biblical originals, suggesting that although Muhammad had some acquaintance with the Bible, he was not well versed in it. The chronology of various biblical figures seems confused in the Quran and is often divergent from the Bible.

The story of Adam and Eve is a case in point. Agreeing with the biblical account, the Quran declares that Adam and his wife were the first human beings. The Quran does not specifically name Adam's wife as Eve, although Muslims agree to use this name (Hawwa, in Arabic). The Quran has its own version of the Garden of Eden story, in which Adam and his wife eat the forbidden fruit together, and she is never singled out as the guilty party. For Muslims, it is Adam rather than Eve who was tempted, and women are not blamed for the disobedience as they are in some Christian circles. (Still, there is a teasing saying of Muhammad: "Had it not been for Eve, woman would never have acted unfaithfully toward the husband.")

In the Quranic view, the tempter was the devil, Satan, a character who does not appear in the Genesis story. The Quran omits the snake. The tree in the Quran is not the Tree of the Knowledge of Good and Evil, but the "Tree of Eternity," probably the "Tree of Life" mentioned in the Bible. The Quran does not give it any particular powers (it just seems to be forbidden), although Satan told Adam otherwise.

In the Quran, Adam and his wife repent their error and are fully reconciled with Allah; Islam has no doctrine of original sin. Adam's fall is considered a lapse in good judgment, and his mistake does not taint the rest of the human race. Nor is there a doctrine indicating that the Fall produced a life of hardship and suffering, or that it brought death into the world. Muslims do not believe that human beings are sinful by nature, although we are naturally weak, needing the help of Allah. Muhammad said, "Every child is born following his natural *Fitrah* [this is interpreted to mean he is by nature a Muslim]. It is the parents who make him a Jew, Christian, or Zoroastrian."

Although Adam and Eve sinned, after he forgave him, Allah bestowed the gift of prophethood on Adam to guide him and his descendants. Here are his last words to Adam: *There shall most certainly come to you guidance from me, and those who follow my guidance need have no fear and neither shall they grieve, but those who are bent on denying the truth and giving the lie to Our messages—they are destined for the fire and therein shall they abide* (2:38–39). The moral is: Allah helps everyone who makes a sincere effort (*jihad*) to keep to the straight path.

The story of Cain and Abel also differs from Genesis. In the Quran, Cain murders Abel, as he does in the Bible, but there are some interesting changes. For one thing, a raven plays a part in the story: *Then Allah sent a raven which began to scratch the ground to show him how he might hide the corpse of his brother. Seeing this, he cried, 'Woe be to me! I have not been able to do even as this raven has done and so devise a plan of hiding the corpse of my brother.' After this he became very remorseful of what he had done.* (5:30–35). This interesting detail appears to be from Jewish legend, and is recounted in the Targum of Jerusalem.

Indeed, the root of many of the differences can be found in rabbinical sources, which frequently provide a bridge between the biblical tale and the Quranic adaptation. However, there are few sustained narratives in the Quran; most of it consists of sayings intended to express the will of Allah and commandments for the faithful. For non-Muslims, much of it seems fragmentary, confusing, repetitive, contradictory, and in many place obscure—perhaps deliberately so.

The Heavenly Quran

Muslims believe that in addition to the earthly Quran, there is a "Mother-Book" (*umm al-kitab*) in Heaven. It resides with Allah on a "preserved tablet" in Paradise, which descended to the lowest heavens (*bayt al-izza*) preparatory to its being revealed. *It is a glorious Quran, on a Preserved Tablet* (85:22). This tablet is open only to Allah, inaccessible to mortals except as revealed in the Quran. *Certainly the Quran is in the Mother of the Book, which is in our Presence, raised high and full of wisdom* (43:4). It is also called the *kalam Allah* or actual speech of Allah.

For most Muslims, the *kalam Allah* is eternal and uncreated, so the Quran also has those qualities. In this regard, it is similar to the Christian idea of Logos, as recorded in the Gospel of John: "In the beginning was the Word, and the word was with God and the Word was God." Its precise nature is a matter of some dispute, however. Whether the Quran is a precise copy of the *umm al-kitab* or an abridged version, for example, is debated. In any case, the Quran says of this book, *Behold it is a truly noble discourse, conveyed unto mankind in a well-guarded divine writ which none but the pure of heart can touch: a revelation from the Sustainer of all the worlds* (56:77–79).

Each verse or sentence of the Holy Book is called an Ayah, which literally means "sign" or "miracle." The Quran even proclaims *itself* to be peerless, divine, infallible, inerrant, and incorruptible, a self-reverent and self-referential claim not present in other holy scriptures. *Indeed,*

We have sent down the Quran, and surely we will guard it from corruption (15:9). However, the Quran itself opens the door for a broader interpretation of itself, and many scholars divide its verses into those considered straightforward, legal, or clearly understood (*muhkamat*) and those of a more allegorical (*mutashabihat*) nature: *He it is who bestowed on you from on high this divine writ, containing messages that are clear in and by themselves, as well as others which are allegorical* (3:7).

But there is a caveat too: *Now those whose hearts are given to swerving from the truth go after that part of the divine writ which has been expressed in allegory, seeking out what is bound to create confusion and seeking to arrive at its final meaning in an arbitrary manner, but none save Allah knows its final meaning.* The problem is that no one agrees precisely on *which* verses are to be taken literally and which should be understood allegorically, or even between just which verses are supposed to be "clearly understood" and those which are not.

Many scholars believe that while Muhammad was alive, the Quran was entirely in oral form. After all, that is the way Muhammad received the word. However, an old tradition asserts that whenever a new verse was revealed, Muhammad would call a scribe to set it down. One source claims there were 24 or 48 such scribes, the most important of whom was Zayd bin Thabit (d. c. 634 or 665). He had been Muhammad's secretary since he was 12 years old and had memorized the entire work and copied it out, comparing what he had to the "leaves" possessed by Uthman's daughter. Some experts, however, blame Zayd for what they consider the incoherent way the surahs are ordered, although, as noted above, it was supposedly Gabriel who oversaw the operation.

The Transmission of the Quran

Early Muslims were extremely careful in copying the Quran, but how it was transmitted is a puzzle. The oral transmission not only was said to come first but also had more prestige than the written version. In the early days, written texts were compared to memorized versions—if there was a discrepancy, the oral version was deemed correct. Today the Quran functions as both a written (*mus-haf*) and an oral (*al-quran*) work. Some tension is generated by the fact that oral and written works have different emphases and reflect the culture in different ways. Whereas a written text "fixes" the revelation and grants it permanency, there are also indications that it represses the original spirit of an entirely oral message. However, as writing became the universal medium of communication across the growing Islamic empire, the written text became inevitable.

What we know "officially" about the collection of the various Quranic passages into a book is recounted in about 22 extant hadith, or reports. Many say that the Battle of Yamamah (633), where many Muslim reciters were killed, spurred the remaining believers to write down and collect the Quran into a single book. The entire Quran was supposedly written down during the reign of Muhammad's successor, Abu Bakr al Siddiq, at least in a provisional collection. Abu Bakr, like Zayd bit Thabit, was a hafiz, one who had memorized the Quran. However, this account is not widely agreed to be historical. Abu Bakr was in office only two years, and that does not seem sufficient time to do the work. In addition, Abu Bakr's purported contribution is left out of some highly respected accounts of the process.

According to yet another tradition, the second caliph, Umar (r. 634–644), ordered that every word of Muhammad's revelation should be collected "whether inscribed on date-leaves, shreds of leather, the shoulder blades of camels, stone tablets, or in the hearts of man." The oldest complete copies were written on parchment made of gazelle skin. (Paper was in short supply, and the Quran was written down on all sorts of unlikely substances.) The entire collection is referred to as *mus-haf*, which literally means "between two covers."

The third caliph, Uthman (579–656, r. 644–656), is also credited with making an early collection, partly from some material saved by Hafsah (d. 665), his daughter and a widow of the Prophet. Uthman became alarmed at the differences he noted in versions recited even by those who were closest to the center of the Muslim faith. "Therefore," he said, "those who are far away in the provinces must be in even greater dispute."

Tradition also tells us that Uthman had all "faulty" copies destroyed. It was Uthman who had six "official" copies of the Quran written down upon the skins of six specially sacrificed goats sent out to the corners of the Islamic empire: Medinah, Mecca, Kufa, Damascus, Cairo, and Sanaa in Yemen. These versions became the basis for the official or "canonical" Quran. The Meccan text was burned in a fire in 683; the Medinah and Kufa books were also eventually lost. All of these stories are suspect; it is likely that the Quran was gathered in increments and over a much longer period of time than the standard account maintains.

The oldest extant Qurans (from before 750 and reportedly ordered by Uthman) are located in the Topaki Museum in Istanbul, Sanaa in

Yemen, and Tashkent in Uzbekistan. The last is a partial copy, heavily mutilated and possibly bloodstained. In 1972, during the restoration of the Great Mosque at Sanaa, some ancient pages were found in a veritable "grave" of early versions. It was the custom to decently "bury" worn-out copies, as the Jews buried outworn Torahs in their genizahs. However, very few scholars have been allowed access to them, so they remain a mystery. Orthodox Islam denies that any "deviant" copies of the Quran ever existed after the text was redacted in Caliph Uthman's time, so the world may never know.

The first copies of Quran had no vowel markings or diacritical marks, and the verses were not separated or numbered. The technical name for this kind of script is *scriptio defectiva*, or "defective writing." Vowel markings and dots were added during the rule of Caliph Malik ibn Marwan (646–705) as an aid to non-Arabic speakers. If there was a doubt about which vowel to insert in a reading, the decision was made to use the one most likely to have appeared in the Meccan dialect of Arabic, the one Muhammad spoke. It was also Malik who declared Arabic to be the official language of his empire, a move that spurred the study of the language, which soon replaced Greek for official business. The Quran was not printed unto the 17th century; before that time every copy had been handwritten.

The current "standard edition" of the Quran was created in 1923, at the request of King Fuad of Egypt, by scholars at al-Azhar University in Cairo. What they created is considered *scriptio plena*, full, errorless, and complete. It is based on Asim of Kufa's (d. 744) reading and today is considered the *only* valid version of the Quran throughout the Muslim world. Therefore, unlike the Bible, there are now no alternate versions (*qiraah*) of Quranic passages admitted by Muslims, although small variations do exist between early versions. (At one time there were seven "allowable" readings or variants of the Quran that could be chanted by the professional chanters. All were recited by Gabriel to Muhammad, who told his companions, "The Quran has been revealed to me in seven different ways, so recite whichever is easier for you.")

INTERPRETING THE QURAN

Formal commentary on the Quran is called *tafsir*. While he was alive, Muhammad was considered the best interpreter of the Quran. Because it was revealed first to him (or, according to a more cynical view, he composed it himself), it only makes sense that he could best decipher its meaning. The formal practice of *tafsir,* or Quranic

interpretation, arose after his death to clarify certain ambigui-
ties within the text. Although *tafsir* began in a desultory, haphazard
fashion, it was soon systematized, and interpretation and clarifica-
tion proceeded verse by verse, indeed word by word, through the
Quran. The most comprehensive compendium of *tafsir* was compiled
by Persian-born, but Sunni, historian Abu Jafar ibn Muhammad ibn
Jarir at-Tabari (839–923), (hereafter Tabari), who wrote more than
30 books of commentary in Arabic, a second language for him. The
title of his best-known commentary is *The Comprehensive Exposition
of the Interpretation of the Verses of the Quran*, which proceeds verse by
verse through the entire Quran.)

Today various types of *tafsir* exist, some focusing on grammar, some
on history, and so forth. Some *tafsir* compare Quranic passages, others examine hadith and recollections of the Prophet's Companions.
Modern scholars are expected to know and understand the whole
1,400-year year history of commentary before adding their own interpretation. A scholar's personal reasoning (*tafsir bi al-ray*) is also
permitted if other sources fail to yield an answer. Famous interpreters
of the Quran include Tabari, Zamakhshari (d. 1144), Razi (d. 1209),
and Baydawi (d. c. 1291).

One division of Muslims, the Shia, considers its leaders, or Imams,
rather than legal scholars, to be infallible interpreters of the book. Indeed, the Sixth Imam, Jafar al-Sadiq, "The Truthful One" (d. 765),
wrote extensively and with great authority on this matter. Jafar was
especially interested in decoding the "ambiguous verses" of the Quran,
which he claimed could be comprehended by none but the Imams. He
said that the Quran could be understood on four levels: the literal level
(*ibarah*) for the common people, allusion (*isharah*) for scholars, the
hidden meaning (*lataif*) for the so-called "Friends of Allah," and the
spiritual truths (*haqaiq*) for the Prophet and the Imams. His allegorical
interpretation of the Quran is called *tawil*. In *tawil* exegesis, the reader
first examines the *zahir*, exterior or literal meaning of the passage, and
then delves into the *batin*, or interior.

As a result of his work, the Shia (especially the Ismaili branch) tend
to interpret the Quran more allegorically and less literally than the
Sunni. One popular 19th-century commentator, Sir Sayyid Ahmad
Khan (1817–1898), known for his rationalism, preferred to divide
Quranic verses into "essential" and "symbolic" verses. The first presented the fundamentals, while the second were more allegorical,
offering multiple interpretations that could be applied throughout the
ages. Sir Sayyid got himself into some hot water with more traditional

commentators, when he declared that certain Quranic events such as Muhammad's ascent into heaven should not be interpreted literally. However, his work was in line with age-old Shia thought.

BEFORE THE QURAN

Muslims believe that Allah gave humankind other holy books before the Quran. *And before this was the Scripture of Moses as a guide and a mercy. And this Scripture the Quran confirms it in the Arabic tongue, to warn the wrong-doers and as a glad tidings to those who do good* (46:12). Muslims maintain that these previous scriptures were intended for a limited period (because human beings had not reached a stage where they could understand the full message), or that they were corrupted and needed to be superseded. (The idea that previous scriptures have been invalidated by a new one is called supercessionism.) The old scripture remains in force until the new one is revealed, and those faithful Christians and Jews who died before the coming of Muhammad will still be saved. The Quran does not teach a new message but carries Allah's original words. In the Muslim view, therefore, Islam is not the newest of the world's great religions, but the oldest.

It is understood by Muslims that when there is a discrepancy between another scripture and the Quran, the latter is always correct. The Quran is the final and universal message. Muslims believe that it is entirely uncorrupted, unlike other scriptures, which are filled with human editions and amendments. Jews and Christians are accused of *tahrif,* or willfully distorting the scriptures that were given to them, especially of editing out those prophetic passages said to refer to Muhammad.

Earlier revealed texts include the Law of Moses (*Tawrat*), the Psalms of David (*Zabur*), the Books of the Prophets (*Suhuf,* which literally means "leaves"), and the Evangel of Jesus (*Injil*). This last book is unknown to Christians and is not the same as the Gospels in the Bible. (Some Muslims have tried to make the case that the *Injil* is the apocryphal Gospel of Barnabas, but their arguments are not convincing to Christian scholars.) In the Muslim view, although these other revelations were once perfect, they have been corrupted. The earliest revelation, that to Abraham, is considered by Muslims to have been lost.

WESTERN VIEWS OF THE QURAN

From the beginning, Westerners' view of the Quran was colored by prejudice. The first complete translation of the Quran into Latin, an international language that made it available to all European scholars, was done in 1143 by the Englishman Robert of Ketton (c. 1110–1160), archdeacon of the church of Pamploma. He worked under the auspices of Peter the Venerable (c. 1092–1156), whose own anti-Islamic writings went under the rubric of "Know your enemy." Robert had earlier penned *Saracen Fables or Lies and Ridiculous Tales from the Saracens*, to show where his sympathies lay. Still, his translation was interesting. He avoided a literal rendering and consulted Muslim commentaries, including those of the great historian and scholar Tabari. His unfortunate title, *The Law of the Pseudo-Prophet Muhammad*, is not encouraging, but his translation was not bad, especially in the earlier surahs.

The early English reformer John Wycliffe (d. 1384), who had read the Quran in translation, found it to be similar to Roman Catholic traditions in what he regarded as its cherry-picking and distortion of biblical passages, thus managing to insult both traditions at once.

The philosopher and theologian Nicholas of Cusa (1401–1464) attempted a careful discussion of the Quran in 1460, *The Sieve of the Quran*. In it he argued that the Quran could stand as an introduction to the Christian Gospel (which might have surprised Muslims). In this work he also honors the ethics and religiosity of Muhammad's followers.

Martin Luther (1483–1546) encouraged the publication of the Quran— only, however, so that what he regarded as its manifest errors and apostasy could be revealed. It was, Luther decided, a "shameful" book full of lies and "abomination."

In 1649 Alexander Ross published a translation amazingly titled *The Alcoran [The Quran] of Mahomet: Translated out of Arabique into French by the Sieur Du Ryer, Lord of Malezair, and Resident for the King of France at Alexandria, and Newly Englished for the Satisfaction of All That Desire to Look into Turkish Vanities, to Which is Prefixed the Life of Mahomet, . . . with a Needful Caveat, or Admonition, for Those Who Desire to Know What Use May Be Made of, or If There Be Danger in Reading, the Alcoran.* The translation bears only a vague resemblance to the original, possibly because Ross knew no Arabic, and his French wasn't very good either.

The first English translation of the Quran was produced in 1734 by George Sale (1697–1736), an English Orientalist and solicitor, along with his *Preliminary Discourse*. This work, commissioned by the Society for the Promotion of Christian Knowledge, presents on the whole a fair and even positive view of the text and of Muslims. But David Friedrich Megerlin (1698–1750), who made the first translation of the Quran into German in 1772, unhelpfully labeled it the "Turkish Bible." He included an etching of Muhammad (in itself automatically an insult to Muslims) titled "Muhammad, the False Prophet."

The veneration given to the Quran led to the art of calligraphy. Because Islam does not permit representational art, Muslim artists turned to calligraphy, which means "beautiful writing," for creative expression. Since the 11th century, most Qurans have been printed using the Nashki style of calligraphy, a flowing, cursive script that adapts well to pen and paper. The earlier, angular Kufic script was much more ornamented and, though very beautiful, was also hard to read, partly because it has no vowel signs.

Veneration was also revealed in Islamic architecture. The Taj Mahal, though most famous as a tomb, is also a tribute to Islam's holy book. The Taj Mahal was begun in 1632 as tomb for Mumtaz Mahal, who died the year before while giving birth to her 14th child. It was finished four years later. The grieving husband, Shah Jahan, spared no expense in making this building the most glorious ever constructed—and studded with quotations from the Quran. In fact, there are more quotes from the book at the Taj Mahal than on any other Muslim tomb. Most of them record the joys of Paradise, whose pleasures are suggested in the glorious garden in front of the tomb. The 99 names of Allah are also featured.

PROPHETS

Belief in prophets is an essential part of Islam. The prophet, by definition, speaks for Allah to others. All these men (and all were men) were specially favored by Allah: *Those are they unto whom We gave the Scripture and Command and prophethood* (6:84). (Many writers traditionally add the phrase "peace be upon him" or the initials "pbuh" whenever they mention Muhammad or any of the prophets.) For Muslims, prophets have three functions: to receive revelations from Allah, to live exemplary lives according to that message, and to teach others to do the same.

The Quran and Islam recognizes prophets prior to Muhammad. According to a widely quoted hadith, there have been 124,000 prophets. (The number 124,000 is probably a symbolic one representing infinity.) All were sent by Allah to teach the same basic message, and all are equal. *Say: "We believe in Allah, and in that which has been sent down on us and sent down on Abraham, Ishmael, Isaac and Jacob, and the Tribes, and that which was given to Moses and Jesus and the Prophets, of their Lord;*

we make no division between any of them, and to him we surrender" (2:136). Muhammad said, "The prophets are brothers by relationship; their mothers are different, but their religion is one."

According to Islamic tradition, a new prophet was raised up when the teachings of the earlier prophets were forgotten or corrupted. It has been suggested that the pre-Islamic Arabs might have felt slighted that they had received no prophetic revelation of their own and that Muhammad's message was one for the Arabs. (Prophets and messengers are both distinguished from mystics, people whose concern is to get knowledge of Allah in a special, intimate way, but who are not commanded to share Allah's message.) Prophets were sent to every people and nation; each brought the same message of *islam* or submission to the will of Allah: *For assuredly, We sent among every people a messenger with the command, "Serve Allah and shun wickedness"* (16:36). Even the prophets before Muhammad are considered "muslims" because they submitted to Allah. Today, Musa (Moses), Ibrahim (Abraham), and Isa (Jesus) are common Muslim names, as is, of course, Muhammad. Because all the prophets speak for Allah, all should be obeyed: *Each and every Messenger who was sent by Us was sent for the sole purpose that he should be obeyed under the sanction of Allah* (4:64).

The usual words referring to these men are *nabi* ("prophet") and *rasul* ("messenger"). All messengers are prophets, but not all prophets are messengers. A *nabi* is not one who foretells the future or soothsays, but one who has given himself completely to Allah and who spreads the word.

A *rasul*, or "messenger," is one who is entrusted with a scripture from Allah. The prophet may have received messages but was not necessarily given a scripture. There are only three recognized messengers in Islam: Moses, Jesus, and Muhammad. To each a scripture was revealed, in the language of the messenger. For Muhammad, therefore, *We have revealed to thee an Arabic Quran* (42:7). And *We have sent you (Muhammad) as a messenger unto mankind and Allah is sufficient as a witness* (4:79). According to Muslim belief, a messenger is assured success in his mission, but only Muhammad's teachings are said to be perfect and final and are fully preserved in the Quran.

BIBLICAL AND QURANIC PROPHETS

The names of prophets in the Bible and in the Quran are similar but do not exactly match up; each includes some names not listed in the other. Twenty-five prophets are mentioned in the Quran, of whom 21 are biblical characters. These include Adam, Abraham (Ibrahim), Lot (Lut), Noah (Nuh), Joseph (Yusuf), Zachariah (Zakariyya), Enoch (Idris), Elisha (al-Yasa), Elijah, Ishmael (Ismail), Isaac (Ishaq), Jacob (Yaqub), David (Dawud), Soloman (Sulyaman) Job (Ayyub), Jonas (Yunus), Moses (Musa), Aaron (Harun), Ezekiel (Dhul-kifl), John (Yahya) the Baptist, and Jesus (Isa). Muslims consider Adam to be the first prophet (*nabi*), because he was the first to whom Allah revealed himself (in Arabic, by the way). Jews and Christians do not consider some of these figures prophets, and it is not certain whether Muhammad was familiar with the biblical prophets Isaiah, Jeremiah, Amos, and Hosea.

The names of other prophets are unknown. *We have sent messengers before you—some of them we mentioned to you, and some we did not mention to you* (40:78). Muslim historian at-Tabari claimed that the Bible actually predicted Muhammad as well as Jesus in Isaiah 21:5–7, which talks about two leaders, one on an ass (Jesus) and one on a camel. No reasonable man, claimed Tabari, could imagine that anyone other than Muhammad could be referred to as a leader on a camel.

The only non-biblical prophets specifically mentioned in the Quran other than Muhammad were Hud, Shuayb, and Salih. Hud (who *may* have been the biblical Eber) was a prophet to the mysterious but materially well-off Ad people, who lived where Yemen and Oman are today; they disbelieved him and were destroyed by a wind. Salih's people, the historical tribe of Thamud of the land of Hajar, were killed off by an earthquake or thunderbolt, when they refused to listen to their prophet. Shuyab, whom Muslims believe to be identical with Jethro, Moses' father-in-law, was sent to the people of Midian. After Shuyab, Moses came. (These stories are mentioned very briefly, as if it is assumed the audience was already familiar with them.) The name Muhammad occurs only four times in the Quran, although "Prophet" is mentioned frequently, usually in the form of direct address.

Muslims believe that the Quran completes the revelations to the early prophets: *We believe in Allah and what had been revealed to us; in what was revealed to Abraham and Ismail, to Isaac and Jacob and the tribes, and in what was given to Moses and Jesus and the prophets from their lord. We do not make a distinction between any of them. For we submit to Allah* (3:84). All prophets were made sinless through the gift of divine knowledge. All were also protected by Allah from physical disabilities such as blindness and disfiguring diseases such as leprosy. While morally perfect, they were also tempted. Muhammad himself was twice tempted to sin, seduced by the thriving nightlife in Mecca.

On the first occasion be became absorbed in watching a wedding procession, which so exhausted him that he fell asleep, and on the second he was stopped by a "divine, sweet melody," and again he slept until the next day. "After that," he said, "I was never tempted to fall into vice."

Noah

Noah (Nuh) is considered a prophet in the Quran. He is mentioned 43 times in 28 surahs. Surah 11 ("Hud") is an account of the Flood, and Surah 71 ("Nuh") contains Allah's order to Noah to preach, Noah's sermon, and Noah's complaint to Allah about the ridicule he met with when he warned people about the Flood. In the Quran, the ark comes to rest on Mount Judi in Turkey rather than Mt. Ararat as in the Bible. The Quran does not include the narrative about Noah's drunkenness, which has a prominent place in the Bible. The Quran also classifies Noah's wife as a nonbeliever.

Abraham

It is Abraham (Ibrahim) who is considered the most important prophet before Muhammad; he is called the "friend of Allah," and he is mentioned in about 25 surahs and 245 verses. Surah 14 is even called "Ibrahim." Abraham is considered the father of the Arabic people through his eldest son, Ishmael (Ismail). Muslims sometimes say that the lives of Muhammad and Abraham are similar.

According to the Quran, Abraham was the first to submit himself to the will of Allah (2:131) and was therefore the "first muslim," although his own father Azar (not Terah as in the Bible) was an idol-maker. The Quran offers a dialogue between the two men, in which Azar points to the evening star Venus and says, "That is my Lord." As the men watch it set, Abraham says, "I do not worship things that undergo decline." (The biblical book of Joshua reports that Abraham's father worshipped "other gods," but not that he was an idol-maker.) It appears Abraham's father met with a bad end: *Neither did Abraham ask forgiveness for his father . . . when it was shown to him that he was enemy of Allah, he declared himself clear of him* (9:112).

Muslims believe Abraham arrived at the knowledge of monotheism through reason, even though he grew up among "idolaters." *I have surrendered myself to the Lord of all the worlds* (2:131). The Quran consistently holds up Abraham as a stern and unrelenting monotheist amidst the paganism of his day, long before the Jewish Torah (Tawrah) or Christian Gospel (Injil) made an appearance.

The Quranic Abraham, like the biblical one, had two sons. However, the Quran gives first honors to the elder Ishmael (Ismail), the putative ancestor of the Arabic people, whereas the Bible favors the younger Isaac, the progenitor of the Israelites. (The Bible acknowledges Ishmael as the firstborn and states that he received circumcision before Isaac.) Both sons were promised a multitude of progeny, and both were said to be present at the burial of Abraham (Gen. 25:9). There is a disagreement about the status of Hagar, Ishmael's mother. According to the Bible, Hagar was a serving maid and not a legitimate wife; her son could therefore *not* be the true heir of Abraham. In Islam, Hagar was a true wife, and her son the rightful heir.

The Quranic story of the sacrifice of Abraham differs from the biblical version. The Quran indicates (although it doesn't actually *say*) that it was Ishmael, not Isaac, who was the near-victim (37:99–113). The Quran also says that Satan tried to persuade them that only a devil would urge someone to sacrifice a son, but Ishmael (a "full-grown youth") and Abraham resisted the temptation. In the Quran the son was aware of the divine demand and acquiesced to it; in the Bible, Isaac was kept in the dark. The event is portrayed in brutal terms in Surah 37: *They both surrendered to Allah's will and the boy was flung down on his face.* This was at Ishmael's request—he did not want to see the pain on his father's face.

The Bible and Quran agree that Hagar and Ishmael were exiled from Abraham's household after Sarah bore Isaac, but from that point the stories differ. Muslims say that Hagar and Ishmael eventually came to Mecca. They almost died of thirst, but a well (Zamzam) sprang up miraculously to succor them. (Its water was said to come directly from Paradise and is used today for the taps in the Grand Mosque.) Abraham learned that Hagar and Ishmael were alive and went to Mecca to meet them. Together Ishmael and Abraham purified and rebuilt the Kaaba (2:124–129), first constructed by Adam. There is even a stone in the courtyard of the mosque called the *maqam Ibrihim*, from which Abraham directed building operations. There is no historical proof of any of this, of course, or that Abraham ever came to Arabia—or even that such a person as Abraham ever existed in the first place.

In Islamic tradition, Ishmael married an Amalakite woman. The marriage was not a success, and he remarried a woman from the tribe of Jurham. This couple became the founders of Muhammad's own tribe, the Quraysh. Ishmael and Hagar are said to be buried beneath a low curved wall called the Rukn next to the Kaaba.

Muslims believe that the descendants of Abraham abrogated their covenant with Allah. *And when his Lord tried Abraham with certain words, he fulfilled them. Allah said, "Surely I will make you a leader (imam) of men." Abraham said, "And of my offspring?" "My covenant does not include the unjust," said he* (2:124). This is clear indication that the Muslims regard the compact between Allah and the Jewish people as provisional, having been broken by the "unjust" behavior of Abraham's descendants.

Joseph

The Quran's 12th surah, the only really sustained narrative in the entire book, is devoted to Joseph, and makes for exciting reading. It includes Joseph's attempted seduction by Potiphar's wife, although with some elaboration and interesting differences from the biblical account, including some detective work to show how Joseph must have been innocent of the charges against him. The Quran and the Jewish Midrash also include a passage about Joseph's being so handsome that some women at the dining table cut themselves with knives in their excitement at viewing so handsome a man. (The Midrash explains that the ladies had had the knives to eat fruit with, although this is not made clear in the Quran.)

Moses

Moses (Musa) is yet another well-known prophet in Islam. Although Moses gets a lot of mention in the Quran, some of the material relating to him would be unfamiliar to Bible readers. For example, Surah 18 relates a long passage in which Moses searches for the confluence of two rivers, an event never mentioned in the Bible. The story actually contains fragments of the Epic of Gilgamesh, the Syriac "Lay of Alexander," and the Jewish legend of Elijah and Rabbi Joshua ben Levi.

Solomon

King Solomon seems to be unlikely prophet. The Quran agrees with Jewish commentary that Solomon could talk to birds (although this is not reported in the Bible). It also reports that Solomon engaged the help of demons to help him build the Temple in Jerusalem, another event omitted in the biblical account.

Mary, Jesus, and John the Baptist

Of greatest interest to Christians, perhaps, is the place of Jesus in the Quran. Many might be surprised to know that Muslims believe in the Virgin Birth and honor Mary. Indeed, Mary is the only woman *specifically* named in the Quran (others are just called the wife of so-and-so, sister of so-and-so, or something similar); the 19th surah is devoted to her. Like Abraham, Mary submitted perfectly to Allah's will. She is regarded as a "woman of truth" (5:75) and a devout servant of Allah (66:12). Indeed, Allah preferred her "above all the women of creation" (3:42). She is considered to be the most perfect woman who ever lived, and the Quran contains more information about her than does the New Testament.

The Quran refers to Jesus 23 times as "Isa ibn Maryam" (Jesus son of Mary), a phrase occurring only once in the New Testament (Mark 6:3). The fact that he is *not* called the son of Joseph underscores Islamic agreement with Christians that Mary was a virgin when she conceived Jesus. *Remember her who preserved her chastity, into whom We breathed a life from us, and made her and her son a token for mankind* (21:91). And further: *O Mary! Allah gives thee good news of a son through a Word from him! His name shall be the Messiah, Jesus son of Mary, honored in this world and in the next, and of those who are granted nearness to Allah!* (3.45)

The Quran details the annunciation in the following way:

She withdrew from her family to a place in the East. . . . Then We sent her Our angel, and he appeared before her as a man in all respects. She said, "I seek refuge from you to Allah Most Gracious! Do not come near me, if you fear Allah." He said, "No, I am only a messenger from your Lord, to announce to you the gift of a holy son." She said, "How shall I have a son, seeing that no man has touched me, and I am not unchaste?" He said, "So it will be." Your Lord says, "That is easy for Me, and We wish to appoint him as a Sign unto men, and a Mercy from Us. It is a matter so decreed." (19:16–21)

This recounting is similar to that found in Luke. Being the product of a virgin birth, however, does not, in the Islamic view, make Jesus a son of God; it means only that he was born by the will of Allah.

The Quran even discusses the pregnancy, not only of Mary but also of her presumed mother, Anna, and Mary's consequent birth. In the New Testament, Mary's mother is not identified, although there is an Anna (the Greek form of Hannah) mentioned in Luke who is described as a prophetess. In the Quran, Hannah has been promised a child by Allah and was expecting a son. However, *When she was delivered, she said: "O my Lord! Behold! I am delivered of a female child!"* However, Allah seemed pleased, saying, *I have named her Mary, and I commend her and her offspring to thy protection from the Evil One, the Rejected* (3:36).

The newborn Mary was also apparently the subject of some angry discussion in Heaven among the angels: *You [Muhammad] were not present with them when they threw their pens to know which of them should be the guardian of Mary, nor were you present with them when they quarreled thereupon* (3:44).

The Quran records Mary's delivery of Jesus in some detail (which the New Testament does not) and shows how Allah provided for her during her ordeal. *And the pangs of childbirth drove her unto the trunk of the palm tree. She said: "Oh, would that I had died before this and had become a thing of naught, forgotten!" But a voice cried to her from beneath the palm-tree: "Grieve not! for thy Lord hath provided a rivulet beneath thee; And shake towards yourself the trunk of the palm-tree: It will let fall fresh ripe dates upon thee"* (19:23–25). Although most women in labor might not be particularly relieved to have fresh dates dropping on them from the trees, it was the thought that counted—the idea that Allah would provide during her severe travail. The source of this story is the apocryphal gospel the "History of, Nativity of Mary and the Savior's Infancy."

In the Bible, Jesus is born in a stable, and he was later attended by Wise Men (Matthew) or shepherds (Luke). There is no mention of palm trees, although curiously, Maya, the mother of the Buddha, was said to have given birth holding onto the branch of a tree.

The Quran also calls Mary the "sister of Aaron" (19:28), thus linking her with the prophet Moses, whose sister was also called Maryam (Miriam) in the Bible. Scholars disagree about whether labeling the Virgin Mary "sister of Aaron" is an honorific or meant to be taken literally (which would be a problem, given there are about 1,400 years separating the two "Maryams"). Mary is also called the "daughter of Imran" (66:12, 3:31), a designation not known in the Bible.

John the Baptist is a prophet whose annunciation seems to paired with that of Jesus. In the Quran, some angels announce to the elderly Zachariah that his barren wife will produce a son to be named John.

The point of the story implicitly seems to be that one is not necessarily divine, even one's advent is announced by angels. By coupling the stories, it lessens the impact of Jesus' "miraculous" birth.

Following the story of John the Baptist is that of Jesus birth (3:45–51)

Here is the story:

When the angels said, "O Mary, Allah gives you the good news of Word from Him: his name is the Messiah Jesus son of Mary—eminent in the world and the hereafter, and one of the intimate. And he will speak with people while his in the cradle and when advanced in years, and will be one of the virtuous. She said, "My Lord how can I have a child when no man has touched me?" He said, "Thus does Allah create what he wishes. When he decides on a matter, all he says to it is 'Be!' and it comes to be. And he will teach him the Book and wisdom, and the Torah and the Evangel."

Similarities between the New Testament and Quran are broad. Both claim that the birth was miraculous. Both claim Mary was a virgin visited by angels (only Gabriel in the New Testament, several in the Quran). She is told in both scriptures that the child will be named Jesus. Mary is quite surprised in both scriptures by the news.

Muhammad seemed fascinated by the story of Jesus and mentions him frequently, although his knowledge seems largely based on apocryphal rather than canonical Gospels. Muslims regard Jesus as a wonder-worker, the greatest of all time. The Quran has the infant Jesus speaking in full paragraphs, exclaiming from his mother's arms: *Verily, I am the servant of God. He hath given me the Book and he hath made me a Prophet* (19:30). The Quran details some of the miracles, including healing lepers and the blind, making the dead rise, and breathing life into clay birds (3:43). This last is not found in the New Testament but was making its rounds in the apocryphal literature. Although not a son of God, Jesus is considered *almost* superhuman; in fact, the Quran calls him the "Messiah," meaning one who is anointed. It also refers to Jesus as "the word of Allah," and Muslims believe him to be a prophet to Israel, which is more than the Jews believe. *We sent other apostles and after those Jesus son of Mary. We gave him the gospel and put compassion and mercy in the hearts of his followers* (57:27). However, the Quran is careful to state that Jesus does what he does by permission of Allah only. (Among Muslims, the mystical Sufi sect holds Jesus in the highest regard.)

Muslims are careful to refer to Jesus as the "servant of God" rather than as his son. They reject the idea of the Trinity, and believe that Jesus never claimed to be the God's son or divine in any way: *Indeed, they disbelieve who say, "God is the third of three (in a trinity)," when there is no god but one God. If they desist not from what they say, truly, a painful punishment will befall the disbelievers among them. Would they not rather repent to Allah and ask His forgiveness? For Allah is Oft-Forgiving, Most Merciful. The Messiah (Jesus), son of Mary, was no more than a messenger* (5:73–75).

And again: *Verily! The Messiah, Jesus the son of Mary, was only a messenger of Allah and His word which he conveyed unto Mary and a soul from Him. So believe in Allah and His messengers "Three!" (The Trinity). Cease! It is better for you! Allah is the only god. It is far removed from his transcendent majesty that he should have a son* (4:171).

And further: *Verily, Jesus was nothing but a slave upon whom We bestowed favor and made an example for the children of Israel* (43:59).

Muslims do not believe Jesus died on the cross. They maintain believe that Jesus either survived the crucifixion or was rescued from it by Allah and then ascended into Heaven like Elijah (3:55, 4:157–158).

> *And for claiming that they killed the Messiah, Jesus, son of Mary, the messenger of Allah: In fact, they never killed him, they never crucified him—they were made to think that they did. All factions who are disputing in this matter are full of doubt concerning this issue. They possess no knowledge; they only conjecture. For certain, they never killed him. . . . Instead, Allah raised him to him; Allah is Almighty, Most Wise. Everyone among the people of the scripture was required to believe in him before his death. On the Day of Resurrection, he will be a witness against them.* (4:157–159)

In Muslim folklore, another person was substituted in place of Jesus, but this theory does not appear in the Quran. This was an idea also floated about by several heretical Christian sects.

Muslims reject the Christian doctrine of atonement. In the Islamic view, no person can suffer for the sins of another, so there is no doctrine of atonement or vicarious suffering. Thus Jesus could not have suffered for us. Nor is there need for a savior because there is no original sin from which to be saved. Thus, Islam (along with Judaism) denies the central tenets of Christianity: the crucifixion and resurrection of Jesus, the Trinity, and the doctrine that Jesus was the Son of God. (The main difference here between Islam and Judaism is that Islam regards Jesus as a prophet; Judaism does not.)

THE DAY OF JUDGMENT

According to Islam, the Judgment Day will come and end life on earth forever. The Quran depicts the Day as a fearsome event, and the Quran gives it a good deal of attention. The Quranic word for it, *qiyamat*, appears about 70 times. Other terms are used as well: the Day of Reckoning, the Day of Separation, Resurrection, Day of Gathering, the Day of Standing Up, and so forth. Together they are mentioned over 300 times. Many of the surahs also have terrifying, apocalyptic titles such as "The Terror" (56), "The Splitting" (82), and "The Earthquake" (99). Muslims do not search the Quran for clues as to when the Earth will end, as some Christians do the Bible, but at the appointed hour, the angel Israfil will sound the note that will bring on Judgment Day; apparently that is his only job. Surah 74 declares, *When the Trump is sounded, that day will be a harsh day, for the unbelievers not easy.* Judgment Day will come once only; there is no notion of cyclical time or a return. When Judgment comes, the books on our lives will be closed forever.

Although the precise timing of the great event is known only to Allah, *what* will happen is clear. Not only is every individual doomed, but the earth itself will come to a crashing end. Sura 81 ("The Darkening"), for example, poetically declares,

> *When the sun shall be folded up*
> *And when the stars shall fall*
> *And when the mountains shall be set in motion*
> *And when the pregnant she-camels are abandoned,*
> *And when the wild beast shall be gathered together,*
> *And when the seas shall boil*
> *And when souls shall be paired with their bodies*
> *And when the girl child that was buried alive shall be asked*
> *For what crime was she put to death*
> *And when the leaves of the Book shall be unrolled*
> *And when the heaven shall be stripped away*
> *And when Hell shall be made to blaze*
> *And when Paradise shall be brought near*
> *Every soul shall know what it hath produced.* (81:1–14)

In a corroborating hadith, Muhammad said (in response to a test question by Gabriel), "The slave girl will give birth to her mistress and you will see barefooted, naked, destitute herdsmen competing in constructing lofty buildings." The precise meaning of these words is disputable, but they indicate an upheaval in the normal course of events.

On that day, there will be a terrible, deafening cataclysm that will destroy the earth and everything on it. There will be no escape: *Wherever you are, death will find you, even if you are in mighty towers* (4:78). And the idea of a pregnant camel, a most valuable possession, being neglected betokens nothing less momentous than the end of the world.

Right before the Last Day will come the Last Days. How many Last Days will come before the Last Day is not revealed, but they will be ushered in by the al-Mahdi, or Rightly Guided One. For the Shia, he is the Twelfth Imam, now in occultation. The Sunni believe that after the al-Mahdi comes, Jesus will return to earth to fight the forces of evil led by al-Dajjal, the Great Charlatan or Antichrist. The forces of good will prevail, and Jesus will rule the world for an undisclosed period of time, after which he will die and be buried alongside Muhammad in Medina. Then the true Last Day will arrive.

On the Day of Judgment, every human being has accountability (*Hisab*) for his own actions. *Do you think that we created you for nothing, or that you would not return and give account?* (23:115). There is no concept of reincarnation in Islam; we are given one life only, a test and preparation for the world to come. To pass the test we must, to borrow a Christian idea, be "in the world but not of the world." Or as Muhammad remarked, "Be in the world as though you were a stranger or a traveler." The Hereafter is of infinite duration, so it looms as much more important than our brief earthly existence.

Everyone will be alone on the Day of Judgment, with no one to intercede for him before Allah. *A man shall flee from his brother and his mother and his father and his wife and his children. Each one of them that day will have enough concern of his own to make him indifferent to the others* (80:33 ff).

THE BOOK OF DEEDS

On the Last Day, everyone will be judged. Each person will receive his "book of deeds," and one's final destiny depends on the relative weight of good versus bad actions. *Those whose balance of good deeds is heavy will attain salvation, but those whose balance is light will have lost their souls and abide in hell forever* (23:102–103). This idea of balance (*mizan*) may have been borrowed from the Zoroastrians, who held a similar doctrine. Gabriel holds the scales, half of which is suspended over Paradise and half over Hell. Good deeds, including acts of worship, are given special bonus points called *hasanat*. As mentioned earlier, every good deed is multiplied by 10, or according to another estimate, 700. Sins, however, are always counted in singles.

Muhammad said, "Fear Allah wherever you are, and follow up a bad deed with a good one and it will wipe it out." He also touches on the role of intent: "He who has intended a good deed and not done it, Allah records it as a full good deed; but if he has intended it and done it, Allah records it as ten good deeds to seven hundred times, or many times over. If he has intended a bad deed and has not done it, Allah records it as a full good deed; if he has intended it and has done it, Allah writes it down as one bad deed." This shows the mercy of Allah, given that a good deed counts more in one's favor than a bad deed counts against it. Muhammad also provided a simple formula for discovering what the good is. He said, "Consider what your ears would like to hear said of you by people after you have left their company and then do that. Consider what your ears would not like to head said of you, and avoid doing that."

If the record book is handed into the right hand, the person will be sent to Paradise; if into the left, hellfire awaits: *We have prepared for the evildoers a fire, whose pavilion encompasses them. If they call for help, they will be helped with water like molten copper that will scald their faces. How dreadful a drink and how evil a resting place* (18: 29).

Everyone is responsible for his or her own actions, and every community will be judged by the revelations brought by its own prophets, all of whom are considered *muslimun*, those who have submitted themselves to Allah (2:136).

Still, it is not always easy to know who will be saved. As an old Islamic story goes, the Muslim humorist Ashab was told to stop making jokes all the time and get serious about the Afterlife. "All right," said Ashab. "I have heard from Nafi, on the authority of Umar, that the Prophet listed two qualities as being essential for salvation."

"By Allah, that would be good to know," said Ashab's companion. "What are the two qualities?"

"I have no idea. Nafi forgot one of them and I forgot the other," replied the inveterate comedian.

On the Day of Judgment, all will rise from the dead and be sent to Heaven or Hell. Rewards and punishments will be handed out, similar to what we know on earth, but unimaginably magnified and lengthened. There is no middle state or purgatory: it is either Paradise or Hell.

For those who doubt the Allah's ability to raise the dead, the Quran offers this analogy: *And among his signs is this: You see the earth barren and desolate, but when we send down rain, it is stirred to life and yields increase. Verily, he who gives life to the dead earth can surely give life to the dead. Lo! He has power over all things (41:39).* And further: *Verily We shall give life to the dead, and We record all that they send before and that they leave behind, and We have taken account of all things in a clear book* (36:12).

JUDGMENT

On the great Day, everyone will be lined up behind the one they followed. Muslims, of course, will stand behind Muhammad. Sun worshippers will line up behind the sun, and moon worshippers behind the moon. Exceedingly evil people will be sent to Hell right away. The rest, when the Judgment is finished, will cross a bridge called Sirat, an image borrowed directly from Zoroastrianism. The most virtuous will skim lightly over the bridge straight into Paradise; the rest will follow. As they walk, the bridge becomes razor thin and jagged. Evil people tumble into the roaring flames of Hell; the rest manage to achieve Paradise.

No matter how terrifying the Last Day may be, however, there is hope: *And never give up hope of Allah's soothing mercy, except those who have no faith* (12:87). And further, *If anyone does a good deed, be they male or female, and has faith, they will enter Paradise and no injustice will be done to them* (4:124). In one place the Quran promises a "tenfold" reward for good deed done (6:160). In another place (2:261) it offers a 700-fold return. However, mercy is apparently limited to Muslims: *Those who give the lie to Our messages and scorn them in their pride, the gates of heaven shall not be opened; and they shall not enter paradise, any more than a twisted rope can pass through a needle's eye* (7:40). Muhammad's wife Aishah reported that some of her nonbelieving relatives had fed the poor, and she asked if that would be of any help on Judgment Day. Muhammad replied that it would not avail. Jews, Christians, and recalcitrant Meccans were equally doomed: *And whoever seeks a religion other than Islam, it will not be accepted from him and he will be one of the losers in the Hereafter* (3:85).

As in Christian doctrine, body and soul will be reunited at the Last Day, and the Quran leaves no doubt about Allah's power to make it happen. Since Allah created mankind from *dust, then a drop, then from a clot, then from a lump of flesh* (22:5), it should be easy to acknowledge that he can raise the dead. *Then how can you reject faith in Allah, seeing that you were without life and he gave you life; then he causes you to die and will bring you to life again, and again, to him will you return* (2:28).

The people of Mecca openly scoffed at the idea of bodily resurrection: *What? When we are dead and become dust and bones, shall we indeed be raised up? And our forefathers of old?* (37:16–17). The nomadic Bedouins were also a hard sell. The Quran marks them as *confirmed in unbelief and hypocrisy* (9:97), reflecting the prejudice sedentary tribes (like Muhammad's) bore the desert peoples. They challenged Muhammad: *That which is ahead of us is our first and only death, and we shall not be raised to life again. So then, bring forth our forefathers as witnesses, if what you claim is true* (44:35–36). They also stated, *There is only our life in the world; we die and we live and nothing destroys us but Time* (45:24). Allah's response was, *Say: Allah creates life in you, then causes you to die and gathers you on the day of resurrection* (45:25–26).

The Quran emphasizes again and again that if Allah can create the world, he can destroy it and resurrect it again as he pleases: *Does man think that we shall not reassemble his bones on the day of Resurrection? No, We are able to remake his very fingertips* (75:3–4). The choice of "fingertips" is significant, for it implies the human beings' entire reach. Finger bones are also among the most delicate bones of the body, so if Allah can remake something that delicate, nothing is beyond his ability. Further, as we know today, each "finger-tip" is unique. It is a powerful and complete image.

The Fate of Christians

Christians, who maintain that God has a son, are singled out for special mention: *And we shall drive the sinners to Hell like thirsty cattle driven down to water. None shall have the power of intercession, except one who has received permission from Allah Most Gracious. They say: Allah Most Gracious has begotten a son! Indeed you have put forth a thing most monstrous! At it the skies are ready to burst, the earth to split asunder, and the mountains to fall down in utter ruin that they should invoke a son for Allah Most gracious* (19:86–91).

According to a hadith,

Then the Jews will be summoned, and it will be said to them: what did you worship? They will say: We worshipped Ezekiel, son of Allah. It will be said to them: You tell a lie; Allah had never a spouse or a son. What do you want now? They will say: We feel thirsty, O Lord! Quench our thirst. They will be directed to a certain place and asked: Why don't you go there to drink water? Then they will be pushed towards the Fire . . . and they will fall into it. Then the Christians will be summoned and it will be said to them: What did you worship? They will say: We worshipped Jesus, son of Allah. It will be said to them: You lie; Allah did not take for himself either a spouse or a son. Then it will be said to them: What do you want? They will say: Thirsty we are, O Lord! Quench our thirst. They will be directed to a certain direction and asked: Why don't you go there to get water? But they will be pushed and gathered together towards the Hell. . . . They would fall into the Fire till no one is left except he who worshipped Allah, be he pious or sinful.

But in another hadith, Muhammad seems of a more generous turn of mind: "If anyone testifies that there is no god but Allah alone, who has no partner, that Muhammad is his servant messenger, that Jesus is Allah's servant and messenger, the son of his handmaid, his word which he cast into Mary and a spirit from him, and that Paradise and Hell are real, Allah will cause him to enter Paradise no matter what he was done."

BARZAKH: THE TIME BETWEEN

The period between one's death and the Judgment Day is Barzakh, or "The Partition," a place where time has no meaning. Muhammad drew a vivid picture of the plight of the deceased person being carried to the grave. "When the coffin is ready and people lift it above their shoulders, if the body is that of a virtuous person, it urges, 'Take me ahead, take me ahead.' But if it is the body of an evil-doer, it says, 'Curses! Where are you taking me?' Its screams are heard by everything except human beings, and if they could hear it, they would faint."

Once buried, the corpse can even hear the departing footfalls of the mourners. In the grave, good people will experience expanded horizons, sweet odors, and dry, comfortable warmth, but the evil will feel cramped, cold, and stinking already. Everyone will encounter Malik ul-Mawt of Azrael, the angel of death, who is responsible for taking the soul away from the body. Virtuous people will have their souls gently removed; the sinful will have theirs ripped out violently. The deceased's soul hovers around the body for a time and can apparently see everything that is going on; however, it cannot communicate with the living. Sometime before the actual moment of resurrection, and while the body is still in the grave, two angels named Nakir and Munkar will question the soul about its activities, faith, and prophet.

HELL

The Quran is clear that Heaven and Hell are physical states—not just conditions of the mind or states of the soul—that existed before the creation of the world. Although ultimately they are beyond our capacity to grasp (32:17), we can grasp something of their nature. Hell is a place of absolute horror. The Quran is much more graphic about Hell than the Bible is. It is hot and smelly and filled with pitch-black flames, blazing winds, and salt wells from which the evil dead must drink without ceasing. It boasts a tree called Zaqqum, whose roots are in the very bottom of the inferno. Zaqqum produces a bitter devil's head fruit that the dead must consume: *Surely the tree of the Zaqqum is the food of the sinful. Like dregs of oil; it shall boil in their bellies, like the boiling of hot water* (44:43–46). Another item on the menu of the damned will be the pus oozing from their own wounds.

Hell is of infinite capacity. It has seven gates and 19 angelic guards, led by the angel Malik, who will supervise the tortures of the damned and who will throw them back if they try to escape, explaining to them that Hell is just what they deserve for the bad lives they have lived. The image of Hell as an ever-burning fire is probably the most potent: *They that deny our revelations we will burn in Fire. No sooner will their skins be consumed than we will give them other skins so that they may truly taste the scourge. Allah is might and wise* (4:56). The worst district of Hell is Al Ghayy, which is so awful that the denizens dwelling in the other six levels pray 400 times a day just to avoid it.

It appears that for some people, including those who commit the sin of *shirk*, the period of Hell-suffering will be permanent, but for others only temporary (11:107–108); Allah in his infinite mercy will release them. Some suggest that believing Muslims may have to endure Hell only as long as it takes to purge them of their sins. This may sound a little like Purgatory, a doctrine Muslims do not accept. Other very serious sins according to the Prophet were to kill one's child for motives of economy and to commit adultery with one's neighbor's wife.

There is a partition called Aaraf between Heaven and Hell: *And between the two is a veil and on al-Aaraf are men who know each other by marks and they shall cry out to the fellows of Paradise, "Peace be upon you!" They cannot enter it although they so desire* (7:44).

The most common term for Hell is *al-nar* ("the Fire"), although other epithets are sometimes employed: *al-hawiya* ("the Abyss"), *jahannam* ("the Depths"), *saqar* ("the Scorching"), *al-Hutama* ("the Shattering") and *Sair* ("the Furnace").

Muhammad was granted a vision of the damned:

> Then I saw men with lips like camels; in their hands were pieces of fire like stones which they thrust into their mouths and would then come out of their posteriors. I was told that these were those who devoured the wealth of orphans. . . . Then I saw men with good fat meat before them side by side with lean stinking meat, eating the latter and leaving the former. These are those who forsook the women which Allah had permitted them, and went after those He has forbidden. . . . Then I saw women hanging by their breasts. These women had fathered bastards on their husbands.

And so on.

Hell also seems to be portable. On the Last Day, Allah will order Hell to be "brought near." Those who reject Allah and his book will be placed in this state of horrific pain; however, they will be forced to recognize the justice of their fate. *When they are cast inside they will hear the terrible drawing in of its breath even as it blazes forth, bursting with fury. Every time a group is thrown in, its keepers will ask, "Didn't a Warner come to you?" They will reply, "Yes. A Warner did come, but we rejected him and said that Allah never sent anything and that he was greatly in error. If only we had listened or used our intelligence we would not now be people of the fire"* (67:7–10).

(Heaven)

Quite naturally, Paradise is the opposite of Hell. It is absolute bliss, both physically and spiritually. Believers will enter *the gardens of Paradise beneath which rivers flow. They will dwell there forever* (98:7–8). As desert folk, the early Muslims considered a garden the very nicest place they could think of. Paradise has eight gates, each representing a major good deed, such as *Salat* (prayer) or *Jihad* (struggle). There is even a gate called Rayan, reserved for people who were most obedient in fasting. Two angels guard each gate, calling to those qualified to enter there. Those who excelled in several areas of endeavor can enter by any gate they choose.

There will be no pain, sadness, illness, or boredom in Heaven. All desires will be fulfilled, and the bodies of the saved will be restored to a perfect, beautiful condition. The resurrected will sit on cushions in a heavenly mansion. They will wear green silk robes with silver buckles, sipping such heavenly beverages as spring water and wine sprinkled with musk. Wine is not allowed to living Muslims, but in Paradise the faithful can indulge all they like. It will not make them drunk, no matter how much they imbibe. Food will be served too: fowl, fruit, honey, and cake. Most wondrous of all is the magical, softly flowing fountain Salsabil (76:17–18). Those who drink of it will undertake a mystical excursion through the mysteries of existence. Muslims often point out that the Gospel of Luke also seems to intimate a Paradise of food and drink: "You shall eat and drink at the table of my father" (22:30).

Most Muslims take the depictions of Heaven literally, like Hell, although the Quran allows room for a more spiritual interpretation: *In Heaven I will prepare for the righteous believer what no eye has ever seen, no ear has ever heard, and what the deepest mind could never imagine* (32:17).

One will be reunited with one's spouses, but there will be no angels; they have their own realm. There are *houris*, however, our companions in Paradise. The word comes from the Arabic *haura*, or "woman with dark eyes." Every once in a while, someone attempts to show that *houri* is related to the English word "whore," but there is no linguistic link between the two terms. "Whore" is derived from an Indo-European word; *houri* is Semitic and comes from an entirely different source. It is usually understood to mean "virgin," but many commentators say that means only that their souls are pure. The "full-breasted" (78:33) *houris* are both voluptuous *and* pure. A rival definition insists that *houris* could be male or female. A few commentators suggest that the term refers to a variety of white raisins, but that is a minority viewpoint, luckily for all but true raisin aficionados. The Islamic Paradise also includes a few blessed animals, including Noah's dove, the ram Abraham sacrificed, and the fish that swallowed Jonah. The mystical creature that bore Muhammad to Heaven is there, and according to tradition, so is Katmir, a legendary guard dog. Other animals may go there also.

The glories of Heaven go beyond the best things that this world can offer: *Made glamorous or people is the love of desirable things— women, sons, gold and silver piled in heaps, branded horses, cattle, and tilled land. This is the provision of worldly life, whereas with Allah lies the good return . . . gardens with streams flowing underneath—in them they will live forever—chaste spouses and Allah's pleasure* (3:14–17).

Getting to Heaven has nothing to do with earthly riches and delights. *Wealth and children are the attractive things of this life, but good deeds are the things which last in the sight of your Lord as the basis for reward and the best thing to rest your hopes on* (18:46). When a Muslim dies, he can take only his faith (*iman*) and the record of his deeds. And despite attempts of certain Muslim and non-Muslim readers, there is not a single verse in the Quran that guarantees "martyrs" in the cause of Islam more privileges in Heaven than the ordinary believer.

CHAPTER 2

Essential Elements of Islamic Practice

All Muslims are expected to put their faith into action (orthopraxy); mere "right belief" (orthodoxy) is not enough. Yet acting rightly was not meant to be difficult, and people are not to go to extremes. Muhammad said, "Religion is easy, and if one exerts himself too much in religion it will overpower him; so act rightly and keep to the mean and be of good cheer and ask for divine help at morning and evening and during a part of the night." The Quran itself has the believers saying, *And our Lord, do not lay on us a burden the way you laid in on those before us* (2:286). To make religion easier to practice, Islam is famously based on its Five Pillars (*arkan al-Islami*). Each pillar serves to deepen understanding, aid faith, and help the believer achieve a disciplined and holy way of life.

THE FIVE PILLARS OF ISLAM

The Five Pillars are listed in various hadith, although not enumerated as such specifically in the Quran. The Five Pillars are (1) the Declaration of Faith (*shahadah*); (2) Prayers (*salat*) five times a day, at dawn, noon, afternoon, sunset, and nightfall; (3) Almsgiving (*zakat*); (3) Fasting (*sawm*) during Ramadan from dawn to dark; and (5) Pilgrimage (*hajj*) to Mecca at least once during one's lifetime. Of the Five Pillars, only the fourth, *zakat*, is dedicated to human beings; all the rest belong to Allah.

DECLARATION OF FAITH (*SHAHADAH*): THE FIRST PILLAR

The First Pillar of Islam is a declaration of faith, or *shahadah*. It underscores the uniqueness of Allah and the centrality of Mohammed as his prophet; it is the call to prayer and is inscribed on flags and coins in Islamic countries. *Shahadah* means "witness" or "testimony," and this is what one testifies: "There is no God but Allah, and Muhammad is his messenger" (*La ilaha illa llah, Muhammadun rasul Allah*). Some say the words "I testify" (*Ash-hadu*) should be inserted before each clause of the *shahadah*. Curiously, these precise words in this order do not show up anywhere in the Quran. The formulation is found *in whole* only in the hadith, although its constituent clauses appear frequently in the Quran.

It is absolutely obligatory to recite the *shahadah* at least once in a Muslim's lifetime and should be uttered at least five times a day during prayer. The more frequently it is said, the better, following Muhammad's advice to his followers to "refresh their faith." When asked how to do this, he responded, "By saying the *shahadah* much and often."

To become a Muslim formally, one of sound mind over the age of puberty must say the *shahadah*, ideally in the presence of witnesses. It does not have to be said in Arabic, but it must be said *sincerely* and with *understanding* of what it means.

The first part of the *shahadah* declares all gods false except Allah. This includes not only idols of stone and wood, but also human beings, ideologies, nations, material goods, or anything else that serves to distract the believer from the true Lord of the universe. The second part declares the centrality of Muhammad as the Seal of the Prophets and role model for humankind. Muslims believe that Muhammad's words and life were constantly guided by Allah and are thus deserving of obedience and emulation.

PRAYER (*SALAT*): THE SECOND PILLAR

In Islam, prayer (singular *salah*, plural *salat*) comes before everything else—before work, before food, before sleep. The command that *salat* be executed five times a day comes directly from the Quran; the manner in which those prayers are to be performed is found in the Sunnah, or tradition of Islam. Islam places more importance on *salat* than on any other ritual. Yet prayer, although a duty, is never regarded as a hardship.

The word *salah* originally means "connection," a wonderful way of thinking about prayer. According to a beautiful hadith, prayer is light. Its purpose is to put the believer in a proper relationship with Allah, so that he or she always remembers the source of the blessings in life.

Muhammad said, "Whoever offers their *salat* regularly and properly will find that it will be a light for him on the Last Day, a proof of his faith and a means whereby he will be saved. But whoever does not offer *salat* regularly and carefully will find that it won't be a light for him, or a proof of faith or a way to salvation." Simple good intentions or even good works are not enough; prayer to the one and only god is at the heart of Islam.

According to the Quran, *Salat restrains from shameful and unjust deeds* (29:45). It also purifies, for the Prophet noted, "The five set prayers are like a stream of fresh water, flowing in front of your house, into which you plunge five times a day. Do you think that would leave any dirt on your body? The five prayers remove sins, just as water removes dirt."

Islam has made prayer into an institution. It was not a matter left to individual choice to decide how many times to pray, or even what to say, although one can pray more than the minimum number of times a day and add one's own words to a *prescribed* prayer. Having the prayers come at times when individuals are likely to be involved with other, more mundane activities, such as sleep, work, and eating, serves to remind the believers that Allah is present in all activities. Pious Muslims over the age of nine pray five times a day: daybreak, noontime, mid-afternoon, sunset, and nightfall. The actual times are not written in the Quran, which says only, *Salat is a prescribed duty that has to be performed at the appointed times by the believers* (4:103). Muhammad was somewhat more specific:

- The dawn prayer (*subh* or *fajr*) time begins when the sky starts to lighten (true dawn); it may be performed until sunrise. For some commentators, this is the most important prayer.

- The noon prayer (*dhuhr* or *zuhr*) is undertaken ideally slightly after the sun has reached its zenith; the prayer window continues until an object's shadow equals its height.

- Mid-afternoon prayer (*asr*) time begins at the end of the noon prayer's time and can last until an object's shadow is twice as long as its height, although the permissible time extends until sunset.

- The sunset prayer (*maghrib*) time begins when the sun has completely set and ends when the red disappears from the sky. This is the only prayer that has no extended "window" of time.

- Nightfall prayer (*isha*) time begins at the end of the sunset prayer time. The best time for its performance ends when a third of the night has passed, although it is permissible to recite it any time before dawn.

It was deemed inappropriate to time prayers *exactly* with noon, sunrise, or sunset, given that early worshippers might get it confused with sun worship. Today Muslims can purchase pocket devices, such as the Prayer Minder, which calculate correct prayer times for their area. In case a Muslim is staying in extreme northerly or southerly latitudes with no true dawn or twilight, the believer is expected to use the prayer times calculated for the nearest city. In some countries, businesses are closed during prayer times; in other places, people are simply expected to halt what they are doing. Under certain conditions, such as during a journey, prayer times may be joined.

If one forgets a prayer, the Prophet declared, "Let him say it when he remembers it." To guard against the possibility that one may make a mistake or let one's mind wander during prayer, it can be made up with extra prayers called *nafl* or "extra merit" prayers. They can be offered before or after regular prayers and are done in the same way as the regular prayers for that time.

It is preferable to pray in the company of others, especially for the Friday noon prayer. But it is not obligatory (although salutary) to pray in a mosque. (For most people, this would be impossible to do five times a day anyway.) Muhammad said, "When a man prays publicly in a good manner and prays secretly in a good manner, Allah most high says, 'This is my servant indeed.'" In Islamic countries, many offices provide a prayer room for their employees.

The Friday noon prayer is a congregational prayer obligatory for all Muslims, especially males; it serves as a replacement for the regular noonday prayer. Muhammad said, "Prayer said in congregation exceeds the prayer said alone by twenty-seven degrees." According to some, a man who does not attend Friday prayers for three weeks is considered to have left Islam. In the Islamic view, however, the whole world is a mosque, and prayers may be offered anywhere, including outdoors. Indeed, the Prophet recommended that people say a part of their prayers at home, so as to not make "graves" of them.

All male believers are expected to gather on Friday for the noon prayer and listen to a sermon, or *khutba*, by the leader of the community. Islam has no formal day of rest; Friday can be a workday like any other, although in many Muslim countries it is designated a holiday. It not a day of rest like the Jewish or Christian Sabbath, but a day of public prayer. Friday was selected as a day of prayer at the mosque after the Muslims had begun to separate themselves from Jews and Christians. Muslims believe that Adam was created on Friday, expelled from the Garden on Friday, and entered Paradise on Friday. It has also been suggested that Friday was chosen because it was market day in Mecca. By noon, the market would be largely sold out, and the merchants had an opportunity to go to the mosque.

A two-part sermon (*khutba*), parts of which are recited in Arabic, precedes the prayer. (Because the ruler's name is traditionally invoked in the sermon, the *khutba* became an important mark of the authority of the ruler, and in early days the *khutba* was largely political.) The first part runs about 20 minutes, after which the speaker (*khatib*) sits down and says a short prayer. Then he stands and delivers another, briefer sermon of about 10 minutes. The *khatib* is usually the imam, or prayer-leader, as well, but this is not a requirement.

Ritual Cleanliness

Prayer is preceded by ritual cleansing, or *wudu*. Muhammad said, "The key to Paradise is prayer, and the key to prayer is purification (*taharah*)." He also declared, "Prayer is not accepted without purification." The concept of purification (both physical and spiritual) is central to Islam, and Muhammad spoke about it in more than 21 hadith.

The purification process is outlined in the Quran: *O you who believe! When you pray, wash your faces and your hands as far as the elbows and wipe your hands and wash your feet to the ankles. If no water is available, betake yourselves to pure earth and wipe your faces and your hands therewith; Allah does not desire to put on you any difficulty but he wishes to purify you* (5:6). Every part of the body subject to *wudu* must be thoroughly, quietly, and reverently washed. Care must be taken to wash between the toes and fingers. It is not necessary to towel dry the body after *wudu*, and some people prefer to let the water evaporate naturally. Fingernail polish prevents water from touching the nails and must be removed before *wudu*, or the procedure will not be effective. Staining the nails with henna, a common Middle Eastern practice, is acceptable.

Muhammad said, "Anyone who performs ablution thoroughly, and says, 'I bear witness that there is no god but Allah, He is One, there is no associate with Him, and that Muhammad is His servant and His Messenger; O Allah! Make me one of those who turn to You again and again and make me of those who purify themselves,' the eight doors of paradise are opened to him; he enters by whichever door he pleases."

Ceremonial cleanliness can be maintained from prayer to prayer if not broken by a bodily discharge such as urination, defecation, eructation, emission of pus, seminal discharge, vomiting, bleeding or by sleeping. If one's feet are properly washed and encased in thick socks, they do not have to be rewashed between *wudus*, if no other impurity has occurred. The socks can just be wiped.

Water is used for purification, as it is believed to be created pure. No other liquid may be used. Only pure, plain, running water is acceptable; it remains pure as long as there is no alteration in color, taste, or odor. The "running water" may issue from a tap or fountain, or even be poured from a bowl, but it is not acceptable to dip one's hands in stagnant water. If the water is poured, no gold or silver vessels can be used. Even silver plating is disallowed, unless it is of very low value. It is permissible to use vessels owned by Christians or Jews, but not presumably by pagans.

Most kinds of pollution can be eradicated by a complete washing with water just once, although three times is better. It is considered wasteful and wrong to do so *more* than three times, except in unusual circumstances involving pigs or dogs. Contact with the saliva or other moist parts of these unclean animals requires washing seven times. Pigs are so impure (*junub*) that even leather made from pigskin cannot be used, and they are to be killed whenever they appear. Biting dogs are also subject to a death sentence. Black dogs are considered creatures of the devil. Dogs are ranked along with pigs as far as impurity goes. People who are touched by dog saliva can be purified only if they wash themselves seven times, including one washing by water to which some earth has been added. However, if one is touched only by the dry part of a *haram* animal, such as the fur, it is sufficient simply to brush it away. Animals who have died from any cause other than ritual slaughter are also impure.

In some cases, sand is an acceptable alternative cleanser. Muhammad allowed those who traveling for three days and nights to simply wipe their boots rather than take them off before ablutions, as long as the shoes were put on in a state of cleanliness. Even if one has water, earth can be used if oneself, one's companions, or one's animal is thirsty and needs to drink. In fact, if one can surmise that such a need will arise in the future (as before a trip across the desert), it is permissible to save water by using sand or earth instead.

While cleansing the face and extremities is usually sufficient, sometimes a full bath (*ghusl*) is required, especially in the wake of the following:

- Sexual intercourse or the emission of sexual fluid (*jima*) by either sex
- Touching a dead body
- Menstruating (*hayz*)
- Childbirth (*nifas*) bleeding

Ghusl can be combined with *wudu* and may be done using a shower, too. Aishah reports, "When Allah's Messenger bathed because of sexual intercourse, he first washed his hands; he then poured water with his right hand on his left hand and washed his private parts." (The right hand is generally considered to be "clean," whereas the left is considered almost unlucky and rather unclean. The same holds true in European culture—the very word "sinister," for example, comes from the Latin word meaning "left," while orthodox means "right." And the word "right" itself means not only "the opposite of left" but also "good," "correct," or "proper.") It is considered offensive to give or receive goods or to eat with the left hand. Toilet duties are expected to be performed with the left hand. One should always enter a privy left foot first and exit it right foot first. The opposite is true for entering mosques.

Women and men were expected to observe the same purification rituals. One of Muhammad's wives, Umm Salama, asked him if women were required to bathe if they had just had a sexual dream. The Prophet replied in the affirmative "if she saw the vaginal secretion." Some hadith report that the Prophet and his wives might have bathed together after sexual intercourse. This should not be interpreted to mean they leapt into a tub together; it simply means they used the same water—in the dark. Full bathing is *recommended, but not obligatory* under the following circumstances:

- Before attending Friday prayers
- Before the feast at the end of Ramadan or during the *hajj*
- On days when there is an eclipse of the sun or moon
- Before reciting the prayer for rain (from an outsider's view, it seems odd to recommend a ritual bath when water is at a premium)
- Formally converting
- Recovering sanity or consciousness
- Before entering a holy place of pilgrimage

Before going to the mosque, participants are expected to bathe, brush their teeth, trim their nails, and remove bodily hair. Muhammad recommended the removal of pubic and underarm hair as well as trimming the moustache. He did want men to wear a full beard, however, to distinguish them from polytheists or "fire-worshippers" (Zoroastrians).

Muhammad was a stickler for cleanliness, and he felt that purity before Friday prayers was especially important. He said, "Taking a bath on Friday is incumbent on everyone who has attained puberty; he should also brush his teeth and use scent if can find it." He continued, "Were it not that it would place too heavy a burden on my community, I would have commanded them to use the toothbrush at every ablution [wudu]." He followed this practice himself, which may explain why his teeth remained in excellent condition throughout his life. Teeth can be brushed at any time except when the sun is setting during Ramadan.

O believers, draw not near to prayer when you are drunken until you know what you are saying, or defiled—unless you are traversing a way— until you have washed yourselves; but if you are sick, or on a journey, or if any of you comes from the privy, or you have touched women, and you can find no water, then have recourse to wholesome dust and wipe your faces and your hands (4:43). Muhammad was careful to wash himself not only after using the privy, but also when he had been ill and vomited.

Muhammad's own *wudu* practice was as follows: "He sent for water and poured it over his hands twice, then he rinsed his mouth and sniffed water into his nose twice, then he washed his face thrice, then he washed his hands up to the elbow twice, then he wiped his head with both his hands so that he carried them from the front and brought them back to the place from which he had started— then he washed his two feet." He cleaned the inside of his ears with his two forefingers, and the backside with his thumbs. He was concerned about nose-cleaning and said that people awakening from sleep should clean their noses three times "because the devil spends the night in the interior of one's nose." He also said, "When you cleanse your nose with water, use a lot, unless you are fasting." He preferred to begin with the right side for all aspects of *wudu*. Muslims follow this practice today. Rinsing the mouth is particularly important because it must be purified before uttering the words that go to Allah's ear.

Some schools maintain that the worshipper should visit the toilet if necessary before prayer so as to remove wastes from the body and so as not to be distracted during the service.

DRESS DURING PRAYER

Not only should the body be clean, but it also should be clothed in clean garments. Shoes are usually removed, but socks and tights stay on. Because they are in contact with the earth, shoes are considered dirty items. (When in December 2008, Iraqi newsman Muntadhar al-Zaidi threw his shoes at visiting U.S. president George W. Bush, it was intended as an extreme insult.)

Men's clothing must, at a minimum, cover the body from the knees up to and including the navel. Women's clothing must cover the entire body (except the face) to the tip of the chin and the hands. Muhammad once said that Allah would not accept the prayer of a woman who leaves her head uncovered. If any untoward parts of the body are left exposed, the prayer must be repeated unless the offending body part is covered immediately. It is preferable for women not to wear makeup. Clothing that is brightly marked or otherwise distracting should be avoided.

A prayer rug (*sajadah*) helps establish an isolated, sacred "clean" place in which to pray. Islamic prayer rugs are typically small and colorful, usually made of cotton or silk. Rugs may be decorated with abstract designs or feature a depiction of a famous mosque, such as the Kaaba in Mecca or the al-Aqsa Mosque in Jerusalem. It may not show humans or animals. Floral designs are permitted and often have symbolic meaning: the cypress tree represents mourning as well as immortality, and the palm and the coconut represent blessing and fulfillment. Prayer rugs are often designed with a "top" to point to Mecca. If no proper prayer rug is available, any suitable mat will do. After prayer, the mat is rolled up and immediately put away so that it will remain clean.

ATTITUDE DURING PRAYER

Because the mind as well as the body must be prepared for prayer, the *niyyah*, or intention, is extremely important. Insincere, halfhearted, or hypocritical prayers are worth nothing. In the same way, one can be guilty of "overpraying." To take one example, Muhammad was informed about a man who spent all his time praying in the mosque. "Then who feeds him?" wondered the Prophet. "His brother," was the response. "Then his brother is the more worthy one," said Muhammad. Still, Muhammad himself spent so much time standing up and praying that his feet swelled.

Prayer should be performed with dignity. Once when the Prophet was leading a prayer in the mosque, he heard the noise of people who came charging out of breath into the mosque. "What is the matter with you?" he asked. When the runners announced that they were hurrying so as not to miss prayer, he counseled them, "Do not do so. When you come to prayer you should be perfectly calm. You can complete it later." Along the same lines, he advised people not to stop eating to say their prayers. It was important for them to take what nourishment they need first.

Muhammad forbade anyone to walk in front of a person seen praying, even if it meant he had to wait 40 days to pass. Usually, of course, you can simply walk behind the one who is praying. More alarmingly, one hadith states, "The Prophet says that the dog, the ass, and woman interrupt prayer if they pass in front of the believer." Aishah brushed off this saying by announcing she had often been between the Prophet and the direction of prayer and simply stayed still so as not to disturb him. She was also distinctly annoyed at women being thrown into the company of asses and dogs, and told Muhammad so.

The barrier surrounding someone at prayer is called the *sutrah*. Muhammad used his staff as a marker, but he placed it just to the right of him, not in front, not wanting anyone to think he was praying to an idol. If one must spit while praying, one should do it to the left.

Prayer Orientation

Today Muslims face Mecca when they pray—but the original direction was toward Jerusalem, probably as a concession to Islam's sister religion. However, when the Jews of Medina rejected the notion of becoming Muslims in 622, the irritated Mohammad ordered the direction of prayer shifted to Mecca. Some experts say that Muhammad changed the direction to mollify the inhabitants of Mecca, but the full truth may never be known.

If one is uncertain about which direction Mecca is, one should pray in a mosque; it is not permissible to rely on another person's opinion without a personal conviction. Most homes, businesses, and hotel rooms in the Islamic world have a marker to indicate the *qiblah*, or proper direction in which to pray. However, real faith has little to do with facing a certain direction. The Quran proclaims, *It is no piety* (birr) *that you should turn your faces to the east or to the west. Piety, rather is those who believe in Allah* (2:177).

The Call to Prayer

The public call to prayer is known as the *adhan*. Early Muslims decided to use the human voice to call the faithful rather than the ram's horn (*shofar*) as in Judaism, the bell as in Christianity, or a fire as in Zoroastrianism. (Muslim tradition accords the idea of using a human being to Umar, Muhammad's companion.) The rules state that the call to prayer must be sounded from a high place and in the loudest possible voice, and Bilal, the Prophet's Abyssinian slave, was famous for his loud voice. So he became the first muezzin, or prayer-caller. Muhammad told Bilal that if he stuck his fingers in his ears while he shouted the call, it would raise the power of his voice.

For Muslims these chanted words are more meaningful than an empty bell ringing or sound of a *shofar.* The spoken *adhan* also serves as a reminder of the basic principles of Islam. Today, those people who do not live within earshot can consult their daily paper for prayer times. Today the *muezzin* (with the help of a megaphone or microphone or by recording) calls to the faithful, "Allah is great" (*Allahu akbar*), four times. The rest of the call, devised by Muhammad, follows (Sunni version):

> I testify that there is no god but Allah.
>> *Ash hadu an la ilaha illallah* (twice)
>> I testify that Muhammad is Allah's messenger!
>> *Ash hadu ana Muhammadar-rasulullah* (twice)
>> Come to prayer!
>> *Hayya ala salah* (twice)
>> Come to salvation!
>> *Hayya ala falah* (twice)
>> Allah is Great!
>> *Allah akhbar* (twice)
>> There is no god but Allah!
>> *La ilaha illallah* (once)

At the dawn prayer, to encourage the groggy Muslims to rise, Bilal added, "Prayer is better than sleep!" Muhammad liked the addition so much that it remains a formal part of the dawn prayer ritual; it is said twice, after the second "Come to salvation."

PRAYER LANGUAGE AND POSTURES

The words and postures (*rakah*) of the prayers are prescribed. *Salat* is a ritualized, formal prayer, not a spontaneous conversation with Allah, although private, non-formulaic prayer (*dua*) is also encouraged. *Salat* consists of selections from the Quran, including the opening surah, recited in Arabic. Thus, many non-Arabic-speaking Muslims do not know exactly what they are saying, as was the case for centuries for some Christians worshipping in a Latin mass.

The prayers are accompanied by specified postures: standing straight with raised hands, bowing, kneeling, touching the ground with the forehead, and sitting. Muhammad was told by Allah to prostrate himself on the "seven bones" of his body: hands, knees, extremities of his feet, and forehead. These movements are intended to express humility, submission, and adoration; many were derived from ancient Arabic custom when a commoner met a king. Every prayer posture is related to a special *dhikr*, or remembrance of Allah, and the worshipper is expected to keep this in mind while praying.

Humility before Allah in no way diminishes one's dignity before other human beings, however. When praying in groups, Muslims stand shoulder to shoulder in straight rows, filling each row before forming a second one. This is in obedience to Muhammad's command: "Keep straight and do not be uneven, for in that case your hearts would disagree." This arrangement emphasizes solidarity, discipline, and equality before Allah. Many mosques have these prayer lines marked out on the carpet. Children are expected to participate from the time they are seven years old; younger children are allowed to roam freely around the worshippers, imbibing their piety by osmosis. Muhammad himself used to pray with his young grandsons on his shoulders.

The prayer begins with the worshippers standing serenely and quietly, facing Mecca, raising their hands and saying, "Allahu akbar!" ("God is most great!"). This is absolutely obligatory. No other words are permissible. Men raise their hand to their ears, women to their shoulders. Then the hands are folded (right hand over left) over the belly or chest (or left at the sides) while Surah 1:2–6 ("The Fatihah") is recited in Arabic: *Praise be to God, Lord of the Worlds; the Beneficent, the Merciful; Master of the Day of Judgment. You alone do we worship and from You alone do we seek aid. Show us the Straight Way, the way of those upon whom You have bestowed Your grace, not of these who have earned Your wrath or who go astray.* Muhammad said, "There is no prayer for him who does not recite the opening chapter of the book." The Fatihah is followed by *Amin,* or "Grant our prayer." Muhammad is reported to have said, "Ask and you will be given. Ask and you will be given."

Muslims then recite another verse of the Quran of their choosing (after the first two *rakahs* only) and bow down, hands on knees, back horizontal, proclaiming three times, "Glory to God in the Highest" and "Our Lord, all praise belongs to you." This was the traditional position in which a servant received orders from his monarch. Women do not bow as deeply as men.

At this, point the worshipper repeats, "Allahu Akbar!" and kneels with his hands and forehead (and preferably the nose) touching the ground. Shia Muslims often place their foreheads directly on the earth or on a clay tablet taken from a holy place.

This position is called *sujud* or *sajda*. It is obligatory to remain thus motionless for at least one moment. The rear should be higher than the head. (This is the main reason that women are generally relegated to being behind male worshippers or in a separate section altogether.) However, in Muhammad's day, women and men prayed without being separated by a wall, as numerous hadith attest. Today, mosques provide a separate entrance and washing facilities for women.

The worshipper then recites, "Glory to the Lord Most High," and the cycle is repeated. This constitutes a full *rakah*, literally an act of worship. Each *rakah* is repeated a varying number of times, depending on which prayer is being recited: twice for the dawn prayer, four times for the noon prayer, four for the mid-afternoon prayer, three for the sunset prayer, and four for the nightfall prayer. It is always laudable to complete more than the minimum numbers of cycles. During a journey, the number of *rakahs* may be halved.

At the end of the second *rakah*, the worshipper sits on his heels for a moment (this position is called *julus* or *jalsah*) and recites the shahadah and the "peace greeting": "Peace be upon all of you and the mercy and blessings of Allah," said twice and spoken to fellow believers on the right and left, although some Muslims believe that they are also, or instead, addressing the angels perched on their right and left shoulders. These angels are the *kiraman katibin*, or "noble writers," who keep a record of our doings. The prayer is often accompanied by a rosary of 99 or 33 beads called *tasbih* or *subhah*. The only way in which the various prayers differ is the number of *rakah* offered at each and the precise Quranic passages selected.

In addition, there is a prayer "makeup" technique called *sajdah sahew*, which the worshipper can use if he thinks he has made an error somewhere in the prayers. In this case, during the last *rakah*, after finishing certain required parts of the prayer, one turns to the right and says, "*Assalamu alayhum wa Rahmatullah*," and then looks forward, saying, "*Allahu akbar*," and continues with two separate *sajdahs*, finally returning to the *jalsa* position and repeating portions of the prayer by way of penance.

The Quran even specifies the loudness of proper prayer: *And be not loud in thy prayer. Not hushed therein, but seek thou for a way between* (17:110). However, the words should be spoken loud enough for the worshipper himself to hear them clearly. In most cases, Muslims do not close their eyes when praying, unless they find that doing so helps them enter into a prayerful mood more easily.

The worshipper may conclude with personal prayers (*dua*) in his own language, although certain Quranic verses are recommended. *Dua* may be offered for oneself, one's acquaintances, or even for one's country. Muhammad said, "A man is granted supplication provided he does not ask for anything sinful or for breaking ties of relationship." According to Muhammad, "There is no doubt that three kinds of prayers will be answered: the prayers of the oppressed, the prayers of the traveler, and the prayers of parents for their children."

For those who need help composing *dua*, entire books have been written, and there are *dua* designed for almost every act imaginable. It is recommended to say a *dua* immediately upon becoming aware that one has committed a sin, for instance. After every prayer, the Muslim says "*Astaghfirullah*" three times. It means, "I ask Allah forgiveness." This phrase is also used regularly in conversation.

Ennobling as it is, Muhammad placed limits on the power of *salat*: "There are three persons whose *salat* does not rise even a single span above their heads [thus not going all the way to Allah]: a man leading a congregational *salat* while the people hate him, a woman passing the night while her husband is angry with her, and two quarreling brothers."

Islam has other prayers besides the Salat. Other institutional prayers include the Prayer of Peril, undertaken during conditions of combat, the prayer on the two Eids (feasts), the Eclipse Prayer, the Drought Prayer, the Funeral Prayer (*Salatul Jamaza*, always performed in congregation), and the Prayer over the Dead. In this prayer there is no bowing or prostrating; the entire prayer is said while standing.

Another prayer is *tahajjud*, offered during the last one-third of the night (17:79). The *tahajjud* is not required but is considered highly laudable and is said to increase one's nearness to Allah. It is said after one has been sleeping (so staying up all night and then saying it does not count). This prayer involves eleven *rakahs* (prayer cycles), although it can be shortened if need be. Another supererogatory prayer is the *tarawih*, consisting of 8 or 20 *rakahs* said during Ramadan immediately after the *isha* prayer.

Another beloved prayer is the *istikhara*, a *salat* of two cycles recited when the worshipper is facing a difficult decision and wishes to be guided by Allah.

Muslims can perform the required prayer even while traveling in a plane or train or riding on a horse or camel, although it may be a little dangerous. If the vehicle switches directions away from the *qiblah* while you are traveling, that is all right; the prayer counts long as the worshipper is not the one steering.

Certain kinds of behavior render *salat* void. Some are sins of omission: Forgetting to make a *niyyah* or intention, omitting the phrase *allahu akbar*, omitting the Fatihah, or forgetting to perform a required posture or gesture. Some are actions: turning the body away from the proper direction or *qiblah*, breaking *wudu*, talking, laughing, eating, or drinking.

The Mosque

Mosques are an integral part of Islamic society. Although primarily meant for divine worship, mosques have also traditionally served as cultural centers. Mosques can be hired out for weddings, birthdays, or even circumcision parties.

While men are required to go mosque, women are certainly allowed to go if they choose. Muhammad said, "When your women ask your permission to go to the mosque at night, give them permission." In general, menstruating women do not enter a mosque to say prayers, although there is no absolute prohibition against it. In ancient times, some women actually set up their own tents within mosques, presumably for protection. However, later it was more customary for women to pray in the privacy of their homes. Today the trend is for them once again to attend the mosque, although they are segregated from men, usually in a balcony or separate room. Where these are not available, women and children pray behind adult males.

Building a mosque is worthy of great merit in the Islamic tradition, and no Muslim can be denied admittance. Early argument raged about whether pagans, Christians, Jews, and Zoroastrians should be allowed in. Today it is agreed that non-Muslims may be invited, but they have no absolute right to visit or worship.

Most mosques include both a dome and minaret, although the latter feature probably did not exist during the life of Muhammad. The dome carries with it a feeling spaciousness, calm, and peace; they are also an acoustical aid. The minaret, or tower, was historically the place from where prayers were announced by the *muezzin*. Both the dome and the minaret are frequently topped by the crescent moon, the symbol of Islam. Most mosques have a place set aside for ablutions before entering, so that people can perform their prayers in a state of ritual purity. It is customary to take off one's shoes before entering, although it is not absolutely required. Special slippers are usually provided. It is traditional for men to wear cologne and dress in white in the mosque. Women, on the other hand, should *not* wear scent when attending.

The only furniture in a mosque is the pulpit or *minbar*, a platform from which the imam delivers his Friday sermon. Many mosques have a "professional" imam deliver the sermon, although any knowledgeable person can do so. When men and women are praying together, the imam must be male. If only women are praying, a woman from the middle of the row leads the prayers. Muhammad said of the prayer leader: "When he prostrates, you should also prostrate, when he rises up, you should also rise up." One should not speak the prayers in a louder voice than the imam, so as not to seem to compete with him. When someone did this to Muhammad, he complained, "I felt as if you were disputing with me." It is also forbidden to get ahead of Imam in the prayer cycle. "Does the man who lifts his head before the Imam not fear that Allah may change his face into that of an ass?" asked Muhammad.

Muhammad said that he had no command to decorate a mosque, although many are beautifully adorned with passages from the Quran. Islamic law does not permit the artistic representation of human beings. In any case, mosques should be kept scrupulously clean and perfumed. In Muhammad's time, a black slave usually undertook this task. There are no chairs or pews; people are expected to simply sit on the floor. The walls are often decorated with quotations from the Quran and are always in Arabic, no matter where the mosque is located. The names of the first four caliphs and that of Muhammad may also be written on the walls in Sunni mosques.

The main interior feature of the mosque is the *qiblah* wall, indicating the wall in the direction of Mecca. It contains the *mihrab*, a special niche cut into the wall intended to focus the worshipper's attention on Allah and Mecca. The imam stand in front of the *mihrab*.

It is forbidden to yell, spit, carry on trade, or recite poetry in this holy place, although formerly the mosque was used as a marketplace where clothing, books, medicine, and even food have been sold, so long as the worshippers are not disturbed. Children are allowed to move about it freely (if quietly). Muhammad declared, "Do not go to the mosque after eating garlic, onion, and so forth, because angels are harmed by the same things as people." (Muhammad had a strong dislike for smelly vegetables.) One cannot take a dog to a mosque, either, although if a dog does happen to wander through, the mosque is not defiled. Cats are welcome.

Tradition recounts the story of a Bedouin who began urinating in the local mosque, presumably because he did not know better. (The Bedouins were not particularly sophisticated.) The Muslims were about to take him into custody, but the good-hearted Muhammad said, "Leave him alone, and just throw some water over his urine, for you have been raised to deal with people gently, not harshly."

Once a mosque is built, it must always remain a mosque and never be diverted to other purposes. It can never be "owned" except by the community itself. Mosques do not need to be consecrated as churches do in some Christian traditions. Prayers can even be offered in a Christian church, so long as the building contains no statues or pictures.

ALMS TO THE POOR (*ZAKAT*): THE THIRD PILLAR

In no way will you attain to righteousness until you spend in the way of Allah out of that which you cherish most (3:91). In Islamic thought, Allah is the true owner of everything, and therefore, humans are just borrowing from the one who really possesses all riches, material and immaterial. *Zakat* is the obligatory giving of alms to the poor, often anonymously. It is more a tax than a voluntary charity, given that it must be collected as public money, and has often been considered an early form of Social Security. The word *zakat* means purification, and giving alms is a way to purify both the soul and one's possessions. Muslims consider it the most important religious obligation next to prayer. All adult, sane Muslims who possess over a certain minimum (called the *nisab*, equal to the value of about three ounces of gold) for a year or more and have met their expenses are required to pay it.

Hoarding is resented in Islam. Money is to be kept in circulation, and people are expected to share their wealth with the poor. *Those who live off orphans' property without having any right to do so will only suck up fire into their bellies, and they will roast in the fires of Hell* (4:10). The Quran labels one who does not feed the orphan as identical to one who denies the Judgment Day (4:1–10). Orphans were of special concern of Muhammad too, possibly because he was one himself.

Even the spoils of war are to go for the care of the needy, not to be cycled among the already rich. This kind of generosity was already a value in pre-Islamic Arabia, where anyone who acquired an "excess" of wealth was encouraged to give it away to the poor.

The *zakat* is levied on all adult Muslims, male and female, at 2.5 percent of capital assets (not just income) once a year. It is not applied to personal-use items, such as clothing, the family car, or the house one lives in. It *is* applied to cash, camels, gold and silver (over a certain amount), goats, grains, investments, jewelry, horses used during a jihad, and for-profit businesses. Even if the tax amounts to half a date, it should be paid, and cheerfully too. Interestingly, there is no *zakat* for farmers on vegetables other than legumes and no *zakat* on fruits other than raw dates and grapes. Merchants who buy and resell these products, however, have to pay the *zakat*. If one happens to find gold or silver treasure on unowned land, an immediate *zakat* of 20 percent is due. If the land is owned by someone, the landowner has the right to the treasure. Money should be paid to members of the local community first. Those who ignore the duty of *zakat* are said to have no right to call themselves Muslims, like those who refuse to pray.

And what about those who default on the tax? One who declines to pay his *zakat* on his camels, for instance, is in trouble on Judgment Day. Then he will be sentenced to be trampled and bitten by camels forever.

Shia Muslims may pay more than 2.5 percent in *zakat* and in addition pay a 20 percent *khums*, or surplus wealth religious tax to an Imam or religious leader for the benefit of the community. Most people pay their *zakat* during Ramadan, the holy month.

Zakat is obligatory (*fard*), but Muslims are also expected to provide charity to those in need. Muhammad said, "The believer is not one who eats his fill when his neighbor beside him is hungry." This kind of charity is called *sadaqah*, a word that can be translated as "righteousness," but literally means "bearing another's burden." Sadaqah is not obligatory like *zakat* but is praiseworthy and recommended. Muhammad said that the hand that gives is better than the hand that receives, but he also expected people to be reasonable and not give away every penny. A man said to him, "I have a dinar." Muhammad responded, "Spend it on yourself." The fellow rejoined, "I have another one." "Spend it on your wife," urged Muhammad. Then the man said, "I have yet another one." Muhammad said, "Spend it on your servant. Then see." Charity is not restricted to monetary payouts. Good deeds and even smiling at people count as charity. There are material as well as spiritual benefits to paying the *zakat*: *The example of the people who spend their wealth in the cause of Allah is like a kernel of corn: it grows seven ears and each ear has a hundred kernels* (2:261).

The proceeds of all charitable giving are to go to *the poor, to widows and orphans, to free slaves and help debtors* (9:60) and to help those working "in support of God," usually construed to mean those who are helping to build mosques, hospitals, and religious schools. However, over time, even in Muhammad's day, the term acquired the meaning of spending in support of military endeavors. Thus, *zakat* money has also gone to militant or violent causes, for according to tradition, among the "deserving recipients" are those engaged in Muslim military operations to whom no salary has been allotted. It may also be given to gain converts by inclining their hearts to Islam (9:60). Other deserving recipients include debtors, slaves purchasing their freedom, *zakat* collectors themselves (an eighth of the *zakat* funds), and travelers in need of money. It is not possible to give *zakat* to a non-Muslim, or to one's own family, whom one is obliged to support anyway. It is also impermissible to give *zakat* to any descendant of Muhammad.

FASTING (*SAWM*) DURING THE MONTH OF RAMADAN: THE FOURTH PILLAR

O you who believe, fasting is prescribed for you, as it was prescribed for those before you in order that you may be conscious of Allah (2:183). Fasting is a traditional part of many religions, and in Islam, Ramadan, the ninth month, is reserved for this purpose. (It is probable that Ramadan was already a holy month in pre-Islamic Arabia.)

The month of Ramadan is that in which the Quran was revealed. . . . Therefore, whoever of you witnesses the month, he shall fast during it, and whoever is sick or on a journey shall fast a like number of days (2:185). This was also the month in which the important Battle of Badr occurred. According a hadith, during *sawm*, "the gates of mercy are opened, the gates of Hell are locked, and the devils are chained."

The fast has multiple purposes, but primary among them is to make the believer more Allah-conscious. It also disciplines the body and serves as a reminder of the many poor and hungry people in the world. Unlike fasting in some religious traditions, the fast is not regarded as a penance for sin, but as a regular religious duty. The spiritual benefits are said to be enormous: "The breath of the one who fasts is sweeter to Allah than the fragrance of musk," said Muhammad.

Fasting and other disciplines are never to be done to the point of harming the body. As Muhammad told a follower who fasted night and day, "Do not do so; keep fast and break it and stand up in devotion in the night and have sleep, for your body has a right over you, and your eye has a right over your and your wife has a right over you, and the person who pays you a visit has a right over you." In other words, everything in moderation; society, family, and one's own body have a justifiable claim upon a person.

The Fast of Ramadan begins at dawn, and in the day before watches, the proper time was deemed the moment when the human eye can detect the difference between a black thread and a white one. Because the Islamic calendar is lunar-based (and about 11 days shorter than the solar year), Ramadan retreats through the solar calendar, appearing 11 days earlier each year. Most people over the age of puberty are to fast, but younger children often participate, at least partly. (The fast is much harder when it occurs during the hot summer months than in winter. There is one story that during the 18th century some Muslim sailors aboard a British merchant ship starved to death when they found themselves in the Arctic Circle in the summer, when night never comes. The historicity of this tale is uncertain.) Before fasting one is expected to make a simple meal called *suhoor* just before dawn, a meal eaten in silence. One must declare, even silently, each day of the month sometime before noon, one's intention to fast for the entire day for the sake of Allah. "The next day's fasting I intend for the month of Ramadan." Muslims are prohibited to fast longer than sunup to sundown, and believers are advised to eat as late as possible before sunrise and to break the fast as soon as it is dark. "Have the meal before dawn," said Muhammad, for there is blessing in the meal before dawn."

FASTING REQUIREMENTS

The fast puts several restrictions on people's activities. During the fast period, the faithful are expected to refrain from eating and drinking, even water. Ideally, one should not even swallow one's own saliva. Licking a stamp could count as breaking the fast if done intentionally. Even nose drops are technically prohibited; however, those who need to take medicine with water or food for their health may do so. It is also forbidden to vomit. However, if a gnat flies into one's mouth by accident and is swallowed unknowingly, that is not breaking the fast. Even if one simply forgets it is Ramadan, the day is credited to him as a fast. It is considered very bad manners to comment on such a lapse, for it is a "covered" fault. It is also bad manners to eat or drink anything in front of someone who is fasting.

Conjugal relationships are also prohibited during the fast, although kissing and hugging are allowed. However, if there is a slipup, the wife is not responsible and does not have to vitiate the act. During this month, Muslims should be especially careful to avoid evil talk and to do righteous acts. Muhammad said, "He who does not give up uttering falsehood and acting according to it, Allah has no need of his giving up food and drink." In another hadith he said, "Five things break one's fast: lying, backbiting, spreading rumors, false testimony, and lustful gaze." Fighting is generally forbidden during Ramadan, but exceptions can be made: They will question you concerning the holy month and fighting in it. Say, "Fighting in it is a heinous thing, but to bar from Allah's way, and disbelief in him, and the Holy Mosque, and to expel its people from it—that is more heinous in God's sight; and persecution is more heinous than slaying." They will not cease to fight with you, till they turn you from your religion, if they are able; and whoever of you turns from this religion, and dies disbelieving—their works have failed in this world and the next; those are the inhabitants of the Fire; therein they shall dwell forever. (2:216 ff)

In all other respects, people are expected to continue their ordinary work as usual.

Believers are also expected to spend a great deal of time in prayer. Some people go into a retreat (*itikaf*) during the last 10 days of Ramadan; during this time, they pray and read the Quran. Family members assist by providing meals and undertaking household duties for the one in retreat. Men usually go to a mosque for the entire period; women separate themselves into another part of the home.

Following the practice of Muhammad, it is traditional to complete a reading (or recitation) of the Quran, which is divided into 30 equal parts (*juz* or *sipara*) for the purpose. One part is recited each night of the month by a *qari* or professional reciter. This division also has helped children all over the world, even non-Arabic speakers, to learn the Quran by heart. Each *juz* is divided into seven sections or *manazil* (singular *manzil*). The divisions are made purely as an aid to memorizations; they do not correlate with the theme or narrative of the text.

At the end of the day, just after the sunset prayer, people may gather for a simple communal supper (*iftar*) of water, dates, and plain fare, as was the habit of the Prophet. (This meal is sometimes referred to as breakfast, given that the observers have indeed broken their fast.) Muslims are not supposed to omit this meal because the fast is not meant to destroy the body, just discipline it. Muslims are expected to share their food with those who have none. The family goes to *maghirb* prayer.

Later on, another larger meal may be served that includes special treats served only during Ramadan. During the night, Muslims may also have sexual relations.

Permitted to you, upon the night of the Fast, is to go in to your wives; they are garment for you, and you are a garment for them. Allah knows that you have been betraying yourself, and has turned to you and pardoned you. So now lie with them, and seek what Allah has prescribed for you. And eat and drink, until the white thread shows clearly to you from the black thread a dawn; then complete the fast unto the night, and do not lie with them while you cleave to the mosques. (Surah 2:187)

Toward the end of Ramadan (usually on the 27th day), Muslims commemorate the night when the angel revealed the Quran to Muhammad. The month ends at the new moon with a special feast call Enid al-Fitr (Ending the Fast Festival). It is also sometimes called the "sugar festival" because it is so sweet. At this feast it is customary for Muslims to wear new clothes. Muslims may also fast during other times of the year, and some make it practice to fast once a week. The Ashura, the 10th day of Muharram, is also a voluntary fast for believers.

A delightful hadith throws light on Muhammad's attitude toward the fast of Ramadan. An unnamed man approached the Prophet and said, "I fear there's no hope for me. I had sex with my wife during Ramadan." "Well, then," responded Muhammad, "Set free a slave in expiation." "I have no slaves," complained the sinner. "Well, then, fast for two straight months," urged the Prophet. "Oh, I couldn't possibly," protested the man. "That's much too hard." "All right, then feed 60 poor people," suggested the Prophet. "I can't afford that," cried the man. At that very moment, someone handed Muhammad a basket of dates. "Well, then, here, take this basket of dates and pass them out to the needy." "Can I give them to my own family?" asked the man hopefully. "I'm as needy as the next person." At that, Muhammad laughed so heartily that his canine teeth showed. "Get along with you, then," he smiled. "You're welcome to them."

The end of the Fast is marked by large feast and a three-day holiday in most Muslim countries. Children are given gifts and money, and special greetings exchanged. Everyone who possibly can do so goes to the mosque to gather together. In the afternoon, visits may be made to the cemetery to remember those who have passed on.

EXEMPTIONS FROM THE FAST

Certain people are exempt from the fast. People who are ill, pregnant, menstruating, recovering from childbirth (*nifas*), or at war are exempt. Travelers are exempt (if they like) if the journey is at least 50 miles one way and one leaves town before dawn. (Of course this exemption was a function of living mostly in a camel-powered society.) All these exempted people are expected to make up the fast later. The elderly are permanently exempt if they choose because they will not be getting any younger. The mentally disabled or chronically ill are permanently exempt also, as are non-Muslims.

Muslims who cannot fast may make it up by feeding the hungry or freeing slaves. If one dies before making up the fast days, a responsible family member can make up the fast for the deceased loved one, either by fasting or by feeding the hungry. Those engaged on *jihad* are rather expected not to fast. Muhammad said, "You are going to encounter the enemy in the morning, and breaking the fast would give your strength, so break the fast." On the other hand, he is also reported to have said, "Every servant of Allah who observes fast for a day in the way of Allah [*jihad*], Allah would remove, because of this day, his face from the Fire of Hell to the extent of 70 years' distance." Curiously, Muhammad seems to have instructed his own wives *not* to fast, as Aishah reports, "due to my duties to the Messenger of Allah."

PILGRIMAGE (HAJJ) TO MECCA: THE FIFTH PILLAR

It is the duty of all believers towards Allah to come to the House a pilgrim, if able to make their way there (3:91). The hajj takes place during the first half of the last month of the Islamic year, the Dhul-Hijja. Like Ramadan, the month rotates through the solar year. Mecca, the birthplace of the Prophet and once the most populous city in Arabia, lies in a valley about 45 miles from the Red Sea. Because of its poor situation in regard to agriculture, Meccans historically relied on trade with Syria, Egypt, Yemen, and Abyssinia along the Spice Road. As shrewd merchants, they had access to many luxuries not available to Bedouins, including finer food, more comfortable bedding, and richer clothes.

Even during pagan days, Mecca was also a place of pilgrimage, it being a longstanding custom to visit the Kaaba, also called *al-bayt al-Haram*, the "Holy House." Other shrines besides the Kaaba existed at Taif, Nakhlah, and Qudayd at one time, but they are gone now. The earliest pilgrimages were possibly autumn festivals organized to celebrate or bring on the winter rains. Some of the same rituals performed today by devout Muslims are pre-Islamic: the long vigil on the Plain of Arafat, touching the Black Stone, throwing stones at the pillars in Mina, animal sacrifice, circumambulating the Kaaba seven times, drinking from the brackish well of Zamzam, running between the two low hills of Marwa and Al Safa, and so on. Human bloodshed was forbidden during four months of the year when the pilgrimage was made.

Today, Mecca is the most sacred city of Islam, a holy sanctuary (*haram*), to which only Muslims may be admitted. Everything inside a *haram* is protected and considered inviolable. Non-Muslims are not allowed in Mecca or Medina at any time. In fact, they are generally prohibited from the entire Hejaz region, with the sole exception of Jedda, a commercial seaport.

For the pilgrimage to "count," the participant must be Muslim, of sound mind, and of the "age of reason." About two million pilgrims make the hajj every year. *All* morally responsible Muslims, especially able-bodied men, are expected to accomplish it, at least once during their lives, if they are physically and financially able. Those who complete the hajj sometimes indicate the fact by wearing a green band around their headgear.

Under certain circumstances, a substitute may be allowed. A woman of the tribe of Khatham came Muhammad and said, "O Messenger of Allah! My father is a very old man unable to sit firmly on a riding-camel; shall I perform a pilgrimage in his behalf?" And Muhammad responded in the affirmative. Of course, in that particular case, the ordinance regarding the pilgrimage was revealed only when the woman's father was elderly, so he had no opportunity earlier in life to make the trip himself.

Nowadays, most pilgrims arrive not by camel, but by air to Jeddah, about 45 miles west of Mecca, although pilgrims from nearby may come by car, train, or bus. Jeddah, a maritime city, rose to prominence from the earliest days as being a gateway to Mecca. The pilgrimage must also be undertaken at the proper time of year: during the last 10 days of the 12th and final lunar month, the month of Zul-Hijjah, 2 months and 10 days after Ramadan. Minor children may be taken along, but it does not count as a hajj for them.

One is expected to pay for one's own pilgrimage. Muslims should not borrow money to go on the hajj; they need to have enough to pay for their fare, food, and lodging. Ideally, all personal debts should be discharged before leaving. Muslims are also expected to make ample provisions for their family while they are gone; going on a hajj while leaving a family in debt is definitely un-Islamic. The hajj has such a strong spiritual component, however, that if someone has saved up for the pilgrimage, but feels the need to donate that money to someone in desperate straits, that charity counts the same as the hajj.

Before going on hajj, one must announce that is one's intention. It is permissible to make this announcement silently ("in one's heart"), but it is preferable to say it aloud. The instant one makes an intention to go on the hajj, one has entered into a state of *ihram*, or ritual purity.

Hajj Clothing

Once they enter Mecca, pilgrims wear special clothing also called *ihram*. The places where it becomes obligatory to wear these garments are called *miqqat*, about three miles away from the Kaaba. Today, many pilgrims choose to wear their *ihram* from the time they board their planes.

Hajj garments are simple clothes intended to remove distinctions of wealth and status, showing that everyone is equal before Allah. Muhammad said, "A man shall not wear shirt nor turban nor trousers nor headgear, not any cloth dyed with *wars* [a plant producing a red dye] or saffron [a yellow dye]; and if he does not find shoes, let him wear leather stockings, cut off so that they are lower than the ankles." For men the costume consists of two white unsewn (meaning untailored) pieces of cloth used only for hajj. The garments cannot be tied with a knot. Snaps are forbidden, but safety pins and belts are acceptable. The clothing cannot be perfumed, although it is recommended to perfume the body. Men may not use any form of head-cover at all, although an umbrella is allowed to guard against the sun. Muhammad said men may also carry a wallet and ring, although nowadays men do not wear jewelry. Once in the state of *ihram*, one may not marry or propose marriage.

Women wear a plain, loose-fitting garment (it may be sewn) that covers everything except the hands and face. As with men, clothing dyed red or yellow is forbidden; women often choose to wear white. Garments of silk are forbidden.

Women may not veil their faces or wear gloves. In Muhammad's day, the veil and gloves were marks of rank, items worn only by the wealthy classes and therefore forbidden to pilgrims. If an unrelated man passes by, and the woman desires to cover her face, she may do so only with an adjoining cloth or loose veil, perhaps suspended from the visor of a cap, but it cannot touch her face. In accordance with a hadith of the Prophet, it should be removed immediately afterward. Women are also forbidden to use perfume, scented soap, or cosmetics. They may wear only a wedding ring for jewelry.

For both sexes, sandals with open toe and heel are required. (Wearing closed-toe sandals requires one to slaughter an animal.) No hairdressing oil can be applied to the scalp or beard; however, it is permitted to "glue" or gel one's hair to prevent it from getting disheveled or dusty.

BEHAVIOR DURING HAJJ

Hajj behavior is regulated. Upon arrival at Mecca, Muslims re-cite the *talbiyah* prayer: "At your command I am here, O Allah! At your command, O Allah without equal! Yours is the kingdom and the power and the glory, O You alone!" As they enter, they say, "Allah, this sanctuary is your sacred place, this city is your city, and this slave [the pilgrim] your slave. I come to you from a distant land, carrying all my sins and misdeeds, as an afflicted person seeking your help and dreading your punishment. I beg you to accept me, and grant me complete forgiveness and give me permission to enter your vast garden of delight."

The Saudi government requires the following from women:

> All ladies are required to travel for Hajj with a Mahram (close male relative). Proof of kinship must be submitted with the application form. Any lady over the age of forty-five (45) may travel without a Mahram with an organized group, provided she submits a letter of no objection from her husband, son, or brother authorizing her to travel for Hajj with the named group. This letter should be notarized.

Pilgrims are also required to pay for their housing in advance.

During the hajj, pilgrims are to avoid sexual relations (this invalidates the hajj) and quarreling and are forbidden to hurt any living creature except for the "five nuisances": a crow, a kite, a scorpion, a deadly snake, or a biting dog. (Muhammad said snakes should be killed "with disgrace.") Another exception is the mandatory sacrifice that takes place at the feast. Hunting in particular is forbidden: *O you who believe, do not kill any game during pilgrimage. Anyone who kills any game on purpose, his fine shall be a number of livestock animals that is equivalent to the game animals he killed* (5:95).

Pilgrims are encouraged to make a full bath, or *ghusl*—even women who are menstruating and in a technically "impure" state—if there is sufficient water. Otherwise, a simple *wudu* is adequate. Many men shave their heads, but some strict observers do not bathe, trim their hair, or clip their nails in order that their physical bodies will not be "lessened" during the hajj. *Truly did Allah fulfill the vision for His Messenger: ye shall enter the Sacred Mosque, if Allah wills, with minds secure, heads shaved, hair cut short, and without fear* (48:27). Other pilgrims wash themselves as usual and even engage in commercial transactions. A hadith records that men may be allowed "to smell sweet smelling plants, look in a mirror, and use medicine made from what he eats, such as olive oil or butter."

STEPS OF THE PILGRIMAGE

The heart of the hajj is the Kaaba. Mecca's cube-shaped Kaaba, housed within the Grand Mosque, is the most sacred structure in Islam, although technically it is the space within it rather than the building itself that is sacred. Most Muslims believe that Adam built the original edifice, but it had fallen into ruin, destroyed by the Great Flood or left to disintegrate by those who had forgotten Allah. Another Muslim tradition maintains there is a model of the Kaaba in Heaven.

The Kaaba is about 33 feet wide by 50 feet long and 45 feet high. It is draped with a black cloth (*kiswah*) decorated with Quranic verses embroidered in gold thread. Each year the cloth is taken down and replaced with a new one. The remnants of the old cloth are sold to the devout; many Muslims frame their piece and hang it in their homes.

The Kaaba contains the sacred Black Stone (*al-Hajar-ul-Aswad*), placed there by Ibrahim (Abraham) and Ismail (Ishmael). The stone itself is only about a foot in diameter and is framed in silver. Stones were an important part of pre-Islamic, Arabic worship; the ones considered sacred were believed to have fallen from the sky. The sacred Black Stone of Islam, once held sacred to the moon god, Hubal, in fact may be a meteorite. Muslims believe it was delivered to earth by the angel Gabriel and was put in its present position, on the eastern

corner of the Kaaba, by Abraham. Originally, the Black Stone was said
to have been white, but it darkened over the centuries. Today pilgrims
try to kiss the stone, as Muhammad once did, but in most cases are
prevented from doing so by the crowds and merely point to it as they
walk about the Kaaba. Muslims do not believe the stone has any sacred
powers, and Caliph Umar said that he would not have bothered kissing
it, except that Muhammad did so.

Muslims circumambulate (*tawaf*) the Kaaba seven times counter-
clockwise during the hajj; this motion is said to imitate the movement
of the angels around the heavenly throne of Allah (and the sun around
the earth). Muhammad said, "The making of the circumambulations
of the Kaaba is like prayer except that you talk during it; and whoever talked in it, let him not talk anything but good." It happened that
Aishah began to menstruate during this time, and began crying with
frustration. Muhammad told her, "This is a matter that Allah has ordained for the daughters of Adam, so do everything the Pilgrims do,
except you shall not make circuits around the house." Such an event
does not invalidate the pilgrimage. Muslims only rarely go inside the
Kaaba; it has remained empty ever since the Prophet cleansed it. Its
only inside decorations are texts from the Quran on the walls.

The circumambulation should begin at the Black Stone. This ancient
rite dates back before Muhammad's day; however, in pre-Islamic times
the participants were naked. Afterward, the believers may say private
prayers, but before leaving, they make two cycles of the *salat*. After
circling the Kaaba, pilgrims go to the underground well of Zamzam,
which is also within the compound of the Great Mosque. This is the
well that Muslims believe gave succor to Hagar and Ishmael. They may
drink of this water, although it is a bit brackish.

The next part of the hajj is called the *say*, in which pilgrims reenact
Hagar's frantic search for water for her son. They run or quickly walk
between two small hills, Safa and Marwah, seven times. At one time,
this reenactment was done in the open, but the area is now safely
enclosed in a marble-lined corridor.

The most important part of the ritual, perhaps, occurs on the ninth
day of Dhul-Hijah, the Day of Arafat. The rite takes place on a plain
that itself is known as the Plain of Arafat, about a dozen miles north
of Mecca. Failure to be on the Plain of Arafat on the ninth day between dawn and dusk invalidates the entire pilgrimage. The required
noon and afternoon prayers are recited (usually in the truncated version permitted to travelers), and the pilgrims spend the day standing
(*wuquf*) in deep personal prayer and meditation between noon and

sunset. Muslims believe that humanity will be raised from this plain on the Day of Judgment to learn their fate. On this day of the Hajj, some people climb up to the Mount of Mercy, where it is said the Prophet delivered his last sermon in 632. It is also the spot where Adam and Eve were forgiven, hence the name Mount of Mercy. Here the pilgrims pray for forgiveness themselves. It is taught that this will be granted, provided that the pilgrims recognize their sins and resolve to end them, with the help of Allah. This counts as a pure *niyya* (intention). Pilgrims also must make restitution to the victims of their sin if possible. Muslims who are not able to make the pilgrimage to Mecca may also spend this day in fasting and prayer.

At sunset, the pilgrims leave the Plain of Arafat and head for Muzdalifah, a barren spot between Arafat and Mina where the sunset and evening prayers are held. They take time to gather pebbles for the next phase of the pilgrimage, although they may rest for two or three days in the vast tent city set up for them.

The next stop is the village of Mina. Here the pilgrims hurl pebbles at three stone columns, just as Abraham (or Ishmael) once did to Satan, saying, "In the name of Allah the Almighty, I do this and in hatred of the Devil and his shame." (This story is not in the Hebrew Scriptures.) The pilgrims spend three days at Mina. On the first day, each pilgrim throws seven pebbles at one pillar, but they return on the two following days to throw pebbles at all three. The stones must actually be thrown, one by one, and not simply placed near the pillar. The best stone throwing time is just after sunrise on the Day of Sacrifice. Unfortunately, this ritual has been accompanied by a lot of overcrowding, and in the past pilgrims have been killed, not by the pebbles, but in the crush of people trying to get closer to the target.

After the first day at Mina, men shave or at least shorten their hair, if they have not previously done so. It considered sufficient to remove as few as three head hairs to complete the requirement of the rite; women cut off a lock of theirs as well.

After this, the pilgrims make a final circumambulation around the Kaaba. This is not officially part of the hajj itself, but a rite that should be performed in any case just before one leaves Mecca.

The close of the hajj is marked by the Eid al-Adha, or Feast of the Sacrifice. This is Islam's most important festival and is sometimes called the "Great Festival" as opposed to the "Little Festival" that marks the end of Ramadan. It is celebrated by Muslims around the world. This feast, which can last for four days, is a more serious feast than the one celebrated at the end of Ramadan, and people are expected to keep

their minds on the importance of submission to Allah by remembering
Abraham and his sacrifice. It is not lawful to fast on this day.

A sheep, goat, or camel is slaughtered in remembrance of Abraham's
near sacrifice of his own son. (In Islamic belief this momentous event
occurred in Mecca, not in Palestine.) The sacrifice of a cow suffices
for five people; that of a camel for seven. In former times, the pilgrims
did the slaughtering themselves; however, nowadays, professional
slaughterers are used to ensure that the animals do not suffer. Prayers
are said throughout the entire process. The sacrificed meat is called
qurban. Some of the meat is roasted and goes to feed the pilgrims, and
the rest is given to the poor. If one is unable to slaughter an animal,
the requisite amount of meat can be bought and given to the poor of
Mecca. Muhammad mentioned four types of animals unsuitable for
sacrifice: those with a limp, those with only one eye, those that are
manifestly diseased, and those that are emaciated. Camels are slaughtered while standing up; sheep and cows are forced to lie down. Since
there is more meat than available mouths to eat it, the unused sacrifice
is frozen and distributed later.

One of the most famous of all hajj pilgrims was Malcolm X, whose
visit to Mecca changed his entire life and attitudes. His experience
there made him understand for the first time that people of all colors
and races could join in a spirit of unity and equality under Allah. Many
pilgrims take the hajj opportunity to visit Medina, Islam's second holy
city, although it is not officially part of the pilgrimage.

The Minor Pilgrimage

Besides the hajj, a minor pilgrimage called *umrah* (visitation) may
be made. It involves viewing many holy sites and can be undertaken at
any time of year, except the 8th, 9th, and 10th days of Dhu al-Hijjah,
the month of pilgrimage, days that are reserved for the hajj. The *umrah*
does not require standing at Arafat, but it *does* include being in a state
of ihram and dressing appropriately, circumambulating the Kaaba,
performing the *say* rite, and clipping hair from the head. Undertaking
umrah does not, however, fulfill the hajj requirement. If both pilgrimages are undertaken in one year, the hajj should be performed first.

OTHER FORMULATIONS

Although the Five Pillars are central, some hadith seem to offer a
slightly simpler road to salvation; the one from which the following

quotation comes mentions only two of the pillars, although it adds a remark about obeying commandments: "A man asked the Messenger of Allah, 'Do you think that if I recite the obligatory prayers, fast in Ramadan, treat as lawful that which is lawful and treat as forbidden that which is forbidden, and do nothing further, I shall enter Paradise?' He said 'Yes.'"

According to most Islamic theologians, true religion (*din*) simply consists of doing what Allah has commanded, avoiding what Allah has prohibited, and accepting what Allah has ordained. Once Muhammad said merely, "Whoever dies while he knows that there is no god but Allah enters Paradise." Some Muslims, based on a reading of Surah 3:110, also add the "three duties" to the beliefs and practices of Islam: *dawah* (calling others to Islam or proselytizing); encouraging good and forbidding wrongdoing; and, most notoriously, jihad.

THE SPECIAL CASE OF JIHAD

Jihad is sometimes considered the Sixth Pillar of Islam. Probably no term in the Islamic lexicon has caused more confusion—and more fear—than the simple Arabic word *jihad*. Muhammad was once asked to name the best deed. "Belief in Allah," he immediately replied. And second best? "Jihad," he answered. It is a central Islamic concept, and every major collection of hadith arranged by topic has a section titled "Jihad."

But what does this really mean? Literally, the word *jihad* means "to strive" (from the Arabic root *jhd*) and in Muslim writing is often followed by the phrase "in the path or cause of Allah" (*fi sabil illah*). *And those who strive hard for Us, We will certainly guide them in Our ways* (29:69).

In the Quran, the opposite of jihad is not "peace," which would be the case if it meant unequivocally "war," but rather *quud*, or idleness—in other words, *not* striving. However, "striving" is an ambiguous concept. When the word occurs in the Quran, it usually refers not to out-and-out warfare, but to argumentation and "efforts" made "in the cause of Allah."

Muslim and non-Muslim scholars agree that the term *jihad* carries two legitimate meanings: inner spiritual effort *and* outer physical struggle against the enemies of Islam. The "inner jihad," sometimes called the "greater jihad," is a believer's effort to live his faith and do his religious duty in the *dunya*, or everyday world. According to a well-attested hadith, a man went to Muhammad, expressing a desire to join in a military jihad. The Prophet asked him, "Are your parents still living?" When the man answered in the affirmative, Muhammad told him, "Then perform your jihad by serving and caring for them."

Muslim writers usually declare that this inner jihad was the *original* meaning of the term and that it remains more central to Islamic faith than the outer, lesser *jihad* (*al-jihad al-asghar*). A few maintain that jihad refers *only* to an inner struggle. Many Western (and some Muslim) scholars disagree, stating that external jihad was first to arrive historically and retains a position of primary importance. In the course of history, it appears that most wars fought by the Muslims, whether called jihad by some of the participants or not, contained elements of both religious and material motives. For example, Ali, the fourth caliph, told his troops on the eve of battle, "Sacrifice yourselves! You are under Allah's watchful eye and with the Prophet's cousin. Resume your charge and abhor flight, for it will disgrace your descendants and put you the hellfire in the Day of Reckoning." He then added a "carrot": "Before you lie the fertile lands [of Iraq] and large tents." Muhammad himself said, "I love that I should be killed in the way of Allah then brought to life, then killed again then brought to life, then killed and then brought to life, then killed again."

The issue remains complex. War against unbelievers is a notable theme in the Quran; however, the word *jihad* is not generally used when referring to it. The term occurs 41 times in the Quran, and when it does, it is usually defined as waging war on behalf of Allah (*fi sabil illah*), although the specific terminology "holy war" does not occur in the Quran at all. To make things more complicated, the term *jihad* has undergone periodic shifts in meaning. Throughout Islamic history, it has been employed to account for everything from a war of liberation to acts of terror.

The Arabic language contains other "war-words" with different connotations: *ribat*, a pious action usually connected with a defensive war (it can also mean a "fort"); *ghazwah*, or raid, as against a caravan; and *harb* or *qital*, both of which mean "fighting" or "war" in a general and non-religious sense. Fighting is especially permitted as means of redressing wrongs. *Fighting in the path of Allah is a worthy response to the activity of oppressor* (4:75). This may be a distinction without a difference, as nonbelievers probably did not care what term was used when the arrows started to fly.

In addition, believers are commanded with some frequency to kill, whether the term *jihad* is used or not. The most troubling war verses are the so-called sword (*ayat al-jizya*) verses, such as the following: *When the sacred months have passed, kill the unbelievers wherever you find them, and take them and confine them and lie in wait for them at every place* (9:5). Some scholars maintain that this verse, which was revealed very late, overrides 124 more peaceful Quranic proclamations. Ibn Kathir (1301–1372) maintained that the Sword Verse abrogated every peace treaty between the Prophet and every "idolater." Ibn Juzayy (d. 1340) went even further, claiming that it nullifies every treaty in the Quran period. However, they can be accused of serious misreading. The ninth surah contains mitigating passages, including, *Announce painful punishment to those who disbelieve, except those of the idolaters with whom you made an agreement, then they have not failed you in anything, and have not supported anyone against you. So fulfil your agreement with them to the end of their term. Surely Allah loves those who are careful in their duty.*

The Quran contains over 100 verses commanding believers to fight against unbelievers. Mercy is to be granted only to those who "repent," "submit," and pay their *zakat*. It is not only anti-Islamic Westerners who have pointed to these passages as important; Islamic extremists and terrorists have used them frequently. For example, Iran's Ayatollah Khomeini said, "Those who know nothing of Islam pretend that Islam counsels against war. Those people are witless. Islam says: Kill all the unbelievers just as they would kill you."

Yet these readings ignore other Quranic verses that present a kinder, gentler approach to conversion: *We have not made you their keeper, nor are you responsible for what they do* (6:107) and *we know best what the disbelievers say. You are not there to force them* (50:45). Most famous perhaps is this: *There is no compulsion in religion* (2:256), although this phrase really refers to people who are already Muslim. More compellingly, an early verse from the Quran establishes this principle: *Say: "O disbelievers! I worship not that which ye worship; not worship ye that which I worship. And I shall not worship that which ye worship. Nor will ye worship that which I worship. Unto you your religion and unto me my religion* (109:1–6).

The problem is that different parts of Quran appear to say different things (the verses were revealed over 23 years under different circumstances, which largely accounts for the discrepancies). To get around the perceived difficulty, Islamic scholars honor the principle of "abrogation," in which a later Quranic verse can trump or cancel out one revealed earlier. However, not all scholars make consistent use of this tool, and it does not help that it is not always possible to know which verses *are* the later ones. At any rate, we can safely agree with those who claim that jihad is not primarily meant to be a "war-cry," and at the same time agree with those who maintain that the Quran condones fighting against unbelievers.

The authoritative *Dictionary of Islam* defines *jihad* this way: "A religious war with those who are unbelievers in the mission of Muhammad. It is an incumbent religious duty, established in the Quran and in the Traditions as a divine institution, enjoined especially for the purpose of advancing Islam and of repelling evil from Muslims." Things could hardly be clearer.

Still, we do not know exactly when the term *jihad* became associated with the doctrine of justified war. When the Quran is studied in a historical context, it appears that in the earliest days, peaceful measures were enjoined whenever possible. However, as the Muslims became more powerful, the earlier restrictions on warfare (by whatever name it was called) were cast off, and the Islamic stance became more belligerent.

This should not be surprising. After all, Islam was born in an unsettled time, where warfare was a way of life and not considered immoral unless innocent children or women were killed. It was much the same ethical climate as the world Homer wrote about in the *Iliad*. Even in modern times, the Muslim stance is that war may be a moral necessity to protect the security of society, the same position held by many Christians.

REQUIREMENTS FOR JIHAD

Fighting should occur only in the "way of Allah"; wars fought for self-aggrandizement, glory, territory, or to oppress weaker people are condemned. To be legitimate, a *jihad* must meet the following conditions, many of which were instituted by the first caliph Abu Bakr (r. 632–634):

- Be led a by spiritual person
- Be declared only in defense in the cause of Allah
- Intend to restore peace and order
- Cease when the enemy surrenders
- Use minimum force necessary
- Non-combatants must not be threatened (ruling out weapons of mass destruction)
- Enemies cannot be deprived of food or water

The practical Muslims added that it should not be undertaken unless there was a good chance of success. The idea of a war fought in defense of some ideal is nothing new in the annals of, for want of a better word, civilization. The West, especially the Christian West, has also developed the concept of the *bellum istrum*, or "just war," as well as the idea of a "holy war." So the idea of a *jihad* is not peculiar to Islam.

The Central Asian Islamic philosopher al-Farabi (870–950) considered the question of just warfare, concluding that war merely serving a ruler's selfish impulses, or whose only purpose was conquest, could never be considered just. The aristocratic Tunisian / Spanish philosopher, statesman, and historian Ibn Khaldun (1332–1406) maintained that there were four kinds of war, but only two of them could be considered just: (1) true divine *jihad* and (2) dynastic wars against rebels who refused obedience to the rightful ruler. Khaldun remarked that when people share a unity of purpose, one for which they are willing to die, nothing can stop them. He also remarked that of the sorts of people in the world, the nomadic Arabs were the least fit to rule—and the most ferocious.

Classical scholars drew a distinction between individual and collective *jihad*. Collective *jihad* is undertaken by the entire community to ward off an invader; however, the individuals who participate in such an endeavor may also be engaged in a personal *jihad*, whose motivation is to store up merit for themselves, rather than the publicly identified goals of defending the community. All males must be ready to participate in such a *jihad* (2:216). Some scholars, such as Albrecht Noth (1937–1999), categorized these types of *jihad* as "holy war" and "holy struggle," respectively. People can support a *jihad* by giving their wealth as well as their persons (49:15), although it is not clear they will receive the same reward as actual fighters. Different traditions provide different answers.

However, the conflicts the Arabs engaged in during Muhammad's time bore little resemblance to the widespread bloodshed of modern warfare. Most of the "wars" were simply caravan raids (*ghazwah*), quickly begun and ended. The first target of the *jihad* was the Quraysh merchants; Muhammad made 17 such raids during his first 18 months after he took over the governorship of Medina. By raiding these unprotected caravans, the Muslims managed not only to enrich themselves, but—equally important—also to weaken their hated rivals, the polytheistic Meccans. The brilliant Muhammad transformed the ancient practice of caravan raiding into a religious endeavor with a sacred goal—the spread of Islam—thus imbuing it with the odor of sanctity.

THE JIHADISTS

A holy warrior is called a *Mujahidin*, who will be rewarded with victory and spoils of war. *For to him who fights in the way of Allah whether he is slain or is victorious, We shall in time grant a might reward* (4:74). And further: *One who fights with his life and possessions is superior to one who stays at home and does not fight* (4:95).

MARTYRS

If the *mujahidin* should die in battle, he or she is considered a martyr (*shahid*, literally "witness"). The linguistic connection implies that the Muslim martyr is literally a witness for his or her faith. The Quran itself provides unsettling details. *When you meet the unbelievers in the battlefield, strike off their heads, and when you have laid them low, bind your captives firmly* (47:4). For jihadists, death is not the final evil, or even an evil at all—it is the gate to martyrdom and the pathway to the ultimate victory of Islam. *And do not think those who have been killed in the way of Allah are dead; they are rather living with their Lord, well-provided for. Rejoicing in what the Lord has given them of his bounty and they rejoice for those who stayed behind and did not join them, knowing that they have nothing to fear and that they shall not grieve* (3:169–170). However, it is reiterated by Muslim scholars that no one can say for certain (unless he or she has received a revelation) whether a person is a martyr or not.

Martyrs face a glorious and sensual afterlife. *They shall recline on jeweled couches face to face, and there shall wait on them immortal youths with bowls and ewers and a cup of the purest wine that will neither pain their heads nor take away their reason; with fruits of their own choice and flesh of fowls that they relish. And theirs shall be the dark-eyed houris, chaste as hidden pearls, a guerdon for their deeds* (56:5–24). According to common belief, they go directly to Heaven and do not have to wait for the Last Day like the rest of us. According to one tradition, the souls of martyrs have the shape of white birds that feed on the fruits of Paradise. Their sins (although not their debts) are forgiven. Those who die at sea are supposed to receive twice the reward of those who die on land. Again, this is according to tradition—nothing of the sort is mentioned in the Quran.

But just who is a martyr? The matter is not clearly defined. The Prophet once asked his companions, "Whom do you count as a martyr?" They answered, "one who is attacked with a weapon and as a consequence of that dies from his injuries." Muhammad rejoined,

"Many persons receive injuries and die in battle but they are neither martyrs nor are their sacrifices laudable. On the other hand, many a man dies a natural death in bed, but in the eyes of the Lord, he is a champion of truth and thus a martyr." Women dying in childbirth, Muslims dying on pilgrimage, and those traveling in the pursuit of learning are also martyrs. Even those dying from certain diseases such a plague are granted martyrdom status.

Another hadith makes the same point even more strongly: "The first person judged on Resurrection Day will be a man killed in battle. He will be brought forth. Allah will tell him, 'You fought in order to be called a hero, and it has already been said.' Then he will be sentenced and dragged away on his face and flung into the Fire." Allah alone knows who is fighting for his sake rather than for some other reason. However, to play it safe, those killed in battle are generally buried as if they were martyrs. This is a special procedure that omits the customary washing of the body.

On a more belligerent note, Muhammad said, "I have been ordered to fight against people until they testify that there is no god but Allah and Muhammad is the Messenger of Allah and until they recite the prayers and pay the *zakat*." War is enjoined even when the combatants may be reluctant. *Prescribed for you is fighting, though it be hateful to you. Yet it may happen that you will hate a thing which is better for you; and it may happen that you will love a thing which is worse for you; Allah knows, and you do not* (2:216).

The concept of martyrdom is especially important in Shia Islam, whose emphasis on death and suffering has always been rather marked. The martyrdom did not, in accordance with Muhammad's teaching, have to take place on a battlefield. Indeed, most of the prophet's descendants through Ali were considered martyrs, but most especially Ali's son Husayn (killed in 680 at Karbala).

Restrictions on Jihad

The Quran puts restrictions on fighting. It specifies that Muslims must not be aggressors, although they are to fight fiercely if wronged. Surah 2:190–192 covers a panoply of military behaviors and the circumstances that warrant them:

And fight in the way of Allah with those who fight with you, but aggress not; Allah loves not the aggressors. Slay them wherever you come upon them, and expel them from where they expelled you; persecution is more grievous than slaying. But fight them not by the Holy Mosque until they should fight you there; then, if they fight you, slay them—such is the recompense of unbelievers—but if they give over, surely Allah is all-forgiving, all-compassionate.

Peacemaking is always encouraged: *If the enemy incline toward peace, incline toward peace also* (8:61). And further: *Allah summons humankind to the abode of peace* (dar al-salam), *both in this life and the next* (10:25). So clearly *jihad* is supposed to be defensive: *Permission is given to those who fight because they have been wronged, and indeed Allah is able to give them victory; those who have been driven from their homes unjustly only because they said "Our Lord is Allah"* (22:39). However, a more offensive stance is permitted if circumstances warrant, within certain limits.

The Quran emphasized that *jihad* must be proportional to the offense: *Whoever transgresses against you, respond in kind* (2:194). Yet forgiveness is better than revenge: *The reward for an injury is an equal injury back; but if a person forgives instead, and makes reconciliation, he will be rewarded by Allah* (42:40). Muhammad said, "Do not kill the elderly, children or babies, or women. Do not steal anything from the booty, but collect it together and do good with it. Allah loves those who do good."

Muhammad forbade the slaying of the enemy's livestock, except those needed for the Muslims to survive. Nor should fruit or palm trees be torched. He generally advocated humane treatment of hostages. In one case, his enemy Suhayl was caught. The man had a cleft lower lip; Umar threatened to knock out his teeth so that his tongue would flop out. Muhammad grew angry: "I will not mutilate him, for if I did, Allah would mutilate me, even though I am his Messenger. Think, perhaps one day he will make a stand for which you will not be able to find fault." And indeed Suhayl converted and became a hero.

One of the most serious jihadist crimes is theft of booty. A slave of Muhammad died fighting in a jihad: normally this would grant him a ticket to Paradise. However, he had stolen an article of clothing from the infidel during the raid, which should have gone to the *ummah*, or Islamic community. Muhammad announced that he saw the man in hellfire.

The classic Islamic tomes of law include a section called "The Book of Jihad," outlining rules for warfare, treatment of noncombatants, collection of booty, and cessation of hostilities. It may not be surprising to find that these authorities do not always agree with one another.

TERRORISM

Most Muslims reject terrorism, although Islamic terrorism remains a significant problem. Islam is neither the most peaceful of world religions nor a front for terrorism. Like members of other faiths, Muslims run the gamut from warriors to peacemakers. Some glory in violence; others deplore it. For example, Sheikh Saalih al-Lehaydaan, the top-ranked jurist in Saudi Arabia, labeled the September 11 attacks a "grave criminal act which Islam does not approve of and which no one should applaud." Other groups, however, such as al-Muhajiroun, founded by Sheikh Oman bin Bakri bin Muhammad, vowed 10 days after the September 11 attacks to "engage in Jihad against [the] USA and target their government and military installations." Also disturbing to Western ears was the shattering silence emanating from certain Muslim clerical circles. Some moderate Muslims seemed more concerned about fancied Western "backlash" and "persecution" than horrified about the actions of the terrorists. Nor did the videos of Palestinians dancing with joy at the news of the attacks do much to allay fears of Islamic jihad. Middle Eastern analyst Daniel Pipes has suggested that between 150 and 200 million Muslims are in sympathy with terrorists, although terms such as "in sympathy with" need to be carefully analyzed.

The Quran has been interpreted in such a way as to legitimize terrorism. But the same can be said of the Bible: one passage, aimed at the Babylonians, is more gruesome than anything in the Quran: "Happy is he who takes your little ones and dashes them against the rocks!" (Psalm 137:9). The Bible also praises Saul who "has slain his thousands" and David who has slain his "ten thousands." However, Christians and Jews are convinced that these passages are historical only, with no relevance today. In any case, "Christian terrorism" is not a factor in the modern world, if it ever was. Yet Islamic terrorist groups have developed multinational apparatus to carry out the Quranic command to "kill the infidels" wherever they are found. These organizations include but are not limited to al-Qaeda, Hezbollah, Islamic Jihad, and Hamas.

WHO ARE THE TERRORISTS?

It is not true that most Islamic terrorists are members of the downtrodden underclass, nor that the leaders of many terrorist groups are highly educated men. Scholars have not been able to draw a connection between poverty, ignorance, and terrorism. If such a link does exist, it is tenuous and indirect. (Such a connection is in force as far as property crimes go, but not terrorism.) A comparison with the Nazis might be in order: Joseph Goebbels, Hitler's Minister of Propaganda, had a PhD from the University of Heidelberg. Shaykh Omar Abdel Rahman, who developed plans to bomb several sites in the United States, has a doctorate in Islamic studies. Osama bin Laden was a college graduate and member of a wealthy family. His chief assistant, Ayman al-Zawahiri, was a surgeon. Ramzi Ahmed Youself, one of the perpetrators of the World Trade Center bombings in 1993, studied engineering at Swansea University in Wales. Bin Laden, who masterminded the September 11 attacks, is an educated person who bases his hate-filled activities on quotations from the Quran. He began in 1996 with a declaration of war against all infidels, among which he includes many Muslims, especially the "apostate" leaders of Saudi Arabia, whom he despises because of their reliance on American "invaders." What would Muhammad say about this? He once commanded, "Help your brother whether he is the wrong-doer or the wronged." Thereupon the people said to him, "O messengers of Allah, we can help the man when he is wronged, but we fail to understand how a wrong-doer can be helped." The Prophet replied, "You can do this by holding his hand back from an act of oppression." Amen. Although Islamic terrorism is a fact today, it cannot be something that Muhammad would have approved.

CHAPTER 3

Muhammad

Islam is indissolubly linked with its founder or revealer, the Prophet Muhammad (whose name may also be spelled Mohammed, a name that means "the praised one"), a powerful figure who fulfilled the roles of Prophet, father, grandfather, husband, friend, ruler, and military leader. Muhammad has been listed as the most influential person in the history of the world, but he has also been a divisive and controversial figure. His character was perhaps too large, too complex, and too strange to be easily captured, although many have tried.

For Muslims, his role was clear: he was sent as a mercy to humankind (21:107) and as a model to all believers (33:21). The Quran repeatedly instructs believers to obey his commandments (3:32, 3:132, 4:13, 4:69, 5:92, 8:1, 8:20, 8:46, 9:71, 24:47, 24:51, 24:52–54, 33:33, 49:4, 58:13, 64:12).

Although there is a wealth of biographical material about Muhammad, the details of his life are recorded in Muslim sources only. Contemporary documents recording events his life are practically nonexistent. Our knowledge is derived from the Quran and the Sunnah (the traditions of the Prophet recorded in the hadith), mostly the latter. This makes ferreting out a historically accurate biography challenging. For many years, even non-Muslim scholars accepted the Islamic version of Muhammad's life and the textual development (if not the initial revelation) of the Quran as basically factual. Most Muslim scholars hold fast to their position that the early biographical material (*sira*) is literally true and that events happened very much as the Quran, *sira*, and hadith say they did. (Islamic studies have always been more resistant to textual criticism than have biblical studies.) Until recently even non-Muslim scholars have adopted this noncritical stance. As French philosopher Ernest Renan (1823–1892) wrote in 1851, Muhammad lived "in the full light of history."

However, recent linguistic, historical, textual, and cultural research has cast doubt on some of the most widely accepted and deeply held facts about Muhammad, including the date of his birth, events of his life, and sayings attributed to him. However, this work is still emerging, and most scholars agree that his traditional biography *sira* (literally "the way") is basically factual. (When Muslims write about Muhammad—or indeed any other prophet—it is customary and recommended to attach the words "Peace be upon him" (*Salallhu alayhi wa sallam*) or the initials PBUH after his name. These words are also often added when the names of other prophets are spoken aloud, although they may be added silently.)

The Quran itself has little to say about Muhammad's life; it talks more about Moses and Abraham. Even the hadith were written down years after Muhammad's death, and like the Gospels and the stories about the Buddha, their historical accuracy is difficult to verify. Still, it is impossible to overestimate their importance for pious Muslims. Muhammad stated, "One who loves my Sunnah loves me and whoever loves me will find himself by my side in Paradise."

The portrait of Muhammad among non-Muslims has been variously drawn. In the West it has often been unflattering. He has been excoriated as a fake, a lecher, a servant of Satan, a demoniac, a heretic, and even the Antichrist. Martin Luther accused Muslims of being servants of the devil and claimed Muhammad was a false prophet driven by lust. The Italian poet Dante, in his epic *Inferno*, consigned Muhammad to the Eighth Circle of Hell as a schismatic. Because Dante regarded Muhammad as sowing the seeds of discord, he is pictured as being cut in half, over and over again, "from the chin / down to the fart-hole."

Humphrey Prideaux (1648–1724), the Dean of Norwich, produced *Mahomet: The True Nature of Imposture*, whose title reveals its bent. Prideaux commented that "for the first part of his Life he led a very wicked and licentious Course, much delighting in Rapine, Plunder, and Blood-shed, according to the usage of the Arabs, who mostly followed this kind of life, being almost continually in Arms one Tribe against another, to plunder and take from each other all they could." He went on to remark that Muhammad's "two predominant passions were *Ambition* and *Lust*." (But it is not only the West that has disparaged Muhammad. The Quran records that Muhammad was vilified by his opponents in his own day, who labeled him a sorcerer and impostor.)

On the other hand, there was a brief frenzy among Enlightenment philosophers to present Muhammad as one of their own, a rationally driven philosopher. The French Voltaire (1694–1778), in his *Les Moeurs et l'esprit des nations* (1756), considered Muhammad an important political thinker and praised Islam as a "rational religion," considering it more tolerant of other faiths than Christianity had been. As a deist, Voltaire appreciated the simplicity of Islamic doctrine: there is one God only, and his Prophet is Muhammad. However, he also declared in his tragedy *Mahomet* (1742), that Muhammad was an "impostor."

Edward Gibbon (1796–1862), a British historian, admired the Muhammad of the early Meccan years, but impugned the Muhammad of the Medina years, noting that the Prophet's personality seemed to undergo an alteration as his role changed from prophet to legislator. The Scottish Thomas Carlyle (1795–1881) made Muhammad a hero in his *Sartor Resartus: Hero-Worship and the Heroic in History*, although he also referred to him as "uncultured" and a "semi-barbarian." Like Gibbon and Voltaire, he seemed conflicted in his opinions.

MUHAMMAD IN ISLAM

For Muslims, Muhammad is the "Seal of the Prophets" (33:40), announcing, "My relationship to the prophets before me is that of a man who had skillfully and beautifully built a house, but there is one brick missing in the corner. People pass by and say, 'If only that brick were in place!' I am that brick and I am the last of the prophets," meaning that he revealed the entirety of Allah's message. Muslims believe that anyone who claims prophethood after Muhammad, or believes in anyone claiming it, is a disbeliever. Interestingly, religious historian Carsten Colpe (b. 1929) identified the first occurrence of the term "seal of the prophets" not in Islamic writings, but in the first century works of the Church Father Tertullian in his *Adversus Judaeos*, referring to Jesus.

Calling Muhammad the "Seal of the Prophets" does not mean that he was greater than the rest, only that his revelations came down uncorrupted and perfectly preserved. No further scriptures will be revealed, no other prophet will arrive. Muslims believe that Muhammad did not speak only to his own tribe or emphasize only one aspect of the divine message, as previous prophets did, but addressed all humanity. *O humanity! I am the Messenger of Allah to you all!* (7:158).

Although Muhammad is not considered a divine figure, his name is honored, and Muslims are sensitive about it. While Muhammad is the most popular name for a Muslim male child, several people have gotten into considerable trouble naming animals after the Prophet. When the American economist John Kenneth Galbraith was ambassador to India (1961–1963), he named his pet cat Ahmed (one of Muhammad's nicknames), and quite a dustup occurred, with protest meetings taking place in several Pakistani cities. The deputy speaker of Pakistan's national assembly announced that such an act, if true, was "much more serious than American arms aid to India." However, it was all a misunderstanding. The cat was not actually named after the Prophet, but after Ahmedabad, the city where the cat was presented to the ambassador's children. To avert an international crisis, the Galbraiths renamed the cat Gujurat.

When, in 2007, British teacher Gillian Gibbons allowed her six- and seven-year-old Sudanese students to name their class teddy bear Muhammad, she was arrested and spent 15 days in jail. By the strong interference of the worldwide community, she was spared the 40 lashes the court originally imposed. According to Isam Abu Hasabu, chairman of Unity High School's PTA, "The whole thing boiled down to a cultural misunderstanding. In our culture we don't know the bear as a cuddly symbol of mercy."

The "Historical Muhammad"

The details of Muhammad's early life are difficult to approach objectively. The traditional biographical material we possess about Muhammad is vast, far exceeding what we have about Jesus, the Buddha, Moses, Socrates, or practically any other figure from his era or before. Pious accounts tell us not only the events of his life but also what he wore, what he said, what he liked to eat, and even his bathroom practices. However, none of the early biographies was composed by anyone who actually knew Muhammad. None were even written during his lifetime (as is the case for Jesus and the Buddha). This, of course, doesn't make them automatically false. Oral records were passed down, and there were probably early written accounts that have not survived. Yet time changes memories, and the written accounts we have are not always in perfect agreement. Three of the most important early biographies are those by Ibn Ishaq (d. 704–768), Abd al-Malik ibn Hisham of Basra (d. 833 or 834), and Ibn Said (d. 845). Ibn Ishaq's biography, the earliest (750), has survived only in an edited version by ibn Hisham. Hisham admits that he omitted certain things from Ibn Ishaq's biography that might "distress" some people; no one knows what they are. Another man, Muhammad ibn Umar al-Waqidi (d. 820), wrote mostly about Muhammad's military campaigns.

Although non-Muslims consider Muhammad the founder of Islam, Islam does not claim to be a new religion. Instead, Muslims believe that Muhammad brought about a restored version of the true faith (*iman*), the primordial religion of humankind. His revelation summed up all previous revelations but did not add anything new. Although some Christians have declared that Muhammad was a Muslim equivalent of their Messiah, Muslims have proclaimed over and over that Muhammad is a mortal rather than a divine being. Muslims do *not* worship Muhammad, and Muhammad himself insisted on his humanity. When people asked him for a miracle, his answer was, *Exalted be my Lord, I am but a mortal, a messenger of God* (17:93). He also said, *I do not say to you, "I have the treasures of Allah with me" nor do I say "I know things beyond human perception" not do I say, "I am angel"; I follow only that which is revealed to me* (6:50 and 11:31). In Surah 7:188 he is exhorted to say, *"I am nothing but a warner* (nadhir), *and a herald of glad tidings to a people who will believe."*

But he remains for Muslims the *ideal* human, with almost (but not quite) superhuman stature. He was also demanding and declared, "None among you is a true believer unless his love for me predominates over love for everything else, including that of family, property, and all humankind." He brooked no opposition. "It was only their excessive questioning and their disagreeing with their prophets that destroyed those who were before you," he said.

Because Muslims believe that Muhammad spoke for Allah, his deeds and words became a guide for holy living second only to the Quran itself. He himself said, echoing the Quran, "What I have forbidden to you, avoid; what I have ordered you to do, do as much of it as you can." The Quran declared his word was law: *Whatever the Prophet gives you, accept, and whatever he forbids you, avoid* (59:7). And further: *Whoever rebels against Allah and His Apostle—verily the fire of hell awaits him, therein to abide beyond the count of time* (72:23). His wife Aishah said that Muhammad's conduct was itself the Quran, and some Muslims have even identified him as the "living Quran." He is their model not only in things that have moral relevance but also in matters of eating, drinking, dressing, grooming, and even sleeping. And the hadith report certain deeds of his that sound fairly miraculous. In one case, for example, his men were digging a trench in readiness for battle but were unable to move a large rock. The Prophet spat some water on it and it shattered.

Muhammad's Early Life

According to tradition, Muhammad ibn Abdullah was born in the trading city of Mecca about 570. The traditional date for Sunnis is April 20; for Shias it is April 26. As if to portend something miraculous about him, 570 was a strange year. It is said that the Christian Abyssinian viceroy to Yemen, a man named Abraha, wanted to turn the Arabs from their faith and convert them to Christianity. He mounted his war elephant and charged with his army into Mecca, promising to raze the Kaaba to the ground. However, mysterious flocks of birds appeared in the sky and began dropping stones infected with some terrible disease on the invaders. Abraha's heart burst, and his fingers fell off one by one, and they were "eaten up." (According to the Quran, the coming of Muhammad was foretold by Jesus himself: *And remember Jesus, son of Mary, said, "O children of Israel! I am the messenger of Allah sent to you, confirming the law which came before me, and giving glad tidings of a messenger to come after me, whose name is Ahmad* [a variant of Muhammad], 61:6.)

The future Prophet was a member of the declining Banu Hashim clan, an offshoot of the wealthy and powerful tribe of Quraysh, which was in control of Mecca. Ultimately, he was a descendant of Abraham. His mother, Aminah bint Wahb, is said to have had visions during her joyful, pain-free pregnancy. "I did not feel that I was pregnant," she said, "nor did I find myself heavy because of it." Once she heard a voice announcing, "You are carrying in your womb the master of the nation. When he is born, say, 'I place him under the protection of the One God, safe from the evil of every envier.' Call him Muhammad," a name not previously used. During the actual birth, a brilliant light came from her body, by which she could see castles in Syria.

Muhammad never knew his father, Abdallah, a caravan merchant, who died in Yathrib (Medina) returning from a journey while Aminah was pregnant. The little information we have about him indicates he was tall and handsome, with a prominent nose, a sign of good looks. One legend says that while he was on the way to his own wedding, a woman rushed out of her home to proposition him. The surprised Abdallah explained he was occupied at the moment but might stop by later. The next day, however, although he walked hopefully by her house, the woman was no longer interested. "When I saw you before," she said, "there was a great light shining between your eyes, a sign that your son would be a great prophet. Now that light it is gone, and I know another woman is bearing this child."

When Muhammad was two years old, he was sent away from Mecca to live in the healthier region of Taif, southeast of Mecca. It was not an uncommon practice among the Quraysh of the time to take children into these uplands. It was intended to strengthen their constitution, improve their manners, and help them absorb the pure Arabic language of the Bedouins. The experience stuck with Muhammad, who was heard to say later in life, "I am the purest Arab among you all."

His foster mother and wet nurse was Halimah, the wife of a poor shepherd. "As soon as I put him to my bosom, my breasts overflowed with milk," Halimah said. The family camel also began giving record amounts of milk, and even the donkey suddenly acquired a new lease on life, outstripping all the others on journeys. Muhammad was definitely good luck to the household.

Even as a child, Muhammad was given to reverie and strange experiences. When he was five years old, he fell down in a field and shouted that two angels wearing white garments had slit open his abdomen and were stirring up his bowels, looking for something. They then cleansed his heart with snow. This scary incident convinced Halimah that it was time to send Muhammad back home, despite his milk-eliciting prowess.

When Muhammad was six, his chronically ill mother died while returning from a visit to her husband's grave. Her son's inheritance consisted of five camels, some sheep, and an Abyssinian slave woman named Baraka, who took him to the home of his grandfather, Abd al-Muttalib. He was a saintly, handsome old man, guardian of the sacred Kaaba and mayor of Mecca. The Meccans did not maintain a separation between "church and state"; the custodians of the holiest shrine in Arabia were also political leaders. It was Abd al-Muttalib who taught the Muhammad the religious rites of the place.

An interesting story attaches to Muhammad's grandfather. As a young man he re-dug the Zamzam well, with the aid of his only son, al-Harith. However, the work proved so arduous that he recognized the need for help and prayed for 10 sons, promising that if his wish came true, he would sacrifice one of them to the gods. Sure enough, 10 fine boys were born, but one of them, Abdullah (later to be Muhammad's father), won his grandfather's heart.

However, a vow was a vow, and when Abd al-Muttalib drew lots to see which son should pay the fatal price, the choice fell on Abdullah. Shades of Abraham! Abd al-Muttalib was ready to carry out his oath, but the Meccans persuaded him that the gods could not really want a human sacrifice. He should substitute camels, of which he owned a large herd. Abd al-Muttalib agreed to test the divine will by drawing lots between his son on one side and 10 camels on the other. The lots pointed to the human sacrifice, so the number of camels was increased, and increased again. Still the lots kept indicating Abdullah as the designated sacrifice. Finally, when the number of camels reached 100, the lots finally switched to the animals. To make sure, Abd at-Muttalib repeated the operation three times, and when he was satisfied that Abdullah was off the hook, the 100 camels were duly slaughtered and their meat given to the poor. Perhaps it was the narrow escape of his father that later set Muhammad so firmly against gambling.

Abd al-Muttalib passed away at the age of 82, and Muhammad was orphaned yet again. Because he was a posthumous child who had not reached the age of maturity when his grandfather died, he was by law excluded from inheriting. Perhaps the deprivations suffered by Muhammad as a youth account for the sympathy he felt for poor and destitute people.

Muhammad's gentle but impecunious uncle, Abu Talib, head of the Banu Hashim clan, took him in. Abu Talib was a cloth merchant who also owned some sheep, and Muhammad took charge of them. During this time, legend says something strange and rather biblical happened. Abu Talib was about to take a caravan to Syria, and the 12-year-old Muhammad begged to go. He had undoubtedly had enough of being abandoned. The party stopped at Bosra, where an old Nestorian monk named Bahira recognized Muhammad as a future prophet by his appearance, his activities, his sleep habits, and his answers to questions. (Muhammad refused to swear an oath by the goddesses al-Lat and Uzzah. "I will swear by Allah alone," he said. "Do not ask me by al-Lat and al-Uzzah, for nothing is more hateful to me than those two.") Of special interest to the monk was the "seal of prophethood" on Muhammad's back, a large mole between his shoulder blades. At his birth this same mole had been said to exude a sweet smell like musk. (The idea that holy persons bear a physical mark of their specialness occurs in many faiths. Special marks, for instance, were also characteristic of the Buddha. It was only when they were discovered by a seer that predictions were made about the Buddha's future career.) Bahira suggested that Muhammad be kept safe from the Jews, who would commit evil against him if they knew who he was. A similar report declares that soon after Muhammad's birth, a Jew spotted the mole and fell into a faint, knowing that the prophethood and scriptures had passed from the Jews to the Arabs. These reports are not absolutely claimed as being true, and they probably throw more light on later Muslim attitudes than on Muhammad's childhood. Muhammad himself never alluded to these experiences.

As he grew, Muhammad became highly respected in all his business dealings, being known as Al-Amin—the "trustworthy or truthful one." He also was a foremost member of the Hilf al-Fudul, or the League of the Virtuous, a chivalrous organization dedicated to safeguarding the rights of the poor and needy. It is partly because of his sterling reputation that he was able to persuade so many people of the truth of his revelations when they did come.

A Verbal Portrait of Muhammad

No physical likeness of Muhammad exists because the Prophet declared that creating likenesses of human beings was an impious act. However, in contrast to Jesus, numerous verbal descriptions of him can be found and we have a very good picture of what he looked like. Indeed, no detail is spared.

He was stocky man of middle height and a good physique, with thick, wavy, shoulder-length hair. He also had a black, curly beard that reached his chest. (When he died, this beard had 17 gray hairs in it.) He had a thin line of hair from the chest to navel, as well as hair on the upper part of his chest, arms, and shoulders; the lower part of his chest and his stomach was hairless. His bones and shoulder blades protruded, according to his son-in-law Ali, who also claimed he had a finer chest than anyone else.

His large dark eyes were enhanced by the use of kohl, an ancient version of eye shadow/liner. It is sometimes remarked that he had a tendency for bloodshot eyes as well, although the word may refer to his eyelashes. His lashes are referred to as being "silky" and heavy.

His skin was as soft as a woman's and rosy. He had a high forehead and a somewhat round head that, although handsome, was a bit too large for his body. He had long tapering fingers. His ankles were thin, although he had fleshy palms and feet.

His teeth were brilliantly white, and when he laughed (which was frequently), his gums could be seen. When he turned, he turned his entire body, not just his head. (Perhaps he suffered from a stiff neck, although an alternative explanation is that he was excessively polite and wished to give his full attention to the person who had called him.) He had a rather odd, lurching walk, as if he were going downhill, which suggests a physical problem, perhaps resulting from his being wounded. Normally, he spoke in a low pleasing voice, but when he yelled, he scared everyone. However, he was not talkative as a rule.

First Marriage

Muhammad became the manager of a caravan owned by a rich, twice-widowed woman and distant relative, also from the Quaraysh tribe. It is said that he doubled her fortune on his first caravan trip. She was so impressed with his ability that she doubled his fee. Her complete name is Khadijah bint Khuwaylid ibn Asad ibn Abd al-Uzza ibn Quasyy, but she is known simply as Khadijah. She was a crucial factor in his life.

Muhammad married her when he was 25 years old, and she was 40. It was Khadijah who proposed the marriage, through a female agent. (Khadijah was not desperate, even if she was at a rather advanced age. She had repeatedly refused offers from others.) The agent suggested slyly to Muhammad, "What prevents you from marrying?" Muhammad confessed he had not the wherewithal to get married, whereupon the agent replied, "What if that difficulty were removed and you were invited to marry someone of beauty, wealth, noble birth, and discretion?"

"Who is she?" inquired Muhammad, his interest piqued by this intriguing picture.

"None other than Khadijah herself," responded the agent smoothly. Muhammad wondered how he could attain such a wife, but the agent assured him she would handle everything. And she did. When they finally met face to face on the balcony of Khadijah's mansion, she said, "O cousin, I have desired to marry you because of our relationship and because of your noble birth and honor among your people, and because of your honesty, your good manners, and the truthfulness of your discourse." And so they were wed. On the day of their wedding, Khadijah gave her husband a Syrian slave named Zayd ibn Harith as a present. This young boy became very attached to Muhammad, who later freed him and adopted him as a foster son.

The couple eventually had four daughters: Zaynab, Ruqayyah, Umm Kuthum, and Fatimah. Fatimah (605–632) is the most famous. She was born in Mecca and married Abu Talib's son, Ali, one of Muhammad's first converts. She bore him four children. She is regarded highly both by Sunni and Shia Muslims, and her life is considered to be an example for both men and women; many Muslim girls are named after her. Sadly, she died only a few months after Muhammad himself. She died in Medina, but the precise location of her tomb is unknown.

Their two sons, al-Qasim and Abdallah, died in infancy, one of the great sorrows of his life. However, his favorite daughter, Fatimah, became famous in her own right; today she is revered by Muslims not only as Muhammad's daughter but also as the wife of his cousin and eventual successor Ali. All Muhammad's children, with the exception of a boy named Ibrahim, who died in early childhood, came from his marriage to Khadijah. Khadijah may also have had three children by a former marriage.

(Direct descendants of the Prophet are called *Ashraf*. Over time the *ashraf* became a social class of their own, distinguished by their noble heritage. They expected deference as a result of their bloodline, and some of them even claimed to possess special and hidden knowledge unavailable to the mass of Muslims. Although some Muslims continued to honor the *ashraf* because of their ancestry, the idea that they were closer to Allah than other believers struck most Muslims as opposite to the egalitarian spirit of Islam.)

Khadijah early recognized that Muhammad was no ordinary man, and all traditions acknowledge the enormous and comforting role she played as Muhammad became aware of his prophetic mission. For this and other reasons, she is sometimes known as Khadijah al-Kubra, or Khadijah the Grand, and is viewed as a perfect woman, one of four in the Muslim tradition. The other three are their daughter Fatimah, the Virgin Mary, and Asiyah, the wife of the Pharaoh who saved the baby Moses from the river.

By all accounts, Muhammad and Khadijah had a close and happy union, and it was not until she died in 619 that Muhammad took other wives, despite the fact that polygamy was extremely common in Arabia. Perhaps it was not something she would have allowed. It is probable that Muhammad loved her above any other woman in his life, and it is known that Aishah, his favorite afterward, was jealous of the Prophet's love for Khadijah, although she had never met her. She recounted that long after Khadijah's death, the Prophet would still send a portion of any sheep he had slaughtered to Khadijah's friends in her memory.

Perhaps because several of Muhammad's own children died before him, he was known to say, "Any Muslim who loses three children will be touched only a tiny bit by the Fire," suggesting that the parent had already suffered enough. When the questioner, a man named Jabir, asked about having lost only two children, he responded, "Even two."

One who was listening said, "By Allah, if only you had said one, he would have said the same." Jabir responded, "I think so too."

Despite the fact that Khadijah was a wealthy woman when she married Muhammad, much of that wealth evaporated over time. It has been suggested that Muhammad was not a very good manager, possibly because he was so honest.

The Call to Prophethood

Muhammad began to receive revelations in about 610, when he was 40 years old. The call did not come out of the blue. It came, just like the Buddha's Enlightenment, only after long mental and spiritual preparation. He had been in the habit, for three years or so, of retreating to Mount Hira for periods of solitary prayerful meditation (*tahannuth*), sometimes for several days or even weeks at a time. This had long been a custom of the Quraysh, so he was honoring a tradition. Khadijah would send up food and water, or even stop by to visit periodically, sometimes bringing along their little girls. Other visitors came as well, for Muhammad, though contemplative, was not a hermit.

It was on Mount Hira that the first verses of the Quran were revealed, during the so-called Night of Power (*Laylat ul-Qadr*), by an angel later identified as Gabriel, although early Muslims believed the figure was Allah himself.

Muhammad's response to the angel's command to "read" seems to have been, "*Ma aqra*," which can be translated as *either* "What shall I read?" or "I do not read," statements that obviously do not mean quite the same thing. In any case, Muhammad seemed confused by the divine command, and it is clearly stated in Islamic tradition that he could not read. In fact, he is known as the unlettered (*ummi*) prophet, although there is increasing dispute about his alleged illiteracy. Because there is no counterevidence, Muhammad's illiteracy can simply be accepted, although it is difficult to see how an illiterate man would have been put in charge of complex business affairs as Muhammad was. The story becomes even more confusing because it is not clear whether the angel even asked him to read in the first place, given that "read" in Arabic can also be used to mean "recite!" It is not possible to learn the truth from the story as handed down. The importance of Muhammad's alleged illiteracy for Muslims is that no one, but especially no one who was illiterate, could be suspected of coming up with the Quran on his own. Therefore it must be divine. Still, a lack of literacy does not mean that one cannot create great poetry.

In any case, when Muhammad denied being able to read (or recite) the angel attacked him. Muhammad felt as if he were being strangled as the angel pressed on him a silken scroll or brocaded cloth, adorned with letters of flame. And then he began to pronounce the words that became Surah 96 of the Quran: *Recite in the name of your Lord who created humankind from a clot of blood . . .* (The term rendered here a clot of blood, *alaq*, may also be translated as "embryo" or germ-cell. More literally, it means "clinging" and refers to some sticky substance.)

Muhammad's famous reaction to the message was one of terror and disbelief. In fact, he seriously considered throwing himself off a cliff, for fear he was mad, possessed, or even worse—a poet. "Never," he vowed, "will the Quraysh say that of me!" (The Quraysh was the elite tribe of Mecca with whom Muhammad had continual difficulties.) He was so bewildered by his unsettling experience that he rushed down the mountainside. Turning around, he saw the entire space between the earth and sky filled by the Angel (widely presumed to be Gabriel) in the form of a man. Gabriel said, "O Muhammad! You are indeed Allah's Messenger!" and then Muhammad became calm again.

Eventually, he was persuaded of the truth of the revelations by his wife Khadijah, who comforted him by covering him with a sheet and holding his hand all night. Being covered with a sheet or cloak was the customary way ancient prophets delivered an oracle, and Muhammad was undoubtedly following in the same tradition. Still, he remained unnerved by the event. "If there's anything I can't stand," he told Khadijah, "it's a soothsayer. Now it looks as if I am turning into one myself."

The angel soon appeared again and said to him, perhaps gently mocking his terror, *You, there, wrapped up in sheets! Stand in prayer at night, but not all night, maybe half. Or a little less or more. Recite the Quran in slow measured tones. Soon We will give you a heavy message. Truly, getting up late at night is powerful for controlling one's soul and the best for forming words of prayer and praise* (73:1–6). These words are some of the earliest revealed verses of the Quran, although they are placed rather late in the text.

According to another tradition, while Muhammad was describing what he had seen (either from the first visitation or a subsequent one), he became aware of angelic presences all about him. Khadijah decided to test the angels by taking off her clothes and having Muhammad sit on her lap. The prudish angels scurried off. "See, Muhammad," she said. "These presences are of God. If they were not, they would have stayed around to see what we would do." Thus, Khadijah convinced her husband that he had received a true revelation. Muhammad continued to receive revelations throughout the rest of his life, line by line and verse by verse.

Muhammad revealed his message only to a small group of followers at first, Khadijah and her elderly cousin Warraqa ibn Nawfal among them. Warraqa was a learned man who was said to have been the first person to translate the Gospel into Arabic; he was reportedly learned in Hebrew also. He at various times declared himself to be a Christian and a Jew, although he eventually returned to his own pagan faith.

Warraqa certified that the angel that Muhammad had heard was Gabriel. He lamented the fact that he himself was not a young man (indeed he died soon afterward) because he wished to offer his help against the time that Muhammad would be exiled from the area. "Will they expel me indeed?" asked Muhammad. Warraqa replied, "Yes, never has a man appeared with something like which you have brought but he has been held in enmity."

After Warraqa died, Muhammad's revelations broke off. This black period of unknown length (different sources give different estimations, ranging from six months to two-and-a-half years) is known as the *fatra*, or "intermission," during which Muhammad sank into a depression. The revelations finally resumed with the surpassingly beautiful Surah 93, the Surah of Morning, and continued sporadically for the rest of his life.

> *By the white forenoon and the brooding night*
> *Your Lord has neither forsaken you nor hates you,*
> *And the Last shall be better for you than the first.*
> *Your Lord shall give you, and you will be satisfied.*
>
> *Did he not find you an orphan and shelter you?*
> *Did he not find you erring, and guide you?*
> *Did he not find you needy, and suffice you?*

THE FIRST CONVERTS

For about three years, Muhammad revealed his message to only a few people, mostly friends and family. (Apparently, Islam was first known by the word *tazaqqah*, a word whose meaning is obscure.) His first converts were Khadijah and Abu Bakr, a 40-year old merchant of high character (and his future father-in-law). Abu Bakr was a respected, well-liked member of the Quraysh tribe—in fact, he knew more about its complex genealogy and interrelationships than did anyone else.

If he had belonged to a more powerful clan, he probably would have achieved a great deal of secular success.

Another convert was Abu Talib's youngest son, 10-year-old Ali (c. 598–661). Once Abu Talib came upon Ali and Abu Bakr praying together, and Abu Talib asked what was going on. "O father," Ali responded. "I believe in Allah and his Messenger, and I declare what he brought was true." Abu Talib responded, "Muhammad would not call you to do anything but good, so cleave to him." Abu Talib himself never converted. When invited to join the Muslims, he sadly told Muhammad that he could not abandon the faith of his fathers. However, he continued to support and protect Muhammad all his life.

Another early follower was the slave Zayd ibn Harith, who was so devoted to Muhammad that he refused his freedom when it was offered. (This Zayd should not be confused with Zayd ibn Thabit, Muhammad's later secretary.) The black slave Bilal ibn Rabah, belonging to a different household, also converted. In retaliation, his master Ummayah tied him up in the desert under the noonday sun with a heavy rock on his chest, telling him that he would stay there until he confessed belief in the goddesses al-Lat and al-Uzzah—or until he died. Bilal steadfastly refused to renounce his faith, muttering "One! One!" for days. Abu Bakr interfered and offered Ummayah a pagan slave in Bilal's place. Eventually Bilal was set free. Another servant convert was Abdallah ibn Masud, who was the first person to recite the Quran in the streets of Mecca. He was known for his red hair, thin legs, and penchant for wearing perfumed garments. Other than these three servants, the great majority of early converts were free people of the Quraysh tribe. (Slaves suffered most from their conversion to Islam, especially because they had no clans to protect them from persecution.)

A colorful conversion story concerns a poet named al-Tufayl ibn Amir, who came from the western regions to Mecca. Having heard about Muhammad's charismatic powers when reciting the Quran, he decided to stuff his ears full of cotton so that he wouldn't be swayed. Then he felt ridiculous and decided to listen. He was converted and went home to his tribe where he converted about 70 families in his tribe.

A most dramatic conversion was that of Umar ibn al-Khattab, a stubborn young aristocrat determined to kill Muhammad with a sword even though his own sister, Fatimah, had become a Muslim. He felt that Muhammad had not only divided the Quraysh tribe, but also mocked its sacred traditions. (He was also a heavy drinker and disliked

Islam's disapproval of alcohol.) However, a friend persuaded him that Muhammad was too well guarded and that he should remonstrate with his sister instead. So Umar went to his sister's home, where he attacked both her and her husband, Said, cutting her ear. She faced him bravely, saying, "We believe in Allah and his Messenger, and you may kill us if you wish!" Umar was taken aback at her courage—and ashamed of the blood he saw on her cheek. The sword fell from his hand.

He asked to see the Quran, and she showed him some verses from Surah 20 ("Ta Ha") written on a palm leaf. Impressed, he asked to take it home. "No," she replied. "You are unclean from worshipping idols. First you must wash yourself." Umar did as requested, took home the palm leaf scripture, and became convinced of its truth when he read, *I am God; there is no god but me. So worship me and keep up the prayer so that you remember me* (20:14). An alternate version of Umar's conversion has it that one time after he had been drinking heavily he crept around the Kaaba and hid under its covering cloth to listen to Muhammad reciting the Quran. Instead of mocking the Prophet, however, he became entranced by the words and converted on the spot. While these stories are at odds and cannot both be true, both make the same point that Umar, blinded by hatred or alcohol, was utterly transformed when he read or heard the Quran.

It is perhaps not surprising that this enemy of Islam became a powerful convert; Muhammad himself was convinced that people who were strong in the state of ignorance would also be strong when rightly guided. Umar became an influential supporter of Muhammad, responsible for leading many people to Islam by his words and example. Ultimately he became Islam's second caliph.

Another disciple was Uthman, the only one among early believers who came from the Meccan hierarchy; he was a leading light of the mighty Umayyad clan. When he converted, his wives deserted him, and Muhammad asked Uthman to marry his daughter Ruqayyah.

All the other converts were people of poor background, some of them outcasts and slaves. They found a road to spiritual freedom in Muhammad's dictum that all believers were equal before Allah.

After gathering together his small group of believers, the revelation went public in 613 or 617: *Therefore proclaim openly that which you are commanded, and turn away from the polytheists* (15:94). Muhammad began to go through the streets of Mecca, relaying his message of hope and doom. He preached strongly against political and social injustice and brought the word that there was only one God, Allah, who promised Paradise to the faithful and eternal Fire to disbelievers.

In fact he did so much warning about future doom that the Quran lists "the Warner" as one of Muhammad's titles. It was probably Muhammad's teaching about the Last Judgment that caused the most reluctance among the Meccans to join his movement. Even the promise of a glorious Paradise was not enough to sway them from their suspicions about a divine plan that weighed their every deed and thought.

Going public put Muhammad in danger, so his uncle Talib hid him in a castle in a gorge east of Mecca and refused all offers to turn him over to the Quraysh. Eventually they "excommunicated" Muhammad and his clan (the Hashim) from their tribe and hung the decree in the Kaaba. This meant that members of the Hashim were forbidden to marry members of other clans or to trade with them. They could not even sell them food. Muhammad remained holed up for about three years, being allowed to walk freely only during the season of pilgrimage, when all hostilities were supposed to cease. At one time, according to tradition, Abu Talib almost buckled under the pressure of keeping his nephew out of harm's way: "Spare me and yourself. Don't place a burden on me greater than I can bear." Muhammad responded sadly that if necessary, he was ready to die. Abu Talib relented and said, "No, go and say what you please; I will never give you up, not on any account."

Early Hardships

Muhammad's early experiences as a prophet were disappointing; the people of Mecca, including his own tribe, the Quraysh, utterly rejected his ideas and ridiculed Muhammad himself.

Rich and powerful clans within the Quraysh, such as the Umayyads and Makhzum, were insulted by the idea that a member of the lowly Hashim clan could presume to dictate to them. They were also displeased with the idea of giving up their other deities, who, as noted earlier, were a sort of cash crop during pilgrimage season. However, they refrained from killing him, knowing that such an outrage would bring about an unending blood feud. Other early Muslims fared less well because they had no powerful family to protect them. Some were beaten and starved; others, such as Bilal, were systematically tortured.

Abu Talib and Khadijah died in 619, only a few days apart (the so-called Year of Sorrow). Muhammad's situation deteriorated. Khadijah had been his main psychological support; Abu Talib had guarded him physically. As long as he remained the head of the Banu Hashim clan, he had protected Muhammad. Now that protection was gone.

The leadership of the Banu Hashim clan was taken over by a man who disliked both Islam and its prophet. This was another uncle, Abu Lahab (d. 624), Abu Talib's brother. Lahab was an interesting character who may have been alone among the early Meccans in realizing the grave threat Muhammad's doctrines would pose to the idol business and Quraysh income if they were widely adopted. He tried everything he could to make Muhammad's ideas seem ridiculous and dangerous. He forced Muhammad to admit that according to his own doctrine, Abu Talib was in Hell because he had refused to convert to Islam. Muhammad replied that although he had found Abu Talib roasting in the lowest part of the fire, he (Muhammad) had brought him to a shallow part. He indicated, however, that Abu Talib was wearing shoes of fire that would boil his brain. This doesn't seem like much compensation for Abu Talib's protection of his nephew during all those years, but according to a Quranic verse revealed at this time, Allah told Muhammad, *O Prophet! Verily, you guide not whom you like, but Allah guides whom He will* (28:56). Poor Abu Talib was stuck in Hell, apparently forever. Muhammad also had to admit that his pagan grandfather, who had maintained the idolatrous Kaaba, was consigned to perdition.

The wife of Abu Lahab, a woman from the hated Umayyad clan, was almost as bad as her husband. She took pleasure in placing thorn branches in the sand along the paths where Muhammad was wont to walk barefoot. This sophomoric trick enraged the Prophet, and Surah 111 is devoted to cursing the pair of them:

> *Cursed be the hands of Abu Lahab: he shall perish!*
> *His wealth and gains shall avail him nothing!*
> *He shall be burned in the flaming fire!*
> *Faggots shall be heaped on his wife,*
> *On her neck a rope of palm-fiber.*

Abu Lahab did eventually die, but not for years. Someone else threw camel intestines on Muhammad's back while he was praying, although the evildoers later got their comeuppance and melted in the sun.

Grief-stricken over the deaths of Khadijah and Abu Talib, tortured by the Quraysh, and disappointed by the lack of converts, Muhammad and his faithful slave Zayd ibn Harith went back to the mountain town of Taif, about 60 miles southeast of Mecca, where the Prophet had spent some comparatively happy days in his childhood. This was in obedience to the following revelation in the Quran: *So proclaim that*

*which you are commanded, and withdraw from the idolaters. Well We know
that your bosom is oppressed by what they say* (94:97).

Perhaps he hoped to make a fresh start, but it was no use. Taif was
a central shrine of the goddess Al-Lat, and the inhabitants were in no
mood to listen to Muhammad. One town leader told him, "I would
tear the curtains off the Kaaba if it were true that Allah chose you as
his Messenger." Another said, "Has Allah found no one other than you
to be his Messenger?" The third sneered, "By Allah, I will never speak
to you. If it is true that you are Allah's Messenger, you are too great
for me to speak to you. If, on the other hand, you are lying, you're not
worth answering."

Being called a liar was one thing Muhammad simply could not stand.
"Attributing lying to me is not like that of attributing lying to other
people, and anyone who dares to commit this offense should seek his
abode in hell," he said. And the Quran proclaims, *Those who charge our
signs with falsehood and proudly reject them, the gates of heaven shall not be
opened to them, nor shall they enter Paradise until a camel pass through the
eye of needle* (7:38), a phrase borrowed from Matthew 19:24, although
used in a different context.

Muhammad was pelted with stones and chased out of Taif by a mob
of teenagers and slaves. He returned to Mecca, where he and his few
followers continued to suffer abuse and persecution. Muhammad was
resigned, however, and the Quran recalls earlier prophets (both biblical and non-biblical) who were also met with scorn and disbelief.

At this time, Mecca was a boiling cauldron of discontent and strife,
not between clans but between the newly prosperous merchant class
and the older artisans. Powerful forces of economic change were
outstripping old political and religious loyalties (poets enjoyed con-
siderably more prestige than priests), but no one was going quietly.
There was also a growing rift between the rich and the poor. The
Meccans regarded Muhammad as someone who was trying to divide
their community further, separating them from their old ways, their
ancestors, and the gods they had worshipped. Muhammad obviously
spurned these deities, which *created nothing but are themselves created,
who neither harm, nor benefit, who have power neither over life, nor death
nor over the resurrection* (25:3).

THE FLIGHT TO ABYSSINIA

In the year 615, 83 of Muhammad's followers fled Mecca to the
ancient Christian country of Abyssinia, where they established a small

colony. The Quraysh tried to get them sent back, presumably for punishment, but the Abyssinian king (or Negus), who was a Christian, nobly refused. The Muslims found a safe haven in Abyssinia until they were established in Medina. Some suggest that the real reason the Muslims went to Abyssinia was not as a result of persecution but to search for an alternative trade route to the rich south, considering that the Quraysh had cut them off from the main roads. The Quraysh did in fact send a couple of emissaries to the Negus complaining about the Muslims, but it did not work. A tradition reports that when the refugees read a passage of the Quran about the conception of Jesus to him, he wept until his beard was soaked, and he said, "For certain, this scripture and what Jesus brought have come from the same niche."

Satanic Verses?

At one point, according to some sources, Muhammad appeared briefly willing to compromise his beliefs. The most famous incident of this nature was the issue of the so-called Satanic Verses, reputedly once part of Surah 53 ("The Star"). The occasion for this surah occurred when Muhammad and his community were under great persecution. During this period Muhammad apparently acknowledged the existence of three goddesses alongside Allah: Al-Lat, Al-Uzza, and Al-Manat. According to Tabari and others, Muhammad was in despair that the Meccans were loath to accept his message and was told (he believed by Allah) that the three goddesses could intercede for him. At the first recitation of this surah, he followed the mention of the goddess with, "These are the exalted females [or 'high flying cranes or herons'] and truly their intercession may be expected [or is acceptable to Allah]." Thereupon, Muhammad bowed twice in reverence. However, although these words (the so-called Satanic Verses) were favorably received by the local polytheists, Muhammad later disowned them as a suggestion from "somewhere else" and replaced them with this: *What? Shall ye have male progeny and God female? That was indeed an unfair partition*, revealing his clear conviction that Allah was male. The Quran continues, *These are only names that you and your fathers have invented. They are mere conjecture and wish fulfillment* (53:23).

The "Satanic Verses" *do not now* appear in the Quran, and whether they were ever there is a matter of controversy. Most Muslims believe they never existed. Things are complicated by the fact that Tabari included two different and conflicting accounts of these verses, so it is hard to know which (if either) is correct. One story suggests that members of the Quraysh tried to make a deal with Muhammad about accepting the goddesses; in the other version, the impression is given that Muhammad himself was searching to find a way to combine his revelation with the received tradition. Tabari may simply have been recounting alternate versions of the history and allowing his readers to choose which if either they wished to accept. The whole controversy heated up enormously in 1988 with the publication of Salmon Rushdie's *Satanic Verses*, which Muslims believe to be an attack on the Quran and which earned Rushdie a notorious *fatwa* calling for his death.

In another incident Muhammad is said to have suggested that those who appealed to the god Hubal were not necessarily excluded from Paradise. The Quraysh merchants were mollified, but only to some extent.

Other passages from the Quran may refer to the compromise between Muhammad and the Arabs and Muhammad's eventual rejection of it. One reads,

> *And they indeed strove to beguile you (Muhammad) away from that wherewith We have inspired you, that you should invent other than it against Us; and then would they have accepted you as a friend. And if We had not made you wholly firm you might almost have inclined unto them a little. Then had We made you taste a double punishment of living and a double punishment of dying, then you have found no helper against Us.* (17:73–75)

THE NIGHT JOURNEY AND ASCENT TO HEAVEN

The Night Journey occurred in 619, the Year of Sorrows, during either the Prophet's final years in Mecca or the following year. It is mentioned only briefly in the Quran, in one verse: *Glory be to him Who transported his servant by night from the sacred mosque to the furthest mosque, whose precincts We blessed, that We might show him some of Our signs* (17:1). However, various hadith provide more details. Muhammad was awakened in the middle of the night, when he was sleeping near the Kaaba, by a brilliant white angel (identified as Gabriel) crying, "Awake, sleeper!" The angel then slit open Muhammad's chest, removed and washed his heart in a golden basin (or, according to another story, in the well of Zamzam), and then filled it with "belief," before returning it to its original place.

Gabriel was accompanied by a white winged creature, smaller than a horse but bigger than a donkey, with a woman's face. It is known in Islamic literature as the Buraq. At first the creature did not seem anxious to be ridden, for when Muhammad placed his hand upon the creature's neck, the Buraq shied away. The exasperated Gabriel then scolded him, "O Buraq, aren't you ashamed of yourself to behave like this? No more honorable person than this Apostle of Allah has ever ridden you!" The guilt-stricken Buraq calmed down and consented to be ridden. When Muhammad mounted, the creature sailed off into the night. With each stride it could travel farther than the eye can see.

Accompanied by Gabriel (and possibly by Michael too), they first touched down at Mt. Sinai and then in Bethlehem, where they prayed. Then they arrived at the Holy of Holies in the ruined Temple (the "farthest mosque") in Jerusalem, where Muhammad dismounted and prayed. A ladder opened miraculously from the sky, and Muhammad leaped back onto his mount. The Dome of the Rock (*Qubbat al-Sakrah*) in Jerusalem still bears Muhammad's footprint. The ascension (*al-miraj*) into heaven occurred in stages, through the seven heavens. When the Prophet asked for the gate to be opened at the First Heaven, a voice cried, "Who is it?" Gabriel answered, "It's I, Gabriel." Then the voice said, "Has Muhammad been summoned?" "Yes," responded Gabriel. The voice answered, "He is welcome. What an excellent visit is this!" When the gate was opened, Muhammad saw Adam standing there. At the Second Heaven, he met Jesus (Isa) and John (Yaya). Muhammad described Jesus as being of medium height, red-faced and freckled, with lank hair that looked as if it were dripping with water, even though it was dry. This is presumed to be a reference to Jesus' being the Messiah or "anointed one."

At the Third Heaven, he met Joseph; at the Fourth, Enoch; at the Fifth, Aaron; and at the Sixth, Moses and Elijah. The Prophet described Moses as tall, with a ruddy face, curling hair, and a hooked nose. Moses wept when Muhammad left. When asked why, Moses replied, "Because after me there has been sent as Prophet, one whose followers will enter Paradise in greater number than mine," an apparent reference to the Jews.

At the Seventh Heaven was Abraham. "Never," the Prophet confessed, "have I seen a man more like myself." Once there he ascended the Tree of the Farthest Limit (the Lote Tree), whose leaves were the size of elephants' ears. Nearby ran four rivers: the Nile, the Euphrates, and two other rivers of Paradise. Only the first two were actually visible, however. Muhammad was offered a container of wine, one of honey, and one of milk, and he took the milk. Gabriel told him, "You've been rightly guided, and so will be your people, Muhammad. Wine is forbidden you." Nothing was said about the honey. They approached the Throne of Allah, although neither Muhammad nor Gabriel was allowed in the immediate vicinity.

However, it is declared that Muhammad was embraced by Allah, although he couldn't actually see his face. He was touched on the shoulder and breast, a touch that froze him to the bone. The visit with Allah put Muhammad (in the eyes of his followers) on a level with earlier prophets such as Abraham, Moses, and Jesus, who also knew their god in a personal way.

During his visit to Heaven, Muhammad got instructions from Allah about prayers. At first Allah enjoined 50 prayers a day. When Muhammad mentioned this to Moses, the older prophet suggested he go back to get the number reduced. "I couldn't get my people the Jews to pray that often," he complained. So Muhammad went back and got the number decreased to 10 and then, after further conversation with Moses, to 5. Moses wanted him to negotiate for a still lower number, but Muhammad claimed he was ashamed to go back and beg, so the number 5 has remained. Muhammad himself, however, was known for praying more than five times a day, often in the middle of the night. To make up for his lost sleep, he would take a midafternoon nap.

After the visit with Allah, Muhammad stumbled away from the brilliant presence and returned via the winged horse to Mecca. For centuries, Muslims have disagreed about whether his ascension was spiritual or bodily. His new wife Aishah, who was only nine years old at the time, said that on the night in question, he was soundly asleep by her side all night). Besides, claimed the skeptics, everyone knew that a journey from Mecca to Jerusalem took two months. Miracles, however, can happen quickly. According to one story, when Muhammad got up to accompany the angel, he knocked over a pitcher of water. By the time he returned, the splash was just striking the floor. In any case, he made it back in time for the dawn prayer.

No similar adventure happened again, but that one was enough to sustain him for the remaining 12 years of his life. Interestingly, the entire narrative is similar to one found in a Pahlavi story called the *Arta Viraf*, composed about 400 years earlier. In that story, Arta Viraf, a young priest, is conducted into Heaven by an angel, where he meets the inhabitants of Heaven and eventually God (Ormazd) himself. The tale also includes the miraculous tree.

The Flight to Medina

During one season of pilgrimage, Muhammad met with about six pilgrims from Yathrib (later called Medina, the "City of the Prophet"), which lay about 220 miles north and several days' caravan trip from Mecca. Unlike the desert trading city of Mecca, the Medina area was an agricultural center, producing barley, vegetables, and date palms. The pilgrims were impressed with Muhammad and his ideas; they began to believe that he might be the Messiah of whom the Jews spoke. Yathrib was home to a large number of Jewish merchants; perhaps a third of the city was Jewish, and certainly, Jewish beliefs were commonplace. The Jews, in fact, may have been the original settlers of the place, arriving there when they fled Roman persecution. There were three main Jewish tribal groups: the Nadir, the Qurairza, and the Qainuqa. When the pilgrims returned home, they had such good words to say about Muhammad that the citizens invited him to relocate there, partly to help settle tribal disputes between two quarreling Arab tribes: the Aws and Khazrai. There were three Arab-Jewish tribes too. Mecca, on the other hand, was basically a one-tribe (Quraysh) town. Muhammad emphasized that the former rivals should owe loyalty to the new *ummah*, or community of believers.

Muhammad left Mecca secretly with about 70 of his followers and, after a 200-mile trek, entered Medina in September, 622. He had wisely sent ahead some converts and a missionary, so that the people of Medina would be Muslims by the time he arrived. Paganism was less entrenched in Medina than in Mecca or Taif, and Jewish and even Christian influence may partially account for Muhammad's message having more success there. This event is known as the hijrah or emigration. It took place in the 12th year of Muhammad's mission, during the month of Muharram. Muslims now commemorate the event by making it the beginning of the Islamic calendar. So the year 622 is year 1 in the Islamic calendar. (As in the Christian calendar, there seems to be no year 0.) Dates after the hijrah are often abbreviated A.H., which is taken from the Latin *Anno Hegira*, "in the year of the hijra." Today the word *hijrah* can also refer to abandoning an evil life to take up a good one. (Each Islamic month is 29 days, 12 hours and 44 minutes long and begins on the night the new moon is sighted. Because of the "leftover" time, some Islamic years have 355 rather than 354 days, just like leap year. The 12 Muslim months are: Muharram, Safar, Rabiul-Awwal, Rabi ath-Thani, Jumada al-Awwad, Jumada ath-Thani, Rajab, Shaban, Ramadan, Shawwal, Dhul Qidah, and Dhu Hijjah.

Great credit should be given to young Ali, who courageously vol-
unteered to act as a decoy, sleeping in Muhammad's bed and wearing his cloak while the Prophet made his getaway. One of the most
miraculous events of the journey occurred when Muhammad spent
three nights in a cave on the Thawr mountain near Mecca. A spider
spun its web quickly across the mouth of the cavern, and a posse of
Meccans passed it by, assuming that no one could be hiding behind
the thick web.

The Early Medina Years

When Muhammad entered Medina, a new era in his ministry began.
Although the trip had been full of perils, the Muslims finally arrived
safely at their destination. Muhammad lived there the rest of his life,
not always in comfort. Despite, or perhaps because of, the fact that it
was an oasis, Medina had a terrible climate—hot, wet, and sticky. The
prophet used to pray that the place would one day become as dear to
him as Mecca was, but clearly, the humidity was not helping.

Those who followed Muhammad on his journey were called the
Muhajirun, or "people of the Hijra." Those who asked him to come
and aided him were the *Ansar*, the "helpers," the formerly pagan Aws
and Khazrai. (In all, the city contained eight clans of Arabs and three
Jewish tribes.) The Medinans, unlike the Meccans, were primed for
belief in Islam, not only on account of the pioneer Muslim missionaries
but also because they were so familiar with Judaism, Christianity, and
the idea of a scripture.

Many people greeted Muhammad warmly and offered him their
homes. Not wanting to choose between his welcomers, Muhammad
allowed his trusty camel to wander around at will. She stopped near
a spot where some dates had been left out to dry, and he selected this
place for his house and that of his wives. To the end of his days, he lived
in a simple hut with walls of unbaked clay and a thatched roof of palm
leaves covered by camel skin. Furniture consisted only of a rope cot,
a pillow stuffed with palm leaves, and an animal skin for a rug. There
were no chairs, of course—they had scarcely been invented. Muhammad simply squatted on the ground. His wives lived similarly.

The Quran states that a house should be merely a protection against
heat, cold, and wild animals, not a luxurious mansion. Houses were not
supposed to be places where one stored up luxuries, and he insisted his
own house be kept free of decorations. A home, thought Muhammad,
should be like a shady tree, a place where one briefly rested, then went

ahead with one's journey, a truly nomadic image. Real riches were of the spirit.

The locals apparently felt free to wander in and out whenever they felt like it, and it may be that this practice sparked the Quranic command to "veil" the prophet's wives. As the unauthorized visitor situation was getting out of hand, Muhammad had a revelation that proclaimed, *O believers! Enter not into the houses of the Prophet, save by his leave, for a meal, without waiting his time. When you are invited then enter and when you have eaten disperse at once* (33:53).

Not everyone in Medina was thrilled with the arrival of Muhammad, however. The city had its share of polytheists, malcontented Muslims whom Muhammad labeled hypocrites, Bedouins, and nervous Jews— all of whom were ready to pounce if something went wrong.

THE FIRST MOSQUE

Muhammad himself helped to construct the first mosque, a simple earthen enclosure with date palms for columns and fronds for the roof. It had three doors—one facing Jerusalem, one "for Gabriel," and one "in the name of mercy." It included none of the accoutrements that became customary later—a niche (*mihrab*) indicating the direction of Mecca, tiled floor, and carpets. It did not even have a pulpit—Muhammad gave his sermons leaning against a palm tree.

Abu Bakr, the first caliph, kept it as it was, but Umar, the second caliph, extended it and rebuilt the columns. Uthman, the third caliph, made major renovations, rebuilding its walls, erecting columns of chiseled stone, and substituting a teakwood roof for the palm fronds. However, he made sure the mosque maintained its simple character. Today it is known as the Masjid al-Nabi, or "Mosque of the Prophet."

MUHAMMAD AS POLITICAL LEADER

Muhammad declared that Medina, like Mecca, was *haram*, or sacred territory. All controversies and disagreements between squabbling parties were to be referred "to Allah and to Muhammad, the messenger of Allah." Indeed, Muslims were at all times to show devotion to one another. Muhammad said, "Religion is faithfulness to Allah and his Messenger and to the leaders of Muslims and Muslims in general."

In Medina, Muhammad's role broadened—he became not only a prophet calling people to follow the one God, but also a governor of a settled community with secular as well as religious concerns. He was responsible for keeping the city safe from external attacks as well as settling internal disputes. His rulership was a great success, as a result of his notable virtue and his ability to make people get along.

THE MUSLIM-JEWISH RIFT

The Muslim-Jewish Rift began during the Medina years, although things looked promising at first. Muhammad drew up a charter with the Jewish citizens of Medina, granting them citizenship. They were recognized as a separate *ummah* (community) allied with the Muslims but with a good deal of autonomy, such as the right to retain their property, religious liberty, and military protection, as long as they took part in defending the city and professed allegiance to the ruling Muslims. They were expected to regulate the conduct of their own members. In the Islamic view it was the Jews' violation of this treaty that eventually caused the rift between Muslims and Jews that has endured to this day.

Before the rift, Muhammad listened to the advice of rabbis and, in an effort to accommodate them, directed his followers to pray in the direction of Jerusalem and to observe the fast of Yom Kippur. Muslims and Jews even prayed together three times a day, not five as became mandatory later. (Back in Mecca, the Muslims prayed only twice a day oriented in a way that aligned them both with Jerusalem and with the Kaaba.) Muhammad also commanded his followers to be circumcised.

Apparently, Muhammad expected the Jews to convert to Islam. However, the Jews, who had strong trading ties with the Meccan Quraysh, felt no inclination to become Muslims. They were satisfied with their own religion. They remained unmoved by Muhammad's early overtures. First, they ignored Muhammad—and then they ridiculed him.

They were displeased by what they regarded as Quranic rewriting of their scriptures, and delighted in pointing out inconsistencies in it. When the Jews did not convert and refused to agree that Muhammad's god had any connection with theirs, Muhammad changed the direction of the prayer (*qibla*) 180 degrees, back to Mecca, and instituted the month-long fast of Ramadan to take the place of the day-long fast of Yom Kippur.

THE BATTLE OF BADR (MARCH 624)

In Medina Muhammad's notion of his mission enlarged and took a more militant turn, and most of the rest of his life was consumed by warfare. Although Muhammad seldom donned armor and fought personally, he was always on hand, giving strategic advice.

The beginning may have been partly economic. His followers, who owned no land in the new city, supported themselves by raiding Bedouin caravans heading north from Mecca toward Syria. This occupation (*ghazwa* or *razzia*) was a time-honored custom, with its own rules, one of which was that bloodshed should be avoided if possible. It was a custom that acquired a rather exalted status in the newly emerging religion. Muhammad called his raiders "strivers in the way of Allah." The raids against the caravans became a sort of holy war, or jihad. Many caravans were controlled by the hated Quraysh merchants, and robbing them weakened the Muslims' idolatrous rivals. Soon the raids exploded into full-fledged battles.

The Battle of Badr, a small oasis town located between Medina and the Red Sea, is so important in Islamic history that the entire eighth surah (*Al-Anfal*, "The Spoils of War") is given over to discussions of it. At Badr, the Muslims raided a very large, very rich caravan, protected by about 900 Meccans and 700 camels, heading from Syria to Mecca. The caravan fought back, and a battle ensued. In the Islamic view, the Muslim victory was made possible by the direct intervention of Allah. *And yet it was not you [the Muslims] who slew the enemy but it was Allah who slew them; and it was not you [Muhammad] who cast terror into them, when you did cast it, but it was Allah who cast it* (8:17).

A strange rain fell during the night that bogged down the Meccans but inexplicably hardened the ground where Muhammad's small army waited. When the morning sun appeared, it seemed to blind the Meccans' eyes. The 300 vastly outnumbered Muslims and their 70 camels—aided, they believed, by a thousand mostly invisible angels—defeated their rivals in a one-day battle, killing many prominent Meccans. *O believers! Remember Allah's favor to you when there came against you hosts, and We sent against them a great wind and hosts ye could not see* (33:9). (One Muslim did report seeing an angel fighting by his side, riding a horse whose hoofs never touched the earth.)

According to one tradition, Muhammad retired to his command tent, praying and sleeping while the Muslims (and the angels) fought the Meccans. Other traditions say he participated in the fighting. Muhammad had already earned some battle experience as a youngster, fighting for his native tribe, the Quraysh, against their rivals, the Banu Hawazin. At one point Muhammad emerged from his tent, throwing some pebbles at the Quraysh and ordering a charge, after which the Meccans departed in confusion.

Fourteen Muslim heroes (most of them Medina natives) were buried with honor, with the bodies of the enemy thrown into a pit. Muhammad then spoke to the dead Meccans, saying, "O people of the pit, have you found that which God commanded is true?" Two of the captured enemy were killed and the rest ransomed. One Quraysh leader named Uqba begged for his life, saying, "Who will look after my children?" The Prophet is reported to have said, "Hell!" and ordered him killed.

The most obnoxious of the Meccans was a leader of the Makhzum clan named Abu Jahl. He would hire thugs to assault converted Muslim slaves in Mecca and do everything he could to make the lives of free Muslims miserable. Earlier, Abu Jahl had tried to assassinate Muhammad while he prayed near the Kaaba. However, as he approached Muhammad with a big rock to smash his head, the angel Gabriel had appeared in terrifying form, a creature with a massive head and sharp, gnashing teeth. But in this battle, Abu Jahl was decapitated, and his head was brought to Muhammad, who proclaimed, "This is more acceptable to me than the choicest camel in Arabia."

One of the hostages was Muhammad's uncle, al-Abbas, who claimed that he had been captured by a giant angel; however, the truth was that his captor was a man only slightly larger than a dwarf. Al-Abbas later became the founder of the dynasty of caliphs named after him—the Abbasids. Of all the spoils of war, the most famous was the legendary double-pointed scimitar called Dhul-Faqr or Zulfiqar, "the Cleaver of Vertebrae," which Muhammad wore during all his subsequent battles. It later became a sort of holy relic that passed on to the Abbasid caliphs. When their line came to an end, the sword disappeared forever.

There was a sad note for Muhammad during the battle. While the arrows were flying, his daughter Ruqayyah, wife of Uthman, died of smallpox. Muhammad was not able to attend her funeral.

The Battle of the Badr opened a rift between Muhammad and the Medinan Jews, who were accused of cooperating with Muhammad's enemies. *Is it not the case that every time they make a covenant, some party among them throw it aside? Nay, Most of them are faithless* (2:100). Muhammad originally planned to kill men of the Qaynuqah tribe (the smallest, weakest group) but was dissuaded by the Khazraj shaykh. Muhammad sent them with their goods into exile. It is worth noting that this tribe had made its living largely in the goldsmithing and armory trade. After each important battle against the Meccans, Muhammad punished the Jews of Medina by exile, death, or enslavement, even those who had remained officially neutral.

It is not completely clear what the main disagreement between the Medinan Jews and Muhammad was, but certainly many Jews felt that Muhammad has appropriated their own prophets and cast them (the Jews) in the role of a discarded people.

THE BATTLE OF UHUD (625)

Another critically important fight was the Battle of Uhud, in January 625. This was another one-day fight, only this time the Muslims did not win. Muhammad and 700 followers joined battle at the foot of Mt. Uhud, three miles north of Medina. The expedition started with 1,000 soldiers, but a third of them defected. Most of the men who did come were untrained and wore no armor. Muhammad suspected treachery in the ranks; to make things worse, he himself had gotten overweight and out of condition. The odds were stacked against the Muslims. Still, Muhammad took the initiative and began giving orders, a complete change of tactics from Badr, when he had stayed in his tent most of the time.

However, this turned out not to have been such a good thing. Muhammad managed the battle poorly, allowing his men to get trapped. He was knocked off his horse (perhaps he was somewhat unwieldy, as he was wearing two coats of mail), was struck in the face, had a tooth knocked out and an eye damaged. Only the sight of his wife Aishah giving water to the distressed soldiers allowed him to pull himself together. Also wounded were his favorite converts, Ali, Abu Bakr, and Umar. His uncle Hamzah was felled by a Meccan javelin, and the wife of Abu Sufyan lopped off his ears and nose, then cut out his liver and tried to eat it. (Later this woman, Hind bint Utbah ibn Rabiah, converted, learning the fundamentals of Islam from Muhammad himself, although she did not immediately reveal her identity.) Hamzah now is sometimes referred to as "lord of the martyrs."

Abu Sufyan's daughter Umm Habibah also joined the faith and became a wife to Muhammad. When her father came to visit her, she would not let him sit on her bed linens because, as an unbeliever, he was impure. Later on, Abu Sufyan himself converted.

Altogether, the defeated Muslims lost 74 men. The Meccans made themselves merry by stringing together the noses and ears of their victims and making necklaces. But they made a tactical blunder: they rode back to Mecca rather than following up on their victory by attacking Mecca. Indeed, the Meccans, although they won a few more skirmishes, were never able to secure further decisive victories against the Muslims.

Still, Muhammad was in despair, attributing the loss to lack of faith and his followers' focus on material gain. He was an embittered man, and the surahs revealed during this period seem exceptionally blood-thirsty. After this battle too, Muhammad took vengeance on a Jewish tribe of Bani al-Nadir. They were accused of plotting to assassinate the Prophet; as punishment he attacked their fortress and burned down their date palms, on which they depended for sustenance. However, he allowed them to leave the area, carrying their weapons and whatever property they could pack on their camels.

In another incident, a certain Jewish poet of Medina named Kab bin al-Ashraf was accused of harming Muhammad (and Allah) "with his po-etry." The Prophet ordered him killed and even allowed the killers to lie and deceive the poet to accomplish their ends. (The murderers pre-tended they only wanted to take a sniff of his perfumed head but used the opportunity to grab his hair and cut his throat.) After Kab's murder, Muhammad said, "Kill any Jew that falls into your power."

KHANDAQ, THE BATTLE OF THE DITCH (MARCH 627)

The final major conflict was the Battle of the Ditch (or Trench). Ten thousand men marched north from Mecca. The Arab preference was always for quick strikes, and when this battle turned into a two-week siege, the disgruntled Meccans, who had no food for their horses and camels, simply went home. The name comes from the ditch that Muhammad ordered to be dug around Medina, in complete violation of the previously established "rules of combat."

After this battle, Muhammad entirely destroyed the largest Jewish tribe—the Qurayzah. They were accused of planning a rear-guard at-tack against the Muslims, and this time Muhammad reacted with utmost severity. He followed time-honored tradition and killed or sold off the members of the last of the offending tribes. Muhammad himself over-saw the massacre, even helping to dig the trenches into which the bodies would spill. Seven hundred Jewish men were taken out in groups of five or six, hands fastened behind their backs, and forced to sit at the edge of the trench; they were then beheaded one by one. After the elimination of this tribe, Muhammad's leadership faced no serious opposition.

Thus it was that after each of the three major battles between the Meccans and the Muslims, a Jewish tribe was liquidated. It didn't mat-ter whether the Muslims lost or won. Although the attacks against the Jews were viewed as a justified response to treason, they set the stage for unfortunate future relationships. As time went on, it was noted that Muhammad's character began to harden. Although still kind and merciful to his intimate friends, he became fearsome and implacable in the face of his enemies.

One untoward incident occurred in 629, when Muhammad raided the Jewish colony of Khaybar, about 100 miles from Medina. It was a rich area known for its fine date palms and even wheat fields. During the siege, Muhammad's son-in-law Ali was suffering from an eye ailment and was unable to fight—until Muhammad reportedly spat in his eyes and healed them, apparently miraculously (much the same story is told of Jesus). Now recovered, Ali led the charge, even wrenching the fortress gate from its hinges and improbably using it as a buckler for the rest of the battle. The battle itself was terrible, with the Muslim soldiers raping pregnant women and eating donkeys. The Jews surrendered, but the treasurer of the city, Kinana ibn al-Rabi, refused to reveal where the treasure was hidden until a fire was lit on his chest to encourage him. Then the Muslims cut his head off. When his 17 year-old widow, Safiyya bint Huyayy, was led past his headless body, Muhammad caught a glimpse of her and fell in love, throwing his mantle over her as a sign of his "protection." He took her to bed with him that night, in apparent violation of his own dictum that the deed should wait until a menstrual cycle had passed. She converted to Islam and became one of his favorite wives (number 11, by some counts) and outlived him by 40 years. After his death, she played an important part in Muslim politics.

Another woman of Khaybar, Zainab, whose relatives had all been killed in the battle, tried to assassinate Muhammad by poisoning the shoulder of a lamb (his favorite part). He spat it out, but one of his followers ate the lamb and died in agony. Muhammad summoned the poisoner, who, remarkably, managed to talk her way out of repercussions. "If you had been a mere king," she said, "you would have died, but since you are the Apostle of God, I knew you would live." Muhammad was so pleased by the response that he let her go.

Treaty with Mecca

In March 628, the diplomatic Muhammad, rather than crush the Meccan spirit, engineered a 10-year nonaggression treaty that allowed Muslims to make a pilgrimage to that city the following year. This was a daring tactic on the part of Muhammad, as pilgrims were expected to go to the holy city completely unarmed, and showed both his strength and his good will to the citizens of his home town. This event became known as the Day of Hudaybiyah, named after the place the treaty was signed, which was about 10 miles from Mecca. It marked the first time that the Meccans acknowledged Muhammad to be a leader in his own right—not an exiled or runaway Meccan. The victorious Muhammad returned peacefully to Mecca in the spring of 628, although he did not make an official, complete pilgrimage at that time, somewhat to the irritation of his followers. The city had been evacuated for three days to avoid any possible conflict.

However, the truce (*hudna*) did not hold. The Meccans reneged on it in November 629; in response the Prophet gathered 10,000 troops outside the walls of Mecca and camped there, threatening but not actually attacking the city. Early the following year, Abu Sufyan and other leading Meccans emerged from the city to meet him and formally surrendered; Muhammad promised a general amnesty, and only four people were executed for treason.

Most Meccans converted to Islam, and Muhammad declared the pilgrimage to Mecca to be a sacred duty. On January 11 Muhammad entered the city at sunrise, accompanied by 30,000 Muslims, both men and women. He was dressed all in white, like a pilgrim, as indeed he was. He rode around the Kaaba seven times, and when he passed the Black Stone, he touched it with his camel stick. On previous occasions he had been seen to run around the Kaaba and kiss the stone; this times he rode slowly and majestically like a king in solemn dignity. He surveyed the 360 (or 365) idols in or around the Kaaba. One story claims they dissolved when he pointed his camel stick at them; another says he simply ordered them destroyed (except, according to another account, pictures of the Virgin Mary and Jesus). In any case, once he had "purified" the Kaaba, he proclaimed,

> There is no God but Allah; there is none with him. Allah has made good his promise and helped his servant. From this day every claim of privilege or blood or property is abolished by me, except the custody of the Kaaba and the watering of the pilgrims. O Quraysh, Allah has taken from you the pride of idols and the veneration of ancestors. Know that man springs from Adam and Adam springs from dust. Know that Allah created you male and female and made you into people and tribes that you may know one another; the noblest of you are those who worship Allah most.

Only a few fights remained against some local tribesmen, the Hawazin and Thaqif. It was a long struggle, but eventually the Muslims prevailed. During the next few years, Muhammad cemented his leadership over all Arabia, although Medina, the "city of the prophet," remained the political capital. Muhammad had an even larger view, continually sending out military expeditions, although they not always successful. When one of his men complained about the desert heat during a foray, he replied, "Hell is hotter." He never gave up his mission to proselytize and conquer. His goal was clear, as he once exclaimed: "One Messenger, one faith, for all the world!"

The Personal Life and Preferences of Muhammad

The Prophet's followers carefully noted almost everything the Prophet did or said, and so his tastes were transmitted along with his spiritual message. He liked children, cats, honey, cucumbers, dates (mixed with milk or butter), pumpkins, and perfumes. His wife Aishah liked to say that Muhammad enjoyed three things most in the world—food, women, and perfume—but managed to get only the first two with any regularity. His followers were apparently not very mindful about bringing him provisions, and he was too proud to beg. In Arabic culture, begging was considered shameful. Aishah remarked that he seldom had even two meals a day. He washed before every meal, and his favorite meat cuts were the neck and flank. He liked to drink sitting down. He ate only with his right hand and only from the side of the bowl with three fingers—never reaching into the middle. He did not use a spoon or knife, and forks were not yet invented. His stepson Hind, son of Khadijah, said, "He never liked to displease or cause offense to anybody. He thanked people even for trifling favors. He took whatever food was placed before him, without making any adverse remark." He also was known never to fill his stomach completely.

He disliked lizards, windy and cloudy days, yellow and discolored teeth, artists, expensive textiles, and the smell of garlic or onions. He said that if one must eat onions, dressing should be put on them to disguise their offensive odor.

He did not like dogs either and made remarks about how "unclean" they were. However, he insisted on kindness to all animals, including canines; cruelty to animals is forbidden in Islam. Once, he and his soldiers passed a mother dog with puppies, and he gave strict orders that they be left undisturbed. He stated, "Verily, there is heavenly reward for every act of kindness done to a living animal." He also declared a certain woman would go to Hell for starving a little cat.

His normal dress, especially early on, consisted of a white shirt and *tamad* (trousers), a cloak, and a turban with one end hanging loose. He never owned more than one set of clothes. He carried a blanket that was well patched; indeed, he patched it himself (and in fact sewed all his own clothes), a job he seemed to enjoy. He also mended his own sandals. Umar reports that he once saw a silk-belted cloth for sale and asked Muhammad if he could buy it to wear to Friday prayers. The Prophet replied, "Such an item is only worn by one who is good for nothing." Later on, Muhammad received a quantity of the same cloth as a gift, and he gave it to Umar. Umar was surprised because Muhammad had forbidden it to him earlier. Muhammad explained, "I did not give it you for you to wear, but for you to sell or give as a gift to someone else."

Cleanliness was very important to Muhammad. He was a stickler for wearing clean clothes and complained when other people wore dirty ones. He was especially insistent about toothbrushing. He regarded it not only as purifying the mouth, but also as a pleasure to Allah. He considered it particularly important to brush one's teeth in the morning after arising from sleep. When it was necessary for him to spit, he used a handkerchief rather than spitting on the ground the way other people did. It grieved him one day to see that someone had actually spat on a mosque wall, and he took great pains to show people a better way to expectorate—by using a handkerchief.

Muhammad washed carefully before going to bed and again if he had to get up in the middle of the night to urinate. For this purpose he would walk as far as necessary to be out of sight, behind a rock or bush, choosing soft ground so he wouldn't be spattered during the process. He was also careful to orient himself correctly before proceeding. Even today it is considered offensive to urinate with one's front or rear facing Mecca, although it is permissible if in a lavatory. The right hand must not touch the penis. The Prophet's modesty extended to bathing, for he always bathed behind a curtain and instructed others not to bathe in the open either.

Privies were of special concern to Muhammad. Whenever he used one, he prayed, "O Allah, I seek refuge in thee from impure deeds and evil habits." More disturbingly, perhaps, is the fact that the Arabic word here rendered "deeds" (*khabithah*) is more frequently translated as "evil female demons." When he needed to evacuate, he had his servant bring him "three pebbles," to use for cleaning his posterior. Although this is more than most people want to know, it serves to show how anxious Muhammad's early followers were to transmit to the world his every action. He also instructed others to use his "three pebble method" for hygienic purposes, in addition to using water. The

- Zaynab bint Khuzaymah
- Hind (Umm Salamah) bint Abu Umayyah
- Zaynab bint Jahsh
- Juwayriyyah bint Harith
- Ramlah (Umm Habibah) bint Abu Sufyan
- Zaynab (Safiyyah) bint Huyayy
- Rayhanah bint Zayd
- Maymunah bint Harith
- Maryam Qibtiyyah (Mary the Copt; she bore Muhammad a son, Ibrahim, who died at age two)

In many cases, the bride was the wife of a fallen comrade of Muhammad, who would have found it difficult to remarry under prevailing Arab custom. His offer of marriage was also an offer of protection. Some marriages were contracted to solidify relationships with a particular clan. Others seem to have been made for love or sexual attraction. In any case, one legend says that Muhammad was potent enough to satisfy all his wives within a single evening.

His most famous marriage, however, was to Aishah, the young daughter of his supporter and friend Abu Bakr (d. 634) and the only virgin among all his brides. Of course she was only six years old when they were betrothed; they waited until she was nine for the actual wedding. The account of her marriage to Muhammad, in her own words, may seem unsettling:

> I was six years old when the Prophet betrothed himself to me in Mecca. Three years later in Medina, I . . . was on a swing playing with my children friends. My mother came and called me. . . . She washed my head and face with water, and took me to a room where there were some *ansar* women, who cried out: "Happiness and blessing and best fortune be upon thee!" My mother handed me over to them and they dressed me up. They had scarcely finished when the Prophet entered suddenly. They gave me over to him.

Muhammad was a little over 50 years old. Aishah's dowry was silver, and the wedding supper consisted only of milk. It has been claimed, perhaps with justice, that this was a politically motivated marriage, contracted to cement the relationship between Muhammad and Abu Bakr.

Still, Muhammad consummated the marriage when the girl was only nine years old; this was not unusual in those times. In any case, Aishah was not only the youngest but also the most beautiful of the Prophet's wives. When Muhammad was asked who on earth he loved most, he answered unhesitatingly, "Aishah." The questioner, perhaps startled that Muhammad liked a woman best, then asked, "Whom do you love most among men?" The Prophet answered, "Abu Bakr—Aishah's father."

Aishah was a remarkable woman. Educated and highly intelligent, she earned Muhammad's trust in her judgment. She argued with others and frequently won. At these times, Muhammad was known to smile and say, "Ah, she is Abu Bakr's daughter!" In fact, she became a respected jurist, and left 2,000 reports about Muhammad's life, more than any other single person. Indeed, one of the companions reported that after Muhammad's death, "whenever a report appeared doubtful to us, we asked Aishah about it, and we always learned something from her about it." Aishah is sometimes called the "mother of the faithful," although this title can be applied to any of the prophet's wives. She never had children of her own.

Close as they were, their marriage was not entirely stress-free. According to an authoritative hadith, Aishah mentioned that Muhammad himself once deliberately struck her "on the chest which caused me pain." Another, less authoritative, hadith, however, claims that "Mohammed never hit anyone, except in battle. He did not hit a servant or woman."

In one famous instance, Aishah accompanied her husband to battle against the Banu al-Mustaliq. (The Prophet's wives drew lots to see who would go.) She stepped behind a sand dune to relieve herself and then realized she had lost her necklace. She stayed to look for it, but the camel driver thought she was safely ensconced in the howdah atop the hump and left with the camel in tow. Aishah was alone in the desert. Unperturbed, she wrapped herself up and lay down for the night, knowing she would be missed and looked for. Soon a soldier who recognized her happened by and transported her back to camp. She was somewhat ill from her ordeal, however, and spent the next few days in bed. She was alarmed to find out that during this time, rumors about her "misconduct" were being circulated, and Muhammad accused her of faithlessness. One of Muhammad's closest friends, the young Ali, advised him to divorce her. Muhammad respected Ali's judgment, but he loved his wife. He asked around, but none of her friends would say a bad word about her. Her worst habit, they said, was being a little neglectful in the preparation of bread (her pet lamb would steal it).

Muhammad openly begged his wife to repent if she had sinned, but Aishah refused to admit to a sin she had not committed. "My duty is to show a comely patience," she responded, echoing some of Muhammad's own words. It was from about this time that the ill feelings between Ali and Aishah began to harden, although they had never been great friends.

Soon Muhammad had a revelation from Allah himself that she was innocent. Aishah was surprised to find herself at the heart of divine intervention but recognized that she was married to a prophet. Afterward, the entire business was called "the affair of the lie." It was this event that prompted the Quranic punishment of 80 lashes to anyone who falsely accused a woman of immoral conduct.

A rather scandalous marriage occurred when Muhammad wished to marry the beautiful Zaynab bint Jahsh; she was already married. The husband was Muhammad's adopted son, and former Christian slave, Zayd ibn Haritha, although the marriage was not a happy one. Muhammad happened to walk in on her when she was undressed and got a sudden revelation that she was to divorce his son and marry none other than himself:

> *Then when Zayd had dissolved his marriage with her, with the necessary formalities, We joined her in marriage to you, in order that in future there may be no difficulty to the Believers in the matter of marriage with the wives of their adopted sons, when the latter have dissolved with the necessary formality their marriage with them. And Allah's command must be fulfilled.* (33:37)

And just in case tongues were still wagging, the Quran says, *No blame shall be attached to the Prophet for doing what is sanctioned for him by Allah* (33:37). His favorite wife Aishah was decidedly not pleased with this revelation and remarked acidly, "It seems to me that your Lord hastens to satisfy your desire." And later she said, "Zaynab was competing with me." The Prophet was also divorced several times, not always on his instigation. One wife, Mary the Copt, accused Muhammad of not being a true prophet because their son Ibrahim had been allowed to die; she wanted to leave Muhammad and return to her own people. He allowed it.

Another unfortunate wife, was Saudah bint Zamah, a pious older woman he apparently married to help him look after his children. She also had several children of her own, perhaps as many as six. However, it is also said that Muhammad wanted to divorce her when she became elderly. She then cried, "O Messenger of Allah! Do not divorce me; give my day to Aishah." Aishah claimed she was a "huge fat lady."

An important wife was Umm Salamah, a particularly intelligent (and even literate) woman. She was one of the first converts to Islam and in fact among those Muslims who had migrated to Abyssinia in the early days. Her first husband, Salamah ibn Abdul-Asad, was mortally wounded during the battle of Uhud. His last words were said to be, "O Allah, please grant my wife a better husband than myself after my death!" She once even prevented a mutiny by her wise advice. In the Treaty of Hudaibiyah, when the Muhammad commanded the Muslims to shave their heads, make sacrifices, and return from Mecca to Medina according to the settlement, many refused. Umm Salamah advised the Prophet: "It is too hard for them to accept the treaty, since they desired victory. You should stand up and go out without uttering a word, then sacrifice and shave your own head, and then they will obey!" It worked.

Another embarrassing incident occurred when his wife Hafsah found Muhammad in bed with Mary the Copt on Hafsah's appointed day. She complained to Aishah, who remonstrated with Muhammad. At first Muhammad agreed that he had made a mistake but soon received another revelation: *Prophet, why do you prohibit that which Allah has made lawful to you in seeking to please your wives? Allah is forgiving and merciful. Allah has given you absolution from such oaths.* The Quran demands that Aishah and Hafsah repent of their complaining and revealing "secrets." It then takes on a threatening tone toward them: *Haply if he put you both away, the Lord will give him in exchange other wives better than you, Muslims, believers, devout, penitent, obedient, observant of fasting, both known of men and virgins* (66:1–9). The Quranic passage taken alone is practically incomprehensible; however, Islamic tradition has filled in the details.

Behavior standards for the Prophet's wives were high. Although all Muslim women were expected to conduct themselves with decency, the bar for the wives of Muhammad was raised. *O wives of the Prophet, if any of you are openly indecent, her penalty will be doubled and this is easy for Allah* (33:30). On the other hand, they were due and accorded extreme respect from other Muslims. They were also not permitted to remarry after the death of the Prophet. *You have no right to annoy the Messenger of Allah or to marry his widows after his passing, ever; for that would be monstrous of you in the sight of Allah* (33:53).

The Death of Muhammad

Muhammad died in Medina on Monday, June 8, 632, after a brief illness he incurred just after returning from a pilgrimage to Mecca. He had received his final revelation only nine days earlier. In this last pilgrimage he had taken all his wives and many of his followers, a number said to have exceeded 124,000. He had shaved his head for the occasion and distributed his hair to the faithful. (Critics argue this practice comes close to relic-collecting, but Muhammad undoubtedly meant it as a simple remembrance gift to those who had stood with him against the world.) In any case, head-shaving has become a practice for pilgrims to Mecca even today.

By many accounts Muhammad's last days were black ones, for he is recorded as saying, "O men, the fire is kindled! Rebellions come like the darkness of the night! By Allah, you cannot lay these things to my charge. I allow what the Quran allows, and forbid what the Quran forbids." In his last sermon, he said, "Know ye that every Muslim is a brother to every other Muslim and that you are now one brotherhood." He concluded, "Verily I have finished my mission, I have left among you a plain command, the Book of Allah, and manifest ordinances. If you hold fast to them, none of you shall go astray." His final revelation was (according to some scholars), *Today I have perfected religion for you and I have completed by blessing upon you, and I have approved Islam as your religion* (5:3).

He lingered for some time with a burning fever and commanded Aishah's father and his most trusted adviser, Abu Bakr, to lead the prayers in the mosque in his place, although Abu Bakr always cried when he read the Quran, making it hard to understand him. At one point in the days leading up to his death, Muhammad wandered off to the cemetery to visit the graves of his departed Companions, saying sadly, "Peace be upon you, O people of the graves! Happy are you, for your lot is better than ours." When he returned, Aishah was complaining about a headache. He told her, "No, you should be complaining about *my* head." Then, as a little joke, he said, "Would it distress you if you were to die before me? If you did, I would pray over you and wrap you in your shroud. And I myself would commit you to the grave."

She responded, "What? And then come back and enjoy a new wife?" He smiled, but Aishah knew he was gravely ill. During his final hours, his daughter Fatimah was at his side. He whispered something to her that made her weep and then something that made her laugh. Later she said that she cried when he told her he was about to pass away but laughed when he said that she would be the first of the family to join him in Paradise. (Indeed, Fatimah did not long survive her father.)

Muhammad died in Aishah's arms—his last request was for a toothbrush. Aishah noted he brushed his teeth more vigorously than she had ever seen before. Then, about noon, he laid his head on her breast and died. She thought his last words were, "The most exalted has entered Paradise." Others reported his saying, "Allah, forgive me, have compassion on me, and take me to the highest heaven." Legend says that as he ascended into Paradise, drops of his sweat turned into roses. Aishah laid his head on a pillow and rose up, beating her breast and slapping her face in her grief. (This was an Arabic custom, but one that the hadith condemn. Extreme grief in the face of Allah's will is frowned upon.) Abu Bakr then came in and uncovered the Prophet's face, saying to him, "Dearer than my father and mother! Alas, my dearest friend! You have tasted the death which God has decreed; a second death will never overtake you." He was buried on Wednesday night. His body lay covered by a cloak in a corner of Aishah's room—everyone was too busy thinking about a successor to wash or attend to its disposal before then.

Muhammad was shrouded in three pieces of clean white Yemeni cotton, without shirt or turban. He was buried in his house, and then a tomb was built over his grave. (Muhammad had once said that a prophet should be laid in the earth where he died.) Later the tomb was incorporated into a mosque, the Masjid al-Nabi ("Mosque of the Prophet"). After Muhammad's death, some of his followers, including Umar ibn Khattab, believed that he was not really dead or that even he was, he would return. Umar even drew his sword in anger that anyone should suggest otherwise. To this, Abu Bakr answered, "If anyone worships Muhammad, he is dead, but if anyone worships Allah, He lives." He then quoted from the Quran: *Muhammad is only a Messenger; other messengers have passed away before him. If he then dies or is killed would you turn about on your heels?* (3:144). Today the Prophet's tomb is visited by faithful Muslims, and Medina is now considered the second most sacred city of Islam.

Successorship

Who would rule the Muslim community after the death of the Prophet? Muhammad had no surviving sons and left no specific instructions as to who was to succeed him. He did not even specify what kind of leader should take his place—military, civil, religious, or all three. He is quoted as once having said that prophets have no heirs. However, obviously someone had to take control of the burgeoning Muslim community. Arguments over the successorship were serious, and the disputants believed the final truth about it would be revealed only in the Hereafter. However, because the disagreement was in good faith, there would be no real losers. According to tradition, "Whoever was right among them will be rewarded twice; whoever was wrong among them will be rewarded once and his or her mistake will be forgiven." Here on earth, it was a different story, and much bloodshed occurred because of a difference in opinion.

Sunni Muslims believe that it was up to Muhammad's Companions (no women participated) to choose his successor; in fact, the title caliph means "successor" or "deputy." Several candidates were available. Primary among them were Abu Bakr and Ali, Muhammad's father-in-law and son-in-law, respectively.

Although Ali had strong support from one group (later known as the Shia), in the end, it was the older and more experienced Abu Bakr who was chosen. Abu Bakr had been with Muhammad for many years; he was also the man whom Muhammad had appointed to lead the Friday prayers in his absence. In addition, he had the support of Aishah, who distrusted Ali and who, naturally, preferred Abu Bakr, her own father. Three days after the death of the Prophet, Abu Bakr was elected as his successor. Muhammad had said of his conversion, "I have not invited anyone to Islam who did not exhibit some hesitation except Abu Bakr. He alone did not tarry when I mentioned it to him, nor did he hesitate." However, although it was Arabic practice to select an elder to lead the "tribe," the choice of Abu Bakr was presented in a preemptory manner that went against old tribal custom. The seeds of resentment were sown, but the bloody harvest would not be reaped for several years.

The First Caliph: Abu Bakr (632–634)

Abu Bakr was a trusting and gentle soul, who continued his profession of selling cloth at the marketplace even after he became caliph, seeing no reason why he should not. He kept the entire treasury of the emerging kingdom in an unlocked box in his house and spent half the night praying to Allah. As caliph he was known as As-Siddiq (Witness to the Truth) and Amirul Muminim (Ruler of the Believers). Abu Bakr also drew up the rules of fair warfare engagement, following the practice of Muhammad. Force was to be used only as a last resort—negotiation was infinitely preferred. Churches and synagogues were not to be touched, and monks and priests were not to be harmed unless they were actively in revolt against Islam.

On the negative side, Abu Bakr got into the habit of collecting a salary and using *zakat* for his own private purposes, clearly in contradiction to what Muhammad wished. During his short reign he seemed somewhat oblivious to the military exploits of his generals, conducted largely against rebellious Bedouin tribes, and probably was not even aware of how fast his empire was growing.

Abu Bakr did not regard himself as being perfect or immune to correction from those who elected him. In a spirit of true democracy and humility, he said, "O people! I have been elected by you as your leader, although I am not superior to you. If I do what is right support me, and if I go astray, set me right. Truth is a trust and a lie is a breach of it. . . . Obey me as long as I obey Allah and his Prophet, and when I disobey them, obey me not." He died of fever (not helped by the fact that he enjoyed taking cold baths). He was 63, the same age at which Muhammad had died, and was buried alongside him. He had been caliph for only two years and was the only one of the "Rightly Guided Caliphs" (the first four caliphs) to die a natural death. On his deathbed, he nominated Umar ibn Khattab to succeed him.

The Second Caliph: Umar ibn al-Khattab (634–644)

Umar was a much harder man than Abu Bakr, with a fierce temper. There is a story that once he visited Muhammad's house, and when he appeared, all the women ran out of the room. He asked Muhammad why he was shown such disrespect. The laughing Muhammad replied, "Umar, if the devil himself were to meet you in the street, he would dodge into an alley!" Umar was as strict with himself as he was with anyone else, living mostly on bread and olive oil and, like Muhammad, patching his own clothes. He introduced harsh punishment for disobedient and traitorous Muslims and put the entire community on a war alert. He also, and in violation of existing treaties, expelled the remaining Jewish and Christian communities from the Arabian Peninsula.

His war-torn reign saw the expansion of Islam. In 638 Jerusalem fell to the Muslims and became the third holiest city in Islam because of Muhammad's association with it. The Christian ruler of the city, Sophronius, declared that he would surrender to no one but Umar himself. Umar showed great respect to the Christian faith by not praying in the Shrine of the Holy Sepulcher—to do so would have turned it into a mosque. In addition Christian churches were left unmolested, and Jews, who had been banished by the Christians, were allowed to return and worship. According to some versions of the treaty, Jews were barred from the city and Christians forbidden to build new churches, display the cross prominently, or carry weapons. They were to wear a special sash, and their houses were to be lower than those owned by Muslims. How many of these regulations are enforced (or even existed) is unclear. It does appear that for 500 years, the three faiths coexisted in Jerusalem in relative peace, until the city was re-taken by Christians in 1099.

Umar is also said to have instituted a strategy that kept the Muslims in control. Whenever the Muslims conquered an area, the lands passed into state ownership, with the conquerors living in garrisoned cities (*amsar*) or armed camps and receiving tribute from the conquered lands. The largest of these camps were in Iraq: Basra in the south (which had good access to the desert trade routes) and Kufa on the site that would later become Baghdad. This was opposed to having the conquerors melt into the conquered areas and assimilate.

Umar forbade non-Arab converts to marry Arab women. Muhammad himself had said, "The survival of the community rests on the hoofs of its horses and the points of its lances, as long as they keep from tilling the fields. Once they begin to do that they will become as other men." Partly because of this policy, Muslims did not achieve a majority of the population in all their conquered lands until about 400 years after the death of the Prophet, but they kept control.

Umar was something of a busybody. One story recounts how he crept over the wall of someone's house and found the man drinking wine and in an inappropriate relationship with a woman. Umar began to remonstrate with him, but the sinner calmly replied, "Look Umar, I may be in the wrong—but yourself have committed three wrongs tonight. First, you were spying on me, and Allah commanded us not to spy; second, you are supposed to enter people's homes through the door and not leap over the walls, and third, you are commanded to ask permission first. You've done none of that, so you're worse than I am."

Eventually Umar was stabbed to death during his dawn prayer by a Persian Christian slave named Firoz (or Abu Lulua) who thought he was paying too much in taxes. (This was the first assassination of a caliph, but it was far from the last.) Firoz then killed himself. Umar's only possessions at death were a mantle and a patched shirt.

On his deathbed, Umar ordered all Arab slaves to be freed; he also initiated a new way of selecting future caliphs—by a committee (*shura*) consisting of Ali ibn Abu Talib, Uthman ibn Affan, Abdur-Rahman ibn

Awf, Sayd ibn Abi Waqqas, Az-Zubayr ibn Al-Awam, and Talhah ibn Ubayd Allah. When Umar died, this committee selected Uthman to succeed him, although in many ways he was undoubtedly the weakest candidate. Perhaps it was because his family had long supported the Prophet, because he was a son-in-law of Muhammad, and because he promised to continue the policies of Umar. At any rate, his election was supported by most Muslims.

The Third Caliph: Uthman ibn Affan (644–656)

Uthman was a member of the rich Umayyad clan. Although personally pious, he was regarded as a weak caliph. He seemed to have no firm principles other than that of appointing members of his own clan to positions of power (unlike Umar, who had allowed local leaders to retain their jobs after the Muslims had invaded). Most of his family promptly took the opportunity to make themselves wealthy and amass large amounts of land. Uthman seems not to have noticed. And despite the fact that he took no salary, he enriched himself through warfare, collecting a great deal of cash, as well as many camels and horses. He also rather enjoyed living the high life. This made many local people hate Uthman and his entire family, even though he developed the laudable habit of freeing some slaves every Friday.

There is some evidence that during his caliphate he expunged Quranic fuming against the Umayyads, his own tribe. He was also accused of introducing dangerous innovations (*bidah*) into the practice of Islam. According to tradition, Uthman achieved one notable feat during his caliphate—he ordered the Quran to be collected and preserved into one document. Also under Uthman, Islam advanced into North Africa, Iran, and Afghanistan.

He was generally considered to be incompetent, with many people demanding that he resign. (He refused.) He was heckled and even had stones thrown at him while he attended the mosque. A group of his opponents from Egypt and Iraq, led by Muhammad ibn Abu Bakr, assassinated him in his own house in Medina on June 16, 656, while he was reading the Quran to his family. He was in his early sixties at the time. (Apparently, Muhammad had predicted this.) His wife tried to protect him by throwing herself on his body, and three of her own fingers were sliced off in the attack. This was the first time a caliph had been killed by someone of his own faith community. His bloody shirt was hung at the Great Mosque in Damascus with his wife's fingers attached to it.

Aishah has been connected to the downfall of this caliph. While the caliphate was being destabilized, she suddenly decided to go on pilgrimage to Mecca, over the objections of many of her followers, who saw that her leaving town just then would only aid the insurgents. Nevertheless, she left. Uthman's death began the first *fitna*, or period of instability, which soon led to out-and-out civil war among the Muslims. The murder of Uthman was a signal that the center of Muslim political power had shifted from Arabia to the "outskirts" of the empire.

The Fourth Caliph: Ali ibn Ali Talib (656–661)

Uthman was followed by Ali, son of Muhammad's protector-uncle, Abu Talib. For Shia Muslims, Ali, whose nickname was "Lion of Allah," is the first rightful caliph, or as they call it, Imam. They believe that the first three caliphs usurped the position unjustly and that Ali was too polite to complain. Ali in fact made no argument at the time he was "overlooked," saying it would be unworthy for him to claim leadership for himself. But the Shia had good reasons for their belief that Muhammad might have selected Ali. After all, he was one of Muhammad's closest associates and fought in all the battles Muhammad did except one. According to Shia thought, Ali was the first person to make the declaration of faith (*Shahadah*) in Islam. He was invited to live with the Prophet when he was only six years old and later married Muhammad's favorite daughter, Fatimah. Together they had two sons, Hassan and Husayn, who in the Shia view were the next rightful Imams.

Muhammad was also heard to remark on occasion that Ali was his *nafs*—his soul or spirit—and the three men later elected caliphs (Abu Bakr, Umar, and Uthman) all heard him say it. In addition, on his last pilgrimage to Mecca, at Ghadir Khum, Muhammad had stopped and raised up the hands of Ali, saying that whoever believed Muhammad to be their leader should regard Ali in a similar light.

Although Ali had the support of most Medinans, members of the old aristocratic Umayyads spread rumors that Ali had had a hand in the murder of Uthman (Aishah may have been behind some of the rumors). Ali felt it advisable to leave the vicinity and establish a new capital in faraway Kufa, Iraq, a garrison city on the banks of the Euphrates, where he had strong support. This was an almost spur-of-the-moment decision and probably was not meant to be permanent, although that is the way it turned out.

At the time Ali was 56 years old, bald, and enormously fat, but he still had the charisma to demand his followers' allegiance. He did have trouble with Muawiya (d. 680), governor of Syria and the son of Abu Sufyan, Muhammad's old enemy who eventually had converted to Islam. Muawiya, the fifth (Sunni) caliph, nephew of Uthman, and founder of the Umayyad Dynasty, refused allegiance to Ali, and a civil war (*fitnah*) ensued, pitting 50,000 of Ali's Iraqis against 50,000 Syrians under Muawiya at the Battle of Siffin (July 657). According to some sources, 70,000 men were killed. Some Syrian soldiers hoisted copies of the Quran on the points of their spears, indicating that the differences should be solved by arbitration rather than war, and Ali agreed under pressure. Eventually the two leaders attempted to establish a truce that essentially divided the empire. This proved to be a divisive error that permanently fragmented the Islamic empire. In the Sunni world, at least, the caliphs were no longer assumed to speak for Allah, as the Prophet had. They were merely administrators of the Islamic state and had no right to modify or add to existing Islamic law, although this rule was frequently misunderstood or even overlooked.

Supporters of Ali who disapproved of the truce left to form their own extreme group, the Karijites.

For Sunni Muslims, these first caliphs (Abu Bakr, Umar, Uthman, and Ali) were the benchmark of Islamic behavior and rulership. They are called the "Rightly Guided Caliphs." *Those whom Allah has guided, follow their example* (6:90). Shia Muslims do not accept the "Rightly Guided Caliph" theory and insist that from the beginning, Ali, the fourth caliph, should have been the heir. (If there was a Rightly Guided Caliph, it was Ali only.) In any case, the caliphs were not prophets (Muhammad was the last prophet), but they were highly respected and had both religious and political authority over the Islamic community (*ummah*). Later in history, the caliphs were granted the right to lead the Friday prayers and to have their names included in those prayers.

THE EXPANSION OF ISLAM

It has been noted that Islam's natural mode of being has never been the nation-state, but the *Dar al-Islam*, the Land of Islam, an empire that transcends national and natural borders and forms an Islamic community or *ummah* based on faith. This is the true motherland for all Muslims and the earthly entity to which they owe their highest allegiance. This has been especially true for Arabic-speaking Muslims, despite the fact that the Arab world has not had anything like an empire since the Middle Ages. The ideal of the world Islamic state remains a dream—but a potent one. Indeed, Islamic legal theory has gone so far as to claim that any land that harbors at least one practicing Muslim is part of the *Dar al-Islam*. Other lands, if there are any, make up the *Dar al-Harb*, or Land of Warfare; there can never be peace between the two. An armistice is the most that can be expected. Partly because of this idea, warfare has always retained a religious quality in Islam.

From its beginning, Islam was an expansionist faith. In his last sermon, Muhammad said, "I was ordered to fight all men until they say there is no god but Allah." And this is largely what happened, bolstered by the words of the Quran: *And he gave you their [People of the Book] land, and their dwellings, and wealth, for a heritage, even a land on which you had never set foot: for the might of Allah is equal to all things* (33:27). Although experts disagree on the ultimate motivations of the Muslim expansion, most believe it was a combination of religious fervor, poverty, nation-formation, and plain old greed that spurred the Arab armies ever onward.

Muslim military campaigns against the "infidels" were so amazingly successful that it was easy for the conquered peoples to believe that the Muslims had God on their side. However, the reasons for the expansion have to do not only with the force of the faith and its practitioners but also with the power vacuum in surrounding areas. The Christian, Greek-speaking Byzantine Empire (the eastern part of the old Roman Empire) and the Zoroastrian, Persian-speaking Sasanian Empire were both in decline. They had been engaged in a protracted war that had left both sides exhausted and ripe for picking, although the Byzantines were technically the "winners." Surah 30 ("The Romans") was said to have been revealed in 615, when Persian soldiers captured Jerusalem from the Byzantines. (The Byzantines took it back in 628. It was this kind of continual give-and-take warfare that was so debilitating.) Even in their prime, however, neither had ever bothered to invade Arabia, considering it a backwater without the water. It is said that the Persian emperor, upon hearing of Muhammad, wrote to his governor in Yemen: "That Arab who has suddenly shown up in the Hijaz has sent me an unacceptable letter. Send two reliable men to bring him in chains before me. . . . If he refuses to come when ordered, take an army and bring me his head." Fifteen years later, Iran would become Muslim. Non-Muslims living under Muslim rule were called the *dhimmi*, a name that means "Protected People." The new Islamic Empire employed both Christians and Jews in important posts for centuries and seemed content to let them retain their religious affiliations. However, their life was not easy. The *dhimmi* in no way held equal rights in Islamic lands. Their place in society was limited by a set of rules that came to be known as the "Covenant of Umar," although in actuality, these restrictions were enacted long after Umar's time. The *dhimmi* were exempt from paying the required alms (*zakat*) but were required to pay a *jizyah*, a head tax, as well as a special land tax. Although the tax was not very large (and it was a common practice among many majority faiths to place a special tax on minority religions), it was still a stigma. And there was more. The *dhimmi* could not carry arms, serve in the military, or even ride a horse. They were required to treat Muslims "with respect" and had to wear distinctive clothing so that they could be identified. According to the Shafii school of law, they could be given Islamic punishment for theft and adultery, but not for drunkenness.

In North Africa, Jews had to wear patches bearing a picture of a pig, whereas Christians were forced to wear monkey patches. In Baghdad both Jews and Christians had to wear yellow stars. Christians were forbidden to build new churches, although they were allowed to repair existing ones. *Dhimmi* sworn testimony against Muslims was not accepted. On the positive side, they were entitled to protection in case of attack. Additionally, the rules against them were variously enforced, and in some countries they had a great deal more freedom than in others. It should also be said that in countries where Christians were the majority, the treatment of minorities was generally worse than in Muslim-majority countries.

As Islam expanded, most Muslims lived under the caliphate, a rule that extended from 632 (when Muhammad died) until 1258, when the Baghdad caliphate was destroyed by Mongol invasions. The caliphate is generally divided into three periods:

- The era of the "Rightly Guided Caliphs," or *Rashidun* (632–661)
- The Umayyad Empire (661–750)
- The Abbasid Empire (750–1258)

Caliphs exerted political, judicial, military, and fiscal control over their communities. (At first, the caliphate was more religious than political, but events forced a change in focus.) During the caliphate, the "capital" of the Islamic Empire moved around to various cities all over the Middle East, depending on who was in charge.

After Muhammad's death, Islam began to grow rapidly, although not without struggle, including rebellion among the Bedouins, who felt their allegiance to Islam ended when Muhammad died. It had been hard enough to convert them in the first place; the Muslim prohibition on wine and nonmarital sex was an attack on pleasures dear to the Bedouin heart. Some said they would remain believers but refused to pay the tax Abu Bakr demanded; others wished to renounce the faith altogether. These wars went on between 632 and 634 and are known as the Wars of Apostasy (*al-ridda*). When they were over, the Muslims had the whole Arabian Peninsula firmly under their control.

Next, Abu Bakr moved into Syria, suppressing revolts there. Then the Muslims invaded Egypt, North Africa, and Khurasan. The Egyptians were rather glad to be conquered because they had been heavily burdened by Byzantine rule. Not all of them converted to Islam, however, and until very recent times, there remained a substantial Coptic Christian minority in the country.

Muslims invaded Spain in 711, where their army of 7,000 defeated 25,000 men under the Visigoth King Roderick. The invading commander was Tariq ibn-Ziyad, a former Berber slave. His name lives on in the name given to the mighty rock rising between Spain and Morocco: Jebel Tariq, or Tariq's Mountain—that is, Gibraltar. This expedition gave birth to the so-called Moorish civilization of Spain. The name "Moorish" actually comes from Mauritania in northwestern Africa, the starting point of the Muslim army. In the ninth century, Muslims conquered Sicily and held it for over 200 years. Eventually, Islam established hegemony over Balkan areas, sub-Saharan Africa, and Indonesia, sometimes through conquest, sometimes peacefully.

Important dynasties include the Umayyads (Damascus and Spain), the Abbasids (Baghdad), the Fatimids (Egypt), the Ottomans (Turkey), the Mughals (India), the Safavids (Persia), and the Alawids (Morocco and West Africa).

THE UMAYYAD DYNASTY (661–750)

The Muslim dynasties are generally reckoned after the passing of the four Rightly Guided Caliphs. Muawiya became the fifth caliph, and the 100-plus-year dynasty he began is known as the Umayyad dynasty, in which Islamic expansion continued.

The handsome, tricky Muawiya was a distinctly different sort of caliph from his predecessors. Descended from a man who had tried to kill Muhammad, he found himself the inheritor of the Prophet's position.

Like Muhammad, he was very approachable, having audiences all day long and inviting people to dinner. Known for his patience, he was an excellent negotiator, diplomat, and conflict resolver, famous for saying, "I do not use my sword when my whip will do, nor my whip when my tongue will do." He began his caliphate as governor of Damascus and never did move to Medina, heretofore the "capital of Islam." Indeed, the caliphate never returned to Arabia. Some were scandalized by Muawiya's decision. Damascus, after all, was a distinctly non-Islamic sort of city, filled with Greek statues and Christian churches. The Iraqis were particularly piqued, feeling dominated by the Syrians, and for a long time that country was the center of anti-Umayyad feeling. The new governor of the country, Hajjaj ibn Yusuf (r. 694–714), did not help matters when he arrived in Kufa, remarking, "I see heads that are ripe for plucking, and I see blood between the turbans and the beards." He wasn't joking.

On the more constructive side, the Umayyads built stone palaces in the Syrian Desert (they sprang from Bedouin stock, after all) and ran the area much like their sheikh ancestors under an Arab military aristocracy. Umayyad Caliph al-Walid I built the Great Mosque of Damascus here between 709 and 715, intended to be a place where the entire Islamic population of the city could worship.

Unlike his predecessors, religion was probably the last thing on Muawiya's mind, although he was regular in his prayers. He was more interested in conquering the world than in purifying his soul. In his 20 years as caliph, Muawiya took on Africa, Byzantium, and areas to the East. He divided his territory into large provinces and appointed his relatives to govern them. In 680 he designated his son Yazid I as the next caliph, rather than leaving the decision to a council or *shura*, as had been the previous practice. Hereditary succession was a less disruptive means of transferring power in a widespread empire without the advantages of modern telecommunications. Still, Muawiya's decision caused dissension among the followers of Muhammad and led to another civil war, during which Husayn, son of Ali, was killed at Karbala in 680. Thus began the separation between the two main Islamic groups, Shia and Sunni, discussed later.

Muawiya died at the age of 80, asking to be buried with a few of Muhammad's hairs and nail parings. His son Yazid I (r. 680–683) was a friendly enough fellow but was more interested in hunting than in being caliph. He was also known to get drunk every day, in distinct violation of Islamic commandments. He was very fond of his singing girls and had what amounted to an obsession with his pet monkey. In fact, when the creature died, Yazid I gave him a state funeral and a proper Islamic burial. Not surprisingly, perhaps, during his reign there were widespread revolts. After a period of uncertainty, the reins of the caliphate were taken over by Abd al-Malik ibn Marwan (r. 685–705).

Under the Umayyads, as we have seen, Muslims conquered North Africa and Spain and even progressed into France as far as Poitiers. (They were stopped by Charles Martel in 732.) What is sometimes called "Moorish Spain" (*al-Andalus*, or Andalusia) was a Golden Age of Islamic scholarship and neo-Platonic philosophy. The first observatories in the world were built in Spain, to plot the movement of the stars. Despite Islamic rule, however, Spain remained a majority Christian nation, with a sizable number of Jews as well. As People of the Book they were not forced to convert to Islam, and Jewish and Christian scholars often worked alongside Islamic ones. This relative harmony between Christian, Jews, and Muslims is sometimes called *convivencia* (living harmoniously together).

The Muslims also made inroads into India and Central Asia. Some got as far as China (via the Silk Road), but their long white robes and perfume temporarily convinced the Chinese that they were dealing with a race of women. The classic Arabic account of this heady time in Islamic history is Tabari's *History of Prophets and Kings*.

In general, most conquered peoples were rather used to being overrun by armies and accepted the Muslim Empire with fairly good grace. The Muslims in many ways were more tolerant than their previous masters had been. The Muslims often allowed the conquered peoples' culture to remain as it was, including most laws regulating marriage, divorce, and inheritance. The Arabic language spread along with the Muslim conquerors, arabicizing the Persian tongue and supplanting Aramaic in Syria and Coptic in Egypt. Arabic itself became the *lingua franca* of the Islamic world, an amazing feat on the part of the Muslim conquerors and one that helped unify the growing empire. One interesting result of the expansion of the Umayyads was the increasing need to find ways to connect Islamic law to local customs and cultures. This led to the development of the *ulama*, or legal scholars, who became adept at translating Islam across cultural divides. Without their efforts, Islamic law would have eventually fragmented into varying local law codes with little or no scriptural basis.

Under Umayyad rule, non-Arabs began to convert to Islam in large numbers, often for political reasons and to avoid the poll-tax (*jizya*) required of nonbelievers, although Muhammad had stipulated that this tax was not required as long as the general peace was not threatened.

There is some evidence that the extra revenue provided by the head tax actually made it rather desirable from the Muslim view that Christians and Jews *not* convert to Islam, although polytheists were forced to do so. In Spain, the Muslim conquerors actually forbade their Jewish and Christians subjects to convert; they wanted to keep the tax money they were due, and mass conversion threatened their fiscal base. Another tax (the *kharaj*) was levied on the land of non-Muslim landowners, and thus, the rural areas suffered more than the urban ones.

One Umayyad ruler, Sulayman, was noted for two things—his girth and his passion for soft silken garments. He was fond of keeping roast chickens in his sleeves and would pull them out occasionally, gnawing ferociously during an audience. When he died of plague in 717, his gentle brother Umar took over. Umar was descended from the first Caliph Umar and was a lot like him. He had been kicked in the face by a mule as a child, and the marks stayed with him for the rest of his life. He was so saintly that talk rose up about his being the Mahdi (literally, "the Guided One") or Islamic "Messiah," but he was not.

The last important ruler of the Umayyad Dynasty was Hisham (r. 724–743), who reigned for 20 years and is said to have been the inventor of the formal sport of horse racing. He was also devoted to craftwork, especially weaving. He had a dark side, though; he is the first person on record to have ordered an execution on a charge of heresy, the culprit being Djad ibn Dirham, in 742. Under Hisham the empire slowly disintegrated: the Berbers, the Persians, the Turks, and others were constantly rebelling, and Hashim simply did not have the wherewithal to fight back. He died at age 53.

The final Umayyad caliphs presided over an increasingly chaotic world, some of which was of their own making. The last of them was Marwan II (r. 744–750), who was killed with a javelin thrust to the stomach by the forces of Abu al-Abbas, who called himself al-Saffah, "The Blood-Shedder." The battle site was the Great Zab, located near the Tigris River. The Umayyads fled west into Spain, where after a time, they managed to recreate their former glory. Marwan's head was sent to Abu Abbas, and his tongue was fed to a cat. So ended the Umayyad Empire. The Muslims (or Moors, as they were called) were finally expelled from Spain in 1492 by Ferdinand and Isabella.

The Umayyads were well known for their architecture. Within a century after the Prophet's death, in 692, the Umayyad Caliph abd-al-Malik (646–705) built the awe-inspiring Dome of the Rock (*Qubbat al-Sakhrah*) on Mt. Moriah in Jerusalem, on the site of Solomon's Temple. Muslims believed that under it was a sweet fountain that produced all the pure water of the earth. Malik hoped the site would eventually prove more attractive to pilgrims than Mecca because he wanted to shift the center of Islam to his own territory. He also wanted to build something that would overpower the nearby Christian site, the Church of the Sepulcher. The Dome of Rock is not itself a mosque, but it is built near one, the so-called Furthest Mosque.

The Dome of the Rock remains pretty much the same today as when it was first built, although some of the mosaics and copper gilt roofing have vanished. It is decorated with quotations from the Quran (in fact, the earliest surviving Quranic text) and other material.

Aside from this feat, Abd-al-Malik is remembered mostly as a brutal tyrant, who on his deathbed told his son, "Don't mourn. When I am dead put on your leopard-skin, gird yourself with your sword, and cut off the head of everybody who gets in your way."

However, his son Walid I (705–715) was different. He built the world's first hospitals for the insane and shelters for the blind. It is also said that he never lost his temper. Like his father, he was interested in architecture; he built the mosque in Medina where Muhammad was buried and built for himself a wonderful mosque in his own capital of Damascus. This mosque has been burned to the ground three times, but it has always arisen from the ashes.

Probably the most infamous Umayyad was Walid II (r. 743–744), a ruler corrupted by power and licentiousness. He took over from his uncle, Hashim ibn al-Malik. In most respects he was a cultivated man, fond of music and poetry. He took care of disabled and blind people, making sure that they had food and money. However, he was a heavy drinker and irreverent. He stuck the Quran on the point of a spear and shot it to pieces with his arrows, reciting his own poetry the entire time. He ruled for less than a year and was killed in battle. His head was cut off by rebels and paraded through the streets of Damascus on the point of a spear, perhaps as a reminder of what he had done to the Quran.

THE ABBASID DYNASTY (749/750–1248)

The last material remnants of Muhammad—his staff, his cornelian finger ring, and his mantle—passed to the new dynasty, which lasted for more than 500 years. The origin of the Baghdad Abbasid line was al-Abbas, a paternal uncle of both Ali and Muhammad. It was the opinion of the Abbasids that only someone "of the Prophet's house" could rightfully assume his mantle.

The first Abbasid caliph, Abu Abbas As-Saffah (r. 749–754), lived up to his terrible nickname mentioned earlier: "Blood-Shedder." He kept his executioner on duty right next to his throne, along with a leather mat for the bloody head to fall on. His excuse for much of this was, as he said in his first speech as caliph, that "it is through us that Allah has guided the people after they had gone astray [under the Umayyads] and showed them the light after their ignorance." He and his successors claimed to be "Allah's Caliph." Abu Abbas clad himself in the mantle of the prophet, wearing it on all state occasions just so that everyone was made aware by whose authority he ruled. (The Umayyad caliphs, by contrast, generally showed up for state occasions in their military outfits.) Just before he died of smallpox, he gave orders for his body to be buried secretly because he was afraid of the desecrations that would be performed on it.

His brother and successor was Abu Jafar (709–775). Also called al-Mansur, the "Victorious," he was a man of better stamp, who brought peace and prosperity to the empire. He tried to establish an Islamic theocracy, with himself, of course, at the head of things and proclaimed himself Imam-Caliph in 760. He was abstemious himself but did not object to others enjoying wine and other non-Islamic pursuits. Still, during his two-plus decades in power, the number of Muslims in the empire rose from 8 percent to 15 percent. His main interest was gathering funds, and his most important project was the building of Baghdad, which was officially named Medina as-slam or "city of peace" (but always simply called Baghdad after the village on top of which it was built). The project took only four years and 100,000 imported workers. Baghdad was built as a circular city, the center of which featured the caliph's "Palace of the Golden Doors" with its notable green dome. The palace was built from the ancient bricks that had been used to build the ancient palaces of the old Iranian empire. Unfortunately, there is nothing left of the palaces built by Harun and Mamun because they were constructed out of mud brick rather than stone, as used by the Umayyads.

The new city replaced Damascus as the capital, becoming the center of the Islamic galaxy and taking advantage of the trade possibilities provided by the Tigris and Euphrates Rivers. Al-Mansur died on his return from making a pilgrimage to Mecca, very much like Muhammad.

Al-Mansur's son, Muhammad, also called al-Mahdi (r. 775–785), was even finer. He freed most of the prisoners, provided for lepers and poor people, and built rest houses along the road to Mecca. He was even good to his enemies. When he defeated a son of Marwan who revolted in Syria, he merely took him prisoner and later pensioned him off. Al-Mahdi died in a hunting accident after a successful reign of 10 years.

His older, rather awful son Musa al-Hadi (d. 786) took over briefly. During his reign, Idris ibn Abdallah (788–791), one of Muhammad's descendants, took himself off and founded his own dynasty, the Idrisids, in Morocco, a loss to the empire that no one paid any attention to. Musa came to a bad end—probably suffocated with the consent of his own mother.

After Musa's death, his younger brother Harun al-Rashid, whose name means "Aaron the Rightly Guided" (786–209), took control. Harun was fictionally immortalized in *One Thousand and One Arabian Nights*, and during his reign, Baghdad reached its pinnacle of civilization. He was noted for dressing like a commoner and wandering around the streets at night "rooting out corruption." However, there was something very unhealthy about Harun. He had four sons, of whom his favorite was the eldest, Jafar. He had Jafar marry his own aunt, Harun's sister Abbasa, but commanded that Jafar never be alone with her. The couple went ahead and had two children anyway, but when the caliph found out, he had both children strangled. He then had the parents killed. Years later, someone dared ask him why. "If I thought even my inmost garments knew the reason, I would tear them apart," he responded, leaving to some terrible speculations. His last act was to order a rebel hacked to bits slowly in front of him; he himself died a few hours later.

The Abbasid dynasty emerged from the outskirts of the Islamic Empire, and it is due to its rise that power eventually shifted away from Damascus and toward Iraq, an ancient center of culture. The Abbasids promised to purify Islam and limit the power of the Arab aristocracy. Under them, Islam ceased to be a de facto "Arab-only" faith and became more truly universal, although Arabic remained the *lingua franca* of the empire.

Under them, the previously underrepresented non-Arabic Muslims (the so-called *mawali*) got their first taste of power. (Under the Umayyads, perhaps only 10 percent of the population converted to Islam; under the Abbasids, the majority were Islamicized.) However, the Abbasids were quite insistent on their own authority, claiming to be caliphs by "divine right" and demanding a new title: "Shadow of God on earth." Abbasid caliphs were impressed by Persian customs and borrowed freely from them, at least in matters relating to obeisance. They expected their subjects to kiss the ground during an audience, something that certainly never would have occurred to Muhammad. The Abbasids employed many Persians in high positions, and the new rulers took on the trappings of the earlier Persian emperors. As one popular saying had it, "Prophecy and the caliphate belong to the Arabs, but kingship belongs to the Persians." They also hired Turks for the army, some of whom, the famous Mamlukes, were slaves. Their name comes from the Arabic *mamluk* or "owned." (The Mamlukes later took things over and ruled until 1517.)

Umayyad and Abbasid scholars made significant advances in optics, astronomy, literature, medicine, architecture, and philosophy. Indeed, it was Islam, not the West, that preserved the teachings of Plato and Aristotle for the world. Muslim scholars even receive credit for inventing the concept of zero, although they actually got the idea from India. The Muslim scholar Muhammad Abu Musa al-Khwarizmi (d. 850) developed algebra (*al-Jabr*), for which school children are not as grateful as they might be. Another, Abul-Wafa al-Busajami (940–998), developed trigonometry. ("Algebra" and "chemistry" are both Arabic words, and the whole world now uses Arabic numerals.) The Muslim physician al-Razi was the first person to accurately differentiate the symptoms of smallpox and measles. The Abbasids also helped develop the Islamic scholarly group called the *ulama*, which developed the Islamic law, or *sharia* (literally a road or pathway).

The 10th and 11th centuries produced a brilliant Islamic culture, even if times were politically chaotic. The Abbasids accumulated great wealth, and the brilliant, half-Persian Caliph Abdallah al-Mamun (r. 813–833), son of Harun, was able to establish the House of Wisdom (*Bayt al-Hikma*) in Baghdad to explore the new learning. Here ancient Greek, Latin, Persian, Syriac, Coptic, and Sanskrit learning was translated into Arabic and preserved for the benefit of the world. (Unfortunately the House of Wisdom was destroyed in 1258 when the Mongols invaded Baghdad. It was said that the Tigris River ran black for six months with ink from the massive number of texts thrown into it.)

Not only that, but the Muslims went further and developed their own sciences and technology, attracting scholars from all over the known world, with Arabic as the language of scholarship. Al-Mamun established a Council of State that included Jews, Christians, and Zoroastrians on an equal basis, with Muslims to advise on matters of state. He claimed that he as Caliph was the only one to decide who was and was not qualified to transmit the traditions of the Prophet, and even began his own version of an inquisition to question religious leaders about their statements. His death was unusual—a servant was bringing in a bowl with a still living fish on it. The fish sprang out of the basin, and the caliph was drenched with cold water, from which he caught a fever and died.

Two of the greatest philosophers of the age were Avicenna (Ibn-Sina in Arabic), who lived from 980 to 1037, and Averroes (Ibn Rushd), who lived from 1126 to 1198. Avicenna (980–1037), born in Central Asia and probably of Persian descent, was both a physician and a prime minister. His text on medicine (*al-Qanun*) was being used in Europe 600 years later. In his spare time he produced an encyclopedia he dictated from horseback. It is reputed to be the longest work ever written by one person. Although he espoused the importance of reason, Avicenna confessed that whenever he got stuck on a particularly knotty problem, he would go to the mosque to pray, and the answer would invariably come. He was a devotee of the belief that faith and reason are completely compatible. Averroes, a member of the scholarly *ulama* and a judge of Cordoba, also attempted to reconcile reason and religion. He was a great student of Aristotle's teaching and helped to clarify that philosopher's thought to the scholars of his age. In fact, his ideas influenced Thomas Aquinas, the great Catholic theologian.

The last great figure of medieval Islamic philosophy was Ibn Khaldun (1332–1406), who was a jurist, historian, theologian, mathematician, and nutritionist. Although he was born in Tunisia, most of his work was done in Egypt, where he taught at al-Azhar University and became a judge in the Maliki school of law. His best-known work is the three-volume *Muqaddimah* (known as *Prolegomenon* in the West), in which he developed a science of history. He concluded that civilizations rise and fall in cyclical manner. He found enough exceptions to his examples, however, to proclaim that only Allah could really know the reasons.

FRAGMENTATION

The Islamic empire was too large to hold together indefinitely. The Abbasids never ruled Spain, for instance, and Morocco seceded from the empire. Soon the Abbasid dynasty was confined to Iraq. Eventually, there were three main caliphates—one in Baghdad (Abbasid), one in Cordoba, Spain (Umayyad), and one in Egypt (Fatimid), as well as some military dynasties in other places. A local dynasty formed in North Africa, the Aghlabids (800–909). The caliphate eventually disintegrated, with the Mongols capturing Baghdad in 1258, although some local sultans continued to call themselves Abbasids for the prestige of the name. The conquering Mongols converted to Islam.

The Fatimid (al-Fatimiyyun) Dynasty (909 to 1171)

The Fatimid Dynasty was born in 909, in modern-day Tunisia and Algeria, although its greatest flourishing was in Egypt, where the dynasty founded the city of Cairo in 969. The first member of the dynasty was Abdullah al-Mahdi Billah, a descendant of Muhammad through Fatimah, hence the name Fatimid. At their height, the Fatimids' realm extended from the Atlantic Ocean to the Red Sea, including Egypt, Algeria, Tunisia, Morocco, Algeria, Libya, Palestine, Lebanon, Syria, Yemen, and the Hejaz region of Arabia.

The ruling Fatimids belonged to the Ismaili branch of Shia Isla, although the Egyptian people remained Sunni. The Egyptian caliphs are also considered part of the line of Sunni caliphs, making the period of the Fatimid Dynasty the only sustained era in Islamic history in which the Shia Imamate and the Sunni Caliphate were essentially the same. For the most part, the Fatimids were tolerant toward other Islamic groups, Jews, and Coptic Christians and established a kingdom of peace in a region that had previously known only war. They established al-Azhar University in Cairo, the world's first such institution, preceding the great European schools of Paris, Oxford, and Bologna by 250 years. It is still the most famous institution of Islamic learning in the world.

The Safavids (1501–1722)

This interesting dynasty was established not through conquest, as were most of the others, but by the Sufi order called the Safaviyeh (which was not originally Shia but instead hailed from among the Shafii Sunnis. Their rulers claimed to be descendants of Muhammad. The most important ruler was Shah Abbas (1588–1629), whose capital at Isfahan was the center of architectural and other marvels. Abbas was a suspicious sort, who so feared assassination that he had one of his sons executed and two others blinded. Despite this small character flaw, Abbas built an empire that at its zenith included Persia, Iraq, Armenia, Azerbaijan, Georgia, and parts of Turkmenistan, Uzbekistan, Afghanistan, and Pakistan.

The Mughul Dynasty

The Mughal Dynasty was based in India. The sultanate of Delhi was founded in 1206. Confined at first to North India, Islam later spread throughout the entire subcontinent. Muslims still make up a large minority in India and a great majority in Pakistan and Bangladesh. The most famous Mughal emperor was Akbar (1565–1605), and he was adept at achieving a cultural synthesis between his Hindu and Muslim subjects. A tolerant ruler, he encouraged close cooperation among scholars of different faiths and always looked for points of commonality rather than differences. The Islamic *ulama*, however, was generally opposed to these moderate moves. After Akbar died, his successor Aurangzeb took apart most of his religious achievements in exchange for a more conservative model.

THE OTTOMANS (1280–1924)

By the time the Middle Ages were drawing to a close, the real center of Islamic culture had shifted to Turkey. This was the home of the famous Ottoman Empire, which finally conquered Constantinople in 1453. (The Muslims had been besieging it on a regular basis since 674.) The name Ottoman derives from an early chieftain, Osman. The Ottomans were not particularly religious, just the opposite. They even sanctioned a strange procedure called the Law of Fratricide, which declared it legal for rival heirs of the throne to attempt to kill each other, so that there would be no quarreling later on about who was the legitimate heir. At their height the Ottomans controlled not only Turkey, but also a large part of southeastern Europe, the Middle East, and North Africa.

Noted Ottoman emperors included Mehmet II the Conqueror (r. 1444–1451), Bayazid II (r. 1481–1512), Selim (r. 1512–1520), and most famously, Sulayman the Magnificent (1520–1566). Mehmet II was the one who chose Istanbul (formerly Constantinople) as his capital. Because it sat astride Europe and Asia, it was an important symbolic choice. The city contained more than 500,000 people, twice the number of any European capital of the time.

The Ottomans were known for persecuting certain Sufi sects, whose holy men had a wild appearance that unnerved the ruling elite. It did not help that a Sufi tried to assassinate Bayazid II.

Although the empire declined after Sulayman, they hung on until they were defeated in World War I, and their remaining territory partitioned. In 1924, Turkey formally abolished the caliphate and sharia (Islamic law) and became an officially secular state under Mustafa Kemal Ataturk (1881–1938). (Ataturk is a nickname that means "father of the Turks.") Ataturk admired Western culture and attempted to establish a secular state in which loyalties would be based on geography rather than religious affiliation. He ordered the Arabic script to be replaced with the Latin one (making most Turks suddenly illiterate). In 1927 Ataturk told the national assembly that it was necessary to abolish the fez and turban, headpieces he declared "emblems of ignorance," and accept the hat, "the headgear used by the whole civilized world." He felt the same way about chadors and ordered them torn from the heads of women to dared to appear on the street with them.

However, the Turkish Constitutional Court issued a ruling on June 5, 2008, annulling the law. Women were then once again permitted to wear headscarves in the universities. (It is believed by some that women who choose to wear the headscarves are receiving financial aid from fundamentalist groups.) Turkey retains the unusual distinction of being one of few Middle Eastern states that was never colonized by European powers.

THE CRUSADES

For both Christians and Muslims, the Crusades were a watershed event that shaped relations between the faiths for centuries. When Turkish armies headed for the Bosphorus, the nervous Byzantine emperor, Alexius Comnenus (1081–1118), wrote to Pope Urban II for help. The Pope was happy to comply, but his ambitions extended beyond an expeditionary force to help his brother ruler. The First Crusade was proclaimed in 1095, when Urban pressed his fellow Christians to "hasten to exterminate this vile race [the Muslims]." He promised Crusaders the rewards of Heaven if they went on this expedition. Many were all too happy to comply—they also exterminated many Jewish communities on their way to the Holy Land. The Pope wanted Jerusalem and in fact conquered it from the Fatimids in 1099. However, that was only the beginning. The Crusades went on and on and on, with more announced in 1147, 1189, 1202, 1217, 1248, and 1269.

The Pope's Crusaders did not hold on to his beloved Jerusalem. Saladin (Salah al-Din, d. 1193) defeated the Christians in 1187 at the Battle of Hattin and reconquered the holy city. Saladin was much kinder to the Christian women and children living there than the Crusaders had been to the Muslim ones. Two years later, Saladin declared, "I shall cross this sea to their islands to pursue them until there remains no one on the face of the earth who does not acknowledge

Allah." (The same sentiment, almost word for word, was echoed by the Ayatollah Ruhollah Khomeini in 1979 and again by Osama bin Laden in November 2001.) The history of the Crusades reads markedly differently from the Islamic perspective; the first scholarly work emphasizing that aspect was Carole Hillenbrand's *The Crusades: Islamic Perspectives*, which was not published until 1999.

Although the Crusades were important to the Middle East, the rest of the Islamic world, especially in Spain, was largely unaffected by them. In more modern times, the brutalities of the Crusades were replaced by the insults and degradation of colonization. Islamic lands lay under European domination for many years; the British and French controlled much of North Africa and the Middle East during most of the 19th and early 20th centuries. They worked not only to consolidate political power but also to convert the people under their domination to Christianity, although with very little success.

THE SCHISM: SHIA AND SUNNI

The division between Shia (Followers of Ali) and Sunni (Followers of the Custom of the Caliphate) dates from the death of Muhammad and persists to this day. The Shia Imamate began with Ali (who is also accepted by Sunni Muslims as one of the "Rightly Guided Caliphs" to succeed the Prophet). For Shia Muslims, Ali is the first in order of succession after Muhammad; for Sunni Muslims he is fourth. Shia call their leaders "Imams"; it should be noted that in English "Imam" with a capital "I" usually designates a Shia leader; "imam" with a small "i" refers to a prayer leader in a mosque. (This distinction serves in English only. Arabic has no capital letters.) Most of the Imams avoided conflict and oppression by living far from the political capitals. In Shia Islam, the power of the Imams is greatly exalted and far exceeds any spiritual authority given to the caliphs by their Sunni counterparts. Whereas Sunnis tend to put more reliance on law and jurisprudence, the Shia place emphasis on the words and teachings of their Imams. Men suitable to be Imams had to possess seven main characteristics: justice; knowledge to render independent judgments about Islamic theology and law; soundness of hearing, vision, and speech; soundness of limb; ability to govern; courage; and not least important—descent from Muhammad.

Ali's entire caliphate was embroiled in a bloody civil war, during which his followers came to be known as "Shiites," which means "partisans." Muhammad's powerful widow Aishah, daughter of Abu Bakr, the first caliph, also opposed Ali, claiming that he had failed to punish the killers of Uthman (although she may have been behind it herself).

This was the first occasion in which a caliph attacked another Muslim army. The most famous event was the "Battle of the Camel" or the Battle of Jamal, fought near Basra. In 656, the 42-year-old Aishah rode at the head of 1,000 armed men to battle, mounted on her camel al-Askar. On the way, many others flocked to her cause. Her party felt that Ali had not done enough to find and prosecute the murderer of the third caliph, Uthman. She supported the claims of two other companions, Talha ibn Ubayallah and al-Zubayr ibn al-Awwam.

Aishah had attempted to get Muhammad's other wives to join her but was not successful, although some accompanied her partway. The battle took place in Basra, in southern Iraq, with some of Ali's people defecting to Aishah's side. In the end, over 10,000 men were killed. Officially, Ali won, although losses were split between the two sides. Ali did not follow up on his victory and commanded that Aishah be escorted home and given utmost respect as the widow of the Prophet. Aishah's reputation suffered a great deal from her interference in this affair, with some Muslim commentators blaming her for the division between Sunni and Shia. Conservative scholars have even claimed that her misguided actions show that women should never be involved in politics.

However, the main struggle was between Ali and the fifth caliph, Muawiya (r. 661–680), Uthman's nephew and founder of the Umayyad Dynasty. Ali, not desiring bloodshed, agreed to meet with Muawiya to negotiate, but certain members of his own party were so enraged by what they perceived as his "giving in" that they left his party. These people became known as the Karijites, discussed in chapter V.

THE DEATH OF ALI

On January 24, 661, in the Iraqi city of Kufa, Ali was stabbed in the brain by a poisoned sword by a certain Abdul Rahman, a Kharijite. He wanted Ali's head for a marriage payment (which also included a good bit of money). Ali lingered on for three agonizing days, and the miscreant was captured, but Ali asked that Abdul Rahman be treated mercifully and not tortured while awaiting trial. "If I do not die," he said, "spare the attacker. If I die and he must be executed, it must be done cleanly with a single sword stroke." Ali did indeed die, and Abdul Rahman had his hands and feet cut off and then red hot nails thrust into his eyes. Finally, he was slowly roasted to death.

According to most historians, Ali is buried in Najaf in Iraq, and the site is more sacred to Shia than the Kaaba. A rival tradition, however, maintains that Ali's body was exhumed by his followers and strapped to the back of a white she-camel. The camel was made to run as far as she could, and the body was buried where the camel collapsed—in Mazar-Sharif in Afghanistan. This tomb, the "tomb of the exalted," is now a pilgrimage spot for Afghanis. Most Muslims then accepted Muawiyah as the Fifth Caliph, beginning the Umayyad Dynasty, but the Shia did not.

The Shia line continued through Ali's sons Hasan (whose name means "pleasant" or "handsome") and Husayn, the grandsons of Muhammad. According to Sunni tradition, Hasan died peacefully from consumption, but Shia believe he was poisoned by a wife or servant who washed his body in a poisoned napkin.

His brother Husayn met with a worse end during the month of Muharram in 680. Husayn and almost all his family (including his year-old son) were traveling from Medina to Kufa when they were ambushed and killed near Karbala during a battle against 4,000 troops supporting the Umayyad Caliph Yazid, son of Muawiya. The Umayyads tried without success to negotiate a surrender. Husayn refused and, after eight days of deadlock, put on the mantle of his grandfather Muhammad and went out to fight.

According to Shia tradition, Husayn was badly wounded in the battle at Karbala in 680. He was tortured by the Sunnis, who denied him water and then beheaded him. The bodies of the family were desecrated. His head was taken to Damascus to show the caliph, but eventually it was returned for burial. The caliph also allowed safe passage back to Medina for the surviving members of Ali's family, including Husayn's sister Zaynab. She actually led the Shia party until Husayn's children Ali Zayn and Muhammad al Baqir came of age and inherited the Imamate.

From that time to this, Shia Muslims observe Muharram as a month of martyrdom. Rites culminate on the 10th of the month, Ashura Day. The faithful enact passion plays (*taziaya*) commemorating the martyrdom of Husayn. To this day, the faithful moan, groan, and call out, "Ya Hasan, ya Husayn!" in heartbroken memory of the fallen leaders. They even beat themselves with chains and scourges and stab themselves with knives. Mourning continues for the entire month. Karbala, where Husayn died, is more important to Shia Muslims than is Mecca.

One caliph, Al-Mamun, attempted to heal the rift between the Sunni and Shia. He invited the Eighth Imam, Ali ibn Musa ibna

Jafar, known as Reza (766–819), who was noted for his virtue, to join him in his capital at Marv, welcoming him with great pomp. He even (apparently) designated him as his successor. The Imam was said to reply, "I will accept this offer to console you, but this will never happen for I will leave this world before you."

Indeed, Reza died on a military campaign in Persia. It has been reliably alleged that Mamun had Reza fed poisoned grapes out of jealousy. A shrine developed around his tomb in Mashbad, which is visited by 12–15 million pilgrims every year. It later became the site of some important theological schools. After al-Reza's death, relations between the Sunnis and Shia became even more strained.

CHAPTER 4

Islamic Law and Cultural Practices

Like Judaism, Islam is a religion of law, and for Muslims, all law comes ultimately from Allah. Islamic law, or sharia, gives concrete guidance for Muslims on how to live their lives. It is supposed to be an expression of divine will. Islamic law holds sway over all aspects of life, including family relations, etiquette, rules for worship, inheritance, punishments, taxation, social interaction, war, purification, and prayer.

Islamic society, by definition, is based on Islamic law. Religion is not simply a personal matter. The Quran states that there must be "no compulsion in [the] religion [*al-din*]" (2:256). Although this widely known statement is often interpreted to mean that people should not be forced to convert, it actually refers to practicing Muslims, who have been shown the truth and who should be allowed to decide whether or not to follow the "straight path" because compulsory obedience is worth nothing. The word *al-din* or "the religion" refers to Islam, not to religion in general. The main point of this particular verse is not to extend tolerance but to make the point that human beings have the freedom to decide whether to follow the commands of Allah.

The basic principle of Islamic law is that anything is allowed except what Allah has forbidden. Human beings do not have the authority to make these judgments themselves; they must rely on the law of Allah as revealed in the Quran. For example, the Ayatollah Khomeini of Iran, who was reviled in the West as an oppressive dictator, had no objection to women voting, for as he said, he saw nothing in the Quran that forbade it. (On the other hand, he consummated marriage with a 10-year-old girl, who miscarried when she was eleven.) It is a matter of dispute among Muslims as to whether Sharia applies to Muslims living outside Islamic lands. Some say yes and maintain they may be dealt with accordingly; others say no, and some attempt a compromise by saying yes, but punishment can only occur if or when the miscreant returns to an Islamic country. The matter is by no means settled. The matter came to international attention when, in 1989 the Ayatollah Khomeini issued a fatwa ordering the death not only of the novelist Salman Rushdie (who lived in London) but also against anyone who helped him in the publication of this book *The Satanic Verses,* including non-Muslims. This unfortunate precedent has been followed by other Muslim clerics since that time.

THE PURPOSE OF THE LAW

For Muslims, law helps to establish Islamic ideal. The Quran clearly sets forth the ideal Muslim:

Truly, men and women who submit, and men and women who believe, and men and women who are patient, and men and women who are truthful, and men and women who are humble before Allah, and men and women who give in charity, and men and women who fast, and men and women who guard their chastity, and men and women who remember Allah, to these Allah has promised forgiveness and a great reward. (33:35)

Thus, patience, truthfulness, belief, and humility before Allah are characteristics to be developed, and fasting, praying, chaste behavior, and giving to charity are actions worthy of reward and forgiveness. Such a person is in possession of *taqwa,* or God-consciousness, or in more Judeo-Christian terms, "fearing God." *O believers, be conscious of Allah and be with the truthful* (9:119). This verse points out the logical connection between "god-consciousness" and truthfulness. The Quran declares, *Believers: Conduct yourselves with justice and bear true witness, even if it be against yourself, your parents, or your kin* (4:135).

Consciousness of Allah is the most important attribute a Muslim can have and is the beginning of worship. It is also the beginning community and of law. Muhammad said, "By him whose hand is in my soul, none of you shall enter Paradise until you believe, and none of you believe until you love one another." The Islamic ideal is just that—an ideal. As in every other religion, most followers never manage to achieve the high standards set for them. Ideals always contrast with practice, on both an individual and a group basis. But the most sincere adherents make attaining that ideal a lifelong goal.

One of the purposes of Islamic law is to guide people in the right direction toward these ideals. Muslims recognize "negligence" or forgetfulness of Allah rather than outright sin as the basic human failing. The devout Muslim believes that Allah is always with him, watching, commanding, helping, and judging. Muhammad paid great attention to the value of fair dealing, kindness, and promises, especially between one Muslim and another. "Do not unnecessarily dispute with a brother Muslim, nor joke with him in such a way that displeases him. Do not promise him something which you cannot fulfill." Further, he noted, "Every man is a mirror to his brother Muslim." The vast majority of Muslim law refers to the way that Muslims treat each other.

Patience and self-control were virtues Muhammad constantly stressed. "Which among you is the best wrestler?" he once asked. He answered his own question in an unexpected way: "The best wrestler among you is the one most capable of controlling himself when angry." The Quran even counsels those who are insulted for their faith to *bear with patience what they say, and when they leave give them a courteous farewell* (73:10). It is for Allah to decide, not human beings.

The opposite of patience is complaining, which is against the strictures of Islam. Bemoaning one's fate is the same as complaining about Allah, which is not allowed. Even complaining about one's food is frowned upon; after all, food comes from Allah, who made all things. Despairing remarks about one's poverty, family, or situation in life are inconsistent with accepting what Allah has determined. Behaving well for the wrong reasons, such as showing off for the neighbors, gives one no credit either. One's inner state is at least as important as outward actions (*amal*).

While Islam is basically a legalistic tradition, morality is also a matter of the heart. Muhammad placed a great deal of trust in people knowing right from wrong and trusting their instincts. According to a hadith, Muhammad asked people to consult their hearts in matters of morality. "Righteousness is that about which the soul feels tranquil and the heart feels tranquil, and wrongdoing is that which wavers in the soul and moves to and fro in the breast even though people again and again have given you their legal opinion in its favor."

Justice in general is extremely important in the Islamic tradition. When an injustice occurs, Muslims are required to set it right if possible. If it is not possible, they are enjoined to speak out against it. If even that is not possible, they must at least not allow the evil to take root in their own hearts.

Sharia

The word *sharia* literally means "path to water" (a track trodden by animals on the way to a water source); for Muslims it is the way to truth and to Allah. Sharia is considered divinely ordered, not man-made law.

Another word used to denote law is *fiqh*, a somewhat earlier term that literally means "understanding." Nowadays it has a narrower connotation than sharia and refers to jurisprudence. In some cases these regulations are laid out in great detail; at other times they are vague and call for careful interpretation. In Islam, the study of law takes the place of theology (*kalam*). More accurately, they are one and the same; Muslim writers often maintain that there is no difference between law and religion. After all, the law is divine, having come directly from Allah himself. Allah's will is made known by his law, which adherents are expected to *joyfully* obey. The Quran is considered to embody Allah's law, although only about 80 verses specifically deal with everyday legal matters. An example is 2:282, which stipulates that loan transactions should be documented in writing. For most quotidian matters, however, human beings had to fill in where the Quran was silent.

Much of sharia was developed by the *ulama* and completed about the year 900. Islam was from the beginning socially oriented, revealed to create a new order on earth, a community of believers. It is not and never has been a solitary path for individual seekers.

However, just because sharia is the ultimate law does not mean it is always invoked. Over time, it has been decreed that for special reasons, Islamic law is held in "abeyance" until such time as it can come fully into force. The divine law is not abrogated in such cases; it is merely not being invoked.

Laws can be divided into *ibadat*, laws respecting the relations between Allah and mankind, and *muamalat*, laws regulating interpersonal conduct. A legal opinion is known as a *fatwa*. It is frequently misunderstood as a "death sentence," but in fact is not.

Sharia is usually considered to be based on (in order of importance) the Quran, words and practices of the Prophet (Sunnah), community consensus (*ijma*), and analogical deduction (*qiyas*) from established rulings. Islamic teachings about beliefs rather than laws are frequently referred to as *al-hikmah* (philosophy) and are not strictly considered a part of sharia.

Although many Muslim countries operate with secular law, the conservative factions of the population often urge a return to sharia. In February 2009, the Pakistan government worked out an agreement with Taliban militants to allow sharia to be implemented in parts of North West Frontier Province. These are the same people who terrorized the area with kidnappings, beheadings, and the destruction of schools to educate girls. The Pakistani Taliban also interprets sharia as forcing women to remain in their homes and the outlawing of all forms of entertainment.

SUNNAH AND HADITH

The Sunnah comprises Islamic practices taught by the Prophet. Originally the Sunnah apparently referred to the practices of all the Companions (sahabah), but its meaning was restricted over time to refer to the practices and words of Muhammad alone. Traditions from the Companions are also considered important, but definitely secondary to those of the Prophet. Closely connected with the Sunnah are the hadith, which are reports by Muhammad's Companions of what he said, did, and approved of.

The Sunnah was originally in oral form and only later committed to writing. The Companions of the Prophet made a prodigious effort to recollect these traditions carefully and would sit in a circle (as many as 60 would join) to share memories and check what each remembered. The Prophet himself was quite strict on this score: "Whoever intentionally ascribes to me what I did not say," he warned, "then let him occupy a place in Hell-fire." (One man supposedly invented about 4,000 hadith and was duly executed.)

The hadith are not mentioned in the Quran, and the Prophet at first was afraid that people would mistakenly attribute them to the Quran. He was particularly concerned that they not be written down on the same piece of parchment as the Quran. They are not considered to be the word of God, like the Quran, but may provide divine guidance for Muslims. However, the hadith are always to be interpreted in the light of the Quran. As Muhammad said, "If you are going to relate a hadith from me, first consider it in the light of the book of Allah."

Some of the early hadith were incorporated into the *sira*, the early biographical material about Muhammad. These brief accounts ultimately go back to Muhammad or to one of his Companions, and all are written in Arabic. Most Muslims regard the hadith as scripture complementary to the Quran; they help explain and clarify it. It is said that without a study of the hadith, a Muslim's knowledge of his faith is incomplete.

The hadith talk about all aspects of Muhammad's life (including hygiene, treatment of others, and ways to pray). They are usually quite brief, making a single point or containing a single observation. Although they contain rules about behavior, they are in narrative form and were transmitted orally before being written down.

Hadith are considered a supplementary rather than a primary source of law. Their study is a specialized branch of Islam, in which the scholar peruses the hadith to discover what regulations may be legitimately drawn from them.

A hadith is divided into two parts. The first part is the *isnad*, or a listing of the chain of authorities by which the hadith in question was transmitted. This is to guarantee its authenticity. Interestingly, the gender of a transmitter was never a consideration—so reports by women and slaves in the chain were as valid as reports by free men. Those considered ineligible to pass along a hadith include mentally deficient persons, habitual liars, those in the grip of passion (who might introduce an innovation), and those who have not mastered the knowledge they are supposed to transmit. The chain of evidence was carefully examined to make sure, for instance, that the links would have known each other.

Over time, various methods of transmitting hadith were employed. In one method (*ard*) the student who had received a work from his teacher by dictation or from a manuscript would read it back carefully for authentication. In another method, *mukatabah*, the manuscript would be received in correspondence and copied. In the *munawalah* method, a written manuscript would be unaccompanied by an oral reading, and in *ijazah* method, a student had a certificate from his master allowing him to transmit his master's material.

The second part of the hadith is the *matn*, or main text. This can only be considered, however, after the *isnad* is authentically fixed. Interestingly, many Muslims scholars have been even more reluctant to translate the hadith into other languages than they have the Quran itself. One explanation has been that the meaning of the Quran is so clear and holy that its main ideas can be understood by anyone with a will; however, the exposition itself of the hadith requires a teacher.

CERTIFYING HADITH

The weight given to a hadith depends on many factors. The most highly regarded are called *sahih* hadith—genuine, rigorously authenticated traditions that meet the following criteria:

- Go back to the time of the Prophet
- Are transmitted by an unbroken chain of upright people known for their accurate memories
- Agree with known historical fact
- Agree with accepted Quranic teaching
- Display basic consistency among different versions
- Agree with general Islamic teaching
- Make no innovations or additions to the existing Islamic law
- Contain material that seems believable coming from the Prophet's mouth
- Are free of grammatical errors and stylistic weaknesses

Less highly rated are the *hasan* or "good" traditions; even less reliable but still acceptable traditions are called *daif* or "weak." Here is a partial list of weak or inauthentic hadith categories:

- Muallaq traditions: Omit one or two transmitters' names in the beginning of the *isnad*
- Maqtu traditions: Reported by a man of second category after the Prophet
- Munqati traditions: Omit one link in the chain
- Mudal traditions: Omit two links
- Mursal traditions: Omit the name of a Companion in the *isnad*
- Muallal traditions: Affected by some weakness or infirmity
- Musahhaf traditions: Contain an error in the words or letters of the *isnad* or *matn* (such as a spelling error in a name)
- Shadhdh ("singular") traditions: Contain a reliable chain of reporters, but have content contrary to similarly attested material accepted by the majority of the collectors
- Gharib traditions: Considered unusual for one reason or another
- Munkar traditions: Considered singular and suspect
- Maudu traditions: Considered fabricated
- Mushkil traditions: Considered ambiguous

If this seems confusing, it may be comforting to know that Muslim scholars themselves disagree over the exact meaning of these terms and argue about what criteria serve to make a tradition unreliable. One scholar may deem a hadith *sahih* that another labels *hasan*, and so forth. Fortunately, the number of really controversial hadith is comparatively small. Although Muslims have always recognized that some of the hadith were inauthentic, or even forgeries, some later scholars, starting with Hungarian scholar Ignaz Goldhizer (d. 1921), suggested nearly all were fabrications or that at least, the elaborate "chains" of transmittal were so detailed that they were in themselves suspicious. The truth is probably somewhere in the middle.

However, since the hadith sometimes directly contradict one another, careful examination is needed to determine which is the correct report. To make a determination about a particular hadith, a scholar must rely on independent evidence, not depend mindlessly of the opinions of earlier scholars. If two hadith conflict, that one most in line with the Quran is considered most authentic. Nothing in a hadith can override anything in the Quran, which is always the primary authority.

If neither is in opposition to Quranic teaching, but are contradictory to each other, the *later* hadith abrogates the earlier one. However, even some hadith not accepted as historically valid are still considered valuable if they report traditions of which the Prophet would have approved; in other words, they still transmit Sunnah.

There are more than 10,000 *sahih* and *hasan* traditions altogether, but no single definitive collection (canon) of them exists. Different schools of Islam have different ideas about which ones to accept. However, there are six widely known collections, those compiled by the following individuals:

- Muhammad Bukhari ibn al Bukhari (810–870)
- Muslim ibn al-Hajjaj (821–875)
- Muhammad Ibn Majah (d. 887 or 896)
- Abu Dawud as-Sijistani (d. 888 or 889)
- Abi Eesaa Muhammad at-Tirmidhi (824–892)
- Ahmad ibn Shuayb an-Nisai (d. 915)

Ahmad ibn Hanbal (d. 855) also collected a veritable encyclopedia of traditions. Of the collections in the preceding list, those of Bukhari and Muslim are held in the highest regard, and a tradition recorded in both is almost assured of acceptance. Bukhari, born as his name indicates in Bukhara, was called the "Commander of the Faithful in

Hadith" (*amir al muminin fi al hadith*), and his collection is considered the first and the most authentic of all. His memory, according to tradition, was the most powerful the world has ever known, and he began studying the Tradition when he was only 10 years old. He traveled all around the Islamic world during his research and is said to have interviewed 1,080 people and looked at 600,000 different traditions by one count (but only 300,000 in another). In the end, he decided to include only 7,397 hadith in his collection, or by another count 2,602. He classified each as "sound," "good," "weak," or "unsound," and arranged them by subject matter. He said, "I entered no hadith in the book before having carried out the ritual purification and prayed twice." His work was heralded, and he became a celebrity in his own day.

Muslim ibn al-Hajjaj, another notable collector, gathered 7,422 authentic hadith. (About 4,000 are simply repetitions of the authentic hadith.) Unlike Bukhari, however, who classified his hadith according to subject matter, Muslim listed his in a willy-nilly fashion, making it difficult to find one apropos to the question at hand. Another highly regarded collection is that of Malik bin Anas (715–801), who gathered the earliest of all the collections.

Hadith Qudsi: A Special Case

These hadith, the Hadith Qudsi, are those in which the Prophet reports what Allah said to him, but in his (Muhammad's) own words, unlike the Quran, which is said to reveal Allah's words verbatim. The style is usually different from that of the Quran. These hadith usually have no relevance to law or creed but encourage the believer's spiritual development.

The Ulama or Scholarly Community

Islam has no official clergy. It does, however, have imams who lead prayers and a scholarly community or *ulama* whose job is it to make judgments about faith and practice. (The authority of any particular *ulama* was based partly on the number of students they could attract.) It was the *ulama* who developed ways to judge the validity of hadith. The original *ulama* were not usually clerics, but laymen. However, they had tremendous influence over the development of Islamic law, and from them specialists in jurisprudence (*fuqaha*), judges (*qadis*) and legal clerics (*muftis*) emerged. The role of the *mufti* was to give an opinion, when asked, about a point of law not covered in the *fiqh* books.

For many functions, such as leading prayers or conducting a wedding or a funeral, any Muslim is empowered.

Who is qualified to be an imam? Muhammad said,

> The man who knows best the Book of Allah shall act as imam, and if there are persons equal in their knowledge of the Quran, then he who has greater knowledge of the Sunnah; and if they equal in their knowledge of the Sunnah, then he who is first in *hijrah*; and if they are equal in *hijrah*, then he who is older; and a man shall not lead another in prayer in the place where the latter is in authority, and no one shall occupy the place of honor in another man's house except with his permission.

One hadith reports that a woman, Umm Waraqah, who had learned the Quran by heart, was commanded by the Prophet to act as imam to her household.

The *ulama* can often be identified by their garb, which is different from that of laymen. Some of Islam's "clerical titles" include:

- Alim (pl. ulama)—legal scholar
- Ayatollah—top-ranked mullah
- Faqih—religious scholar or judge
- Imam—prayer leader who delivers Friday sermon
- Khadi: One who reads the sermon
- Muezzin—one who calls Muslims to prayers
- Mufti—men of extremely high learning empowered with issuing legal amendments; can issue a *fatwa* or personal judgment
- Muqri—one who reads the Quran
- Mullah—religious teacher
- Mutjahid—one entitled to interpret Islamic law using independent reasoning, or *ijtihad* (literally, "effort").
- Pir—Sufi master
- Qadi—judge who hears cases and administers law, originally appointed by the Umayyad caliphs

None of these offices is really analogous to the position of "priest," however, and Muslims believe that the idea of priests or saints detracts attention from the one and only Allah. (In practice, however, things are a little different—certain figures, dead or alive, command allegiance. which seems to lift them above the status of mere mortals. This is particularly true in Shia Islam but can also been seen in the Sunni branch of the faith, especially among certain Sufi orders, who venerate their *shaykh* (master of the order) as a being almost divine.

The term *sunnah* originally referred to tribal traditions, and Arabian society was (and is) highly conservative. Later on, the Sunnah or traditions of the tribe were replaced by the Sunnah of Allah. Change has seldom been welcome (evidenced by the resistance Muhammad met), and even today innovation (*bidah*) in religion is frowned on. One scholar, Asad ibn Musa (d. 827), even claimed that fighting innovation was more important than prayer, fasting, and pilgrimage. Innovations were often equated with temptations by the devil, although innovators were not called apostates so long as they continued to follow the dictates of Islam.

One who contravenes basic laws or institutes unacceptable practices is considered to have committed a blameworthy innovation. Muhammad said, "Beware of newly invented matters, for every invented matter is an innovation and every innovation is a straying away, and everyone straying away is in hellfire." One who violates this principle must be rebuked and, according to some scholars, his company avoided. However, certain innovations, such as writing down the Quran when it was feared that it might be forgotten, were considered obligatory, and others, such as building schools for the study of Islamic law, were considered laudatory, if not actually required.

Doubtful Activities

Muhammad remarked, "That which is lawful is plain and that which is unlawful is plain; between the two are doubtful matters about which not many people know." He recommended that when in doubt, it was best to avoid the dubious action, for "he who falls into doubtful matters falls into that which is unlawful." One who avoids doubtful matters, however, "clears himself in regard to his religion and his honor." The hadith concludes, "Truly in the body there is a morsel of flesh which, if it be whole, all the body is whole and which if it be diseased, all of it is diseased. Truly this morsel is the heart."

Moral Categories

Islam divides actions (*amal*) into specific moral categories. Muslim "jurisprudence" (*fiqh*) applies to cases about which the sharia does not refer specifically. (An expert in Islamic law is a *fiqih*.) *Fiqh* represents opinions from legal scholars over time and in various locations; the different ways scholars have interpreted *fiqh* have produced several legal schools. Most famously, *fiqh* has established five categories of deeds:

- *Fard* (obligatory): This category includes all commanded actions, such as the five daily prayers, and Ramadan fast. Performance of these actions is considered a good deed to be rewarded by Allah, in this life or the next. Failure to perform such an action is a sin and will be punished. Most Islamic scholars use the term *wajib* as a synonym for *fard*, except for Abu Hanifah, who lists *wajib* as a separate, somewhat lower, category.

- *Mandub or masnun* (recommended or meritorious): This category includes extra prayers, visiting the sick, saving a life, and other good deeds. *Not* doing *mandub* deed is not a sin, but performing a *mandub* action will be rewarded.

- *Mubah or jaiz* (permitted): This category is morally neutral. No punishment or reward accrues in relation to it, although one's intention (*niyyah*) in performing such a deed may change its value. According to one hadith, "Actions shall be judged on by intention."

- *Makruh* (detested, disapproved, or offensive): These actions are "hated" but not actually forbidden. Not performing a detested act counts as a good deed and will be rewarded, although performing it does not count as a bad act and will not be punished. Some interesting examples of *makruh* included sleeping on one's stomach, smoking tobacco, or growing long fingernails. (Muhammad instructed Muslims to keep their nails short in the interest of cleanliness.)

- *Haram* (Prohibited or unlawful): This category includes all forbidden actions such as lying, drinking alcohol, or stealing. Committing a *haram* act is a sin and will be punished; not doing so counts as a good deed and will be rewarded.

- Abu Hanifah inserts another category between the *makruh* and the *haram* called *karahah tahrimiyyah*, which means "hated" almost (but not quite) to the level of *haram*. It should be added that whatever may lead to prohibited things is also prohibited.

Another category of deeds is communally obligatory (*fard al-kifaya*) deeds; they must be undertaken by *someone* in the community, but not by all members. For example, *someone* must recite the ritual funeral prayer, but not everyone has to do so. Someone must undertake the job of memorizing the Quran, but this is not required of everyone. Some matters may fall into more than one category, depending on the specific circumstances; in that case, one's conscience should be the guide.

Because many Muslims feel that Islamic society reached a peak during the life of Muhammad and his first followers or "Companions," some aspects of modern life are rejected as unwholesome. Western society's materialism, open display of sexual imagery and behavior, and use of alcohol and drugs are seen as destroying the fabric of civilization.

SOURCES OF LAW

Although the Quran and Hadith remain the bases for Islamic law, over time, religious scholars developed other guidelines as well. For example, a scholar might use *analogy* to decide a case where the Quran did not specifically apply. To take a mundane example, let's say that an old law book, written before the advent of the automobile, states carriages should drive to the right. By analogy, one could assume that cars should follow the same plan. A scholar might also use his independent reasoning, or *ijtihad*, based on his knowledge of the Quran and hadith, to discover how Quranic maxims should be applied to post-Quranic times. (*Itjihad* is contrasted with *taqlid* or mere imitation without the application of independent thought.) It is quite agreed that decisions reached through *ijtihad* are not infallible and hence cannot be regarded as final. Most Muslims say that *ijtihad* is limited to legal scholars, not just anyone who happens to pick up a Quran or hadith. The ideal scholar is defined as having both depth and breadth—that is, he not only can read deeply into the question at hand but also has knowledge of all other relevant texts. In the Hanbali school, this was estimated to be 400,000 hadith! The Prophet himself was heard to remark that those who do not know should ask one who does, and scholars say that to make an Islamic ruling without sufficient knowledge is a crime. Muhammad even said that a man who makes a judgment for people while ignorant of the law would go to Hell, the same as one who knows the truth but rules unjustly. By about the 10th century, most Sunni scholars were of the opinion that all major problems in the texts has been resolved and independent reasoning was no longer needed. This decision is sometimes called "closing the gates of *ijtihad*." This notion has been rejected by Shia scholars, although in actual practices it is not used much by them either.

Legal "Schools" (MADHAHIB)

There are four major Sunni "schools" (*madhahib*, *sing. madhhab*, literally "path") of jurisprudence: Maliki, Hanafi, Shafii, and Hanbali; the Wahhabis are an offshoot of the last. All are accepted, orthodox schools, not different sects within Islam. Muslims do not have to associate themselves with any particular legal school, although all must obey sharia. However, it is accepted that all *scholars* follow one of these schools, although it does not really matter which one. It is similar to the idea that all children must attend a certified school, although it doesn't matter, from the law's point of view, which.

The first major school of "dogmatic theology" to develop was the Mutazili school in the early part of the eighth century. It has three main tenets: (1) absolute unity of God (*tawhid*)—hence, anything besides God, including the Quran, could not be coeternal with God and was therefore considered to be temporal or created; (2) God's justice (*adl*), allowing for human free will; and (3) divine reward and punishment (*al-wad wa-al-waid*) in the Afterlife (*akhirah*).

Today, Islam recognizes the following schools:

- The Maliki school is the oldest, founded by Malik ibn Anas (712–795), a tall, balding Medinan who may have known the last surviving companions of the Prophet. He was so careful of tradition that he would transmit his teachings only when he was in a state of *ihram*, or ritual purity. His main work, the *Muwatta*, is the earliest surviving textbook of the law, and contains 2,000 hadith. His school developed in Medina, but today is found mostly in north and west Africa, and parts of Egypt. This was also the major school in Moorish Spain.

- The Hanafi school, founded by Abu Hanifah (d. 767), a non-Arab native of Kufa, Iraq. A cloth merchant by trade, Abu Hanifah was lauded not only for his scholarship, but for his humility and good works. He was offered the post of judge in Baghdad, but turned it down, fearing the job was too political and would interfere with his scholarly studies. None of his writings have survived, but two of his disciples included his teachings within their own works. The Hanafi school is the most liberal and flexible of the schools, depending heavily on reason and logic. It was closely connected with the early Abbasid dynasty and was always concerned with practical as well as theoretical questions. It is more likely than the other schools to admit a change or reinterpretation of the sharia. Because Hanifah was reluctant to condemn any professed Muslim, his school tended to separate faith and works, considering faith more important. One of its major articles of faith (*Fiqk Akbar*) states, "We do not consider anyone to be an infidel on account of sin, nor do we deny his faith." Abu Hanifah was inclined to let Allah make decisions about who should be punished and who should be rewarded. The school originated in Kufa, Iraq but became established in the Ottoman Empire and is the official school throughout much of the Middle East (except Saudi Arabia). It is also found in Afghanistan, Pakistan, and the Islamic communities of India. However, its influence is probably waning.

- The Shafii school was founded about 800 in Cairo by Abu Abdullah Muhammad ibn Idris al-Shafii (767–820), who was descended from the Prophet's own Quraysh tribe. There is a legend that he was born on the very day Hanifah died. He originally was a student of Malik ibn Anas at Medina, but also practiced law in Baghdad in the Hanafi school. It is the Sahfii school that listed the four accepted sources of law: the Quran, the Sunnah, consensus of the community (*ijma*), and analogical reasoning (*qiyas*). The Shafii school relies heavily on integrating the hadith with the Quran for support of its doctrine. This was the official school of the Abbasid caliphate in Baghdad and is found today in Egypt, East Africa, Yemen, Southeast Asia, and Indonesia. Al-Shafii's tomb is still preserved in Cairo.

- The Hanbali school, founded by Ahmad ibn Hanbal of Baghdad (780–855), who was born and died in Baghdad. This school formed largely in reaction to what it considered the excessive liberalism of the other three, attempting to return to a purer form of Islam. It particularly opposed the early rationalist school, the Mutazilites. (See Chapter V for more about the Mutazilites.) Found today mostly in Saudi Arabia, alone among the schools it recommends the full punishments of the law, such as cutting off the hands of thieves, as the Quran enjoins (5:38). Hanbal supposedly memorized a million hadith and collected 40,000 of them into a major work, *The Musnad*.

THE WAHHABIS

An important sub-school of the Hanbali is the ultraconservative Wahhabi group, founded by Sheikh Muhammad ibn Abdul al-Wahhab

(1703–1792) in the desert province of Najd. He was descended from a long line of Hanbali legal scholars, of whom his grandfather was most famous. The Wahhabis are similar to the ancient Kharijites in that they believe anyone who does not completely agree with them is not a true Muslim.

Wahhab strongly believed that religion should dominate both public and private life; all worldly power was understood to have been given by Allah. Wahhab was also committed to social justice. Although not by modern standards a feminist, he believed that women had rights in Islam that had been usurped and should be restored. He demanded a strict adherence to sexual morality, making no provisions for sex outside marriage. He was also quite firmly against the notion that anyone (except Muhammad to a limited degree and in certain circumstances) could intercede with Allah, as granting too much power to mortal and too little faith in Allah's mercy.

Most important to him, however, was the concept of *tawhid*, or the unity and uniqueness of Allah, and he rejected any elements of Muslim practice that seemed to violate this principle. Wahhab's most famous book was even titled *Kitab al-Tawhid* or *The Book of Monotheism*, a scholarly, heavily annotated work of 66 chapters. He denounced the adoption of un-Islamic habits borrowed from other religions, such as praying to saints, a practice deemed threateningly similar to polytheism. He regarded the Shia habit of saint-veneration and invoking the aid of holy men as *shirk*, or idolatry. He rejected all innovations (*bidah*) that occurred after about 950, calling them a form of paganism. (One visible example of the Wahhabi rejection of innovations is Wahhabi mosques, which lack minarets.)

The Wahhabis objected to what they deemed a servile attitude of scholars to the classic commentaries (*tafsir*) on the Quran, commentaries that had come to be regarded almost as authoritative as the Quran. Wahhab, a scholar himself, did not reject the idea of commentaries but wanted fresh ones based on a real understanding of the scriptures, not slavish imitations of past scholarship. He believed that the *tafsir* were reflective of the time and place they were written, as opposed to the eternal and everywhere-valid Quran. Thus, the Wahhabis favored a "back to the Quran" approach, much as present-day Christian fundamentalists want to "return to the Bible" and for pretty much the same reasons.

Wahhab considered study of the Quran to be more than simply memorization, urging that Muslims study its meaning as well as its words. Indeed, he supported *ijtihad*, or individual interpretation of scripture to arrive at the truth. He insisted that every Muslim, male and female, read and study the Quran on a personal level. *This is the book we have revealed to you, full of blessing so that you may reflect upon its verses* (38:29).

Wahhab also regarded the hadith as an important source of law, and was more interested in their content than in the chains of transmission attached to them. The practical effect of all this was to limit the power of the *ulama* or scholarly community, who had a vested interest in remaining *the* experts on the Quran. That was fine with Wahhab, who thought the *ulama* was getting too close to claiming for itself infallibility, something that belonged to Allah and the Quran alone. His ideas were resisted by the local *ulama*, of course.

During Wahhab's life three events occurred that became hallmarks of the Wahhabi movement and that branded it as extremist. The first was the cutting down of some trees in his hometown of al-Uyaynah. These trees had long been revered by the populace, who had the habit of hanging gifts on them to achieve intercession with the powers that be. This smacked of idolatry, and the trees came down, much to the displeasure of the locals. They agreed in theory with monotheism, but perhaps not *that* much.

A second disquieting note was the destruction of the tomb of Zayd ibn al-Khattab, Muhammad's companion and secretary. Wahhab thought people were paying entirely too much attention to it—another example of idolatry. So the tomb was destroyed, by Wahhab's own hands. (Other venerated tombs were razed as well.) He forbade the practice of venerating gravesites in general as well as the largely female profession of "bewailers" at funerals.

The third case involved the stoning of an adulterous (or fornicating— the distinction is not clear) woman. She came to Wahhab of her own free will and confessed her sin. Wahhab told her she could be forgiven but that she must stop her behavior. She refused and continued her activities. Reluctantly, after numerous interviews with the unrepentant woman and repeated infractions, Wahhab ordered her to be stoned in accordance with Islamic law. However, he was clearly troubled by the case and appeared to do everything he could to avoid implementing the death sentence.

However, the original Wahhabis were not violent revolutionaries. They favored reform from the grassroots up and supported education and debate. They expected Wahhabism to be a gradual movement that would eventually establish true Islamic law, based on the Quran and hadith, over Arabia.

The alliance between the Wahhabis and the Sauds goes back to 1744 when Wahhab and Muhammad ibn Saud swore a mutual oath of loyalty that stipulated that Wahhabis were responsible for religious matters, and ibn Saud would control the political and military side of things. This agreement was strained (especially over activities such as *jihad*, which both could lay claim to), and it remains unclear as to how much each partner supported the activities of the other. In addition, the Sauds adopted a luxurious lifestyle not at all approved by Ibn Wahhab. They also skipped prayers and failed to pay the *zakat* required by Islamic law. Right after the Saudis captured Riyadh, the present capital of Arabia, in 1773, Ibn Wahhab resigned his position of imam and retired to a largely private life.

When the Wahhabi Sheikh Ibn Saud took over Arabia in 1932, he instituted Wahhabism as the official brand of Islam in the country. It still is.

Wahhabis exported their puritanical brand of Islam around the world and were undoubtedly the guiding force behind the Taliban in Afghanistan. However, many Muslims around the world reject the Wahhabi interpretation of Islam and especially the Saudi royal house, calling the king a "pirate" of Islam. Objections to the Wahhabi come from both liberal and fundamental factions of Islam. In fact, one of the leading opponents of the Wahhabis is Osama bin Laden.

Shia Jurisprudence

The Shia Muslims were later coming to developing codified jurisprudence because they had their Imams to consult. In general, Shia jurisprudence is more dependent on the opinions of the Imam than on those of legal scholars or consensus. However, the famous Sixth Imam, Jafar al-Saiq, developed rulings that were expanded into a school of law named after him, the Jafari school, the school adhered to by the Twelver Shia. Another Shia school is the Zaydi school (Fivers), followed by that branch of Shia; this school has a distinct rationalistic bent. The Ismaili Shia (Seveners) have divided into several groups, each with its own school.

CRIME AND PUNISHMENT

The Most Serious Crime

The most serious offense in Islam is apostasy. Two Arabic words for apostasy are *ridda* and *irtidad*, although they are not exact synonyms.

Ridda is a reversion to complete nonbelief, whereas *irtidad* refers to conversion to another faith. The Arabic word for an apostate is *murtadd*, referring to one who has "turned back" from Islam. If one is born a Muslim and later rejects Islam, he is known as a *murtadd fitri* ("native-born apostate"), whereas a convert who later renounces Islam is called a *murtadd milli*, one who betrays the *milla*, or religious community. One of the first apostates on record was Ubaydallah ibn Jassh, who converted to Islam during Muhammad's lifetime and then renounced it for Christianity at a time when many Muslims had escaped to his country (Abyssinia) to avoid persecution in Arabia. (The refugees included Muhammad's daughter Ruqayya and her husband Uthman.) Ibn Jassh died a Christian, but his wife, Umm Habiba, remained true to Islam, and after Ubaydallah's death, Muhammad married her himself.

Apostasy can occur even if one does not formally renounce Islam. The early Islamic scholar Al-Shafii (d. 820) was precise in his definition: "Apostasy consists in the abjuration of Islam, either mentally, or by words, or by acts incompatible with faith. As to oral abjuration, it matters little whether the words are said in joke, or through a spirit of contradiction, or in good faith." Examples of apostasy include worshipping in a Christian church, treating the Quran with disrespect, insulting Muhammad, doubting the truth of Islam, announcing disbelief in Allah, or asserting Muhammad or any prophet was an imposter. Minors, lunatics, and those acting under compulsion are exempt from charges of apostasy. Apostates should be exhorted to repent; it is a duty to try to convince disbelievers to follow the correct path: *Invite others to the way of your Lord with wisdom and inspiring speech. Reason with them in a superior manner. Certainly, your Lord knows who has strayed from the path and who is guided* (16:125).

It is Islamic opinion that whoever claims that any religion other than Islam is acceptable, including Judaism or Christianity, is a nonbeliever and should be asked to repent. In the Quran, opponents of Islam are dealt with harshly: *This is the recompense of those who fight against Allah and his Messenger, and hasten about the earth, to do corruption there; they shall be slaughtered or crucified or their hands and feet shall alternately be struck off, or they shall be banished from the land* (5:33–34). However, a nonbeliever is in a different class from an apostate, for the unbeliever has never claimed to be Muslim in the first place. As "People of the Book," Christian and Jewish nonbelievers are to be allowed to practice their religion in peace in an Islamic country, although pagans may be forced to convert. Apostates, who have left Islam, are in worse trouble.

The "Awful Doom" of Apostates

Who disbelieves in Allah after his belief—except for him who is forced thereto and whose heart is still content with the Faith—but whoever finds ease in disbelief: On them is the wrath from Allah. Theirs will be an awful doom (16:106). It is unclear from this passage who will be the punisher, however. Some authorities state that the punishment will be meted out only in the next world; others, such as al-Shafii, maintain earthly authorities can apply the death penalty. (Even today, Pakistan has a blasphemy law with a death penalty attached.) *They would have you disbelieve as they themselves have disbelieved, so that you may all be alike. Do not befriend them until they have fled their homes for the cause of Allah. If they desert you seize them and put them to death whenever you find them* (4:89). It is passages such as this that make many who have converted from Islam to other faiths nervous. In Afghanistan, one can face a death sentence for converting to Christianity, a sentence that has been imposed (and then lifted) even in the 21st century.

Believers vs. Nonbelievers

Muslims see the world as divided between believers on one hand and disbelievers (*Kafirs*) and hypocrites (*Munafiqin*) on the other. Unbelievers and hypocrites belong to the "party of Satan." *The believers fight in the way of God, and the unbelievers fight in the idols'. Fight you therefore against the friends of Satan* (4:76). And again: *Allah is the Protector of the believers; He brings them out of the darkness into the light. And the unbelievers—their protectors are the idols, that bring them forth from the light into darkness deep; those are the inhabitants of the Fire, therein dwelling forever* (2:257). The image of unbelievers drowned in darkness is a common theme: *The state of unbelievers is like the layers of darkness in a vast deep ocean. Overwhelmed by waves on top, of which are dark clouds. Depths of darkness, some of which are over the others. If the unbeliever put out his hand, he can hardly see it. For he whom Allah has not given any light, has no light* (24:40).

Those who do not believe in God as conceived by Muslims are labeled unbelievers and doomed to hellfire. This includes Christians who believe in the trinity or who venerate the Virgin Mary. In fact, they are guilty of *shirk*, the unforgivable sin. *Allah does not forgive anyone for associating something with him, while He does forgive whomever He wishes to forgive for anything else* (4:48). Still, Muhammad was often restrained in his attitude to unbelievers. When he was asked to invoke a curse on the polytheists, he responded, "I was not sent as one given to cursing; I was sent only as mercy."

Unbelievers should be fairly easy to spot, but how about hypocrites, those who claim they believe but do not really? The Quran refers to them as *propped up pieces of wood* (63:4). Muhammad said, "There are four signs of a hypocrite: when he speaks he lies, when he makes a promise he breaks it, when he is trusted with something he betrays his trust, and when he argues he insults." The Quran says sternly: *Among people are some who say We believe in Allah and the Last Day. But they don't really believe. They try to fool Allah and others, but only fool themselves without realizing it. Their hearts are diseased, and Allah increases their disease because they were false to themselves* (2:8–10).

Punishment for Apostates

Different schools of thought offered different consequences for apostasy. According to a compendium of Hanifa thought, the *Hidaya*,

When a Muslim apostatizes from the faith, an exposition thereof is to be laid before him, in such a manner that if his apostasy should have arisen from any religious doubts or scruples, those may be removed. . . . There are only two means of repelling the sin of apostasy, namely destruction or Islam. . . . An apostate is to be imprisoned for three days, within which time if he return to the faith, it is well: but if not, he must be slain.

Most Muslim traditions allow that apostates may be given a chance to repent, although often males are given less leeway than females. Underage apostate boys could be imprisoned until they reach the age of majority—at that time they are subject to the death penalty (usually by the sword) if they do not recant. Mentally incompetent people, those under the influence of drugs and alcohol, and those who have been forced into apostasy are not punished. The husband or wife of an apostate is granted an automatic divorce. According to tradition, apostates are denied a Muslim burial, and their property is confiscated by the believers.

Capital Punishment

All Muslim countries currently retain capital punishment, as does the United States. *Take not life, which Allah has made sacred, except by way of justice and law. Thus does he command you, so that you may learn wisdom* (6:151). Today methods of execution include stoning, hanging, and beheading, as well as the more modern firing squad. Many executions are performed in public, ostensibly to act as a deterrent. Crimes subject to capital punishment include murder as well as other crimes called "spreading mischief in the land," defined as activity that undermines social structure and produces unstable, immoral conduct in others. These crimes can include treason, apostasy, terrorism, piracy, rape, adultery, and homosexual activity.

Historically, those who committed multiple sins were punished cruelly, as this hadith reports:

> A group of people from the tribe of Uki came to the Prophet and accepted Islam. Then they became ill in Medina and he ordered them to drink camel urine and milk as medicine. They did, and were cured. Then they renounced their religion, killed the herdsmen and stole the camels. Muhammad sent trackers after them and they were captured. And he cut off their hands and their feet and burnt out their eyes and did not cauterize their wounds, so that they died.

Many people in Islamic countries around the world have called for an end to capital punishment, especially by stoning, but the practice still continues in some places.

Quranic Punishments *(Hudud, Sing, Hadd)*

Crimes singled out in the Quran include unlawful intercourse, theft, consuming wine, highway robbery, and accusing someone falsely of adultery or fornication. For some crimes, such as theft, the Quran orders amputation of the hand—*As for the man or the woman who is guilty of theft, cut off their hands to punish them for their crimes. That is the punishment enjoined by Allah* (5:38)—although this penalty is seldom meted out. In countries employing this method, the right hand is generally amputated first, and if the miscreant continues in his thievish ways, other limbs are amputated one by one. Quranic punishments are usually meted out in public for maximum effect.

The first caliph, Abu Bakr, was told that a singing girl had had her hands cut off for making up satirical songs about him. Abu Bakr wrote a stiff note to the man who had ordered this punishment, Muhajir:

I have learned you laid hands on a woman who showered abuses on me, and therefore got her hand amputated. Allah has not sought vengeance even in the case of polytheism, which is a great crime. He had not permitted mutilation even with regard to manifest infidelity. Try to be considerate and sympathetic in your attitudes towards others in the future. Never mutilate, because it is a grave offence.

For adultery, the punishment is clear: *The adulterer and the adulteress shall each be given a hundred lashes. Let no pity for them cause you to disobey Allah, if you truly believe in Allah and the Last Day; and let their punishment be witnessed by a number of believers* (24:2). In another place, the Quran also enjoins that fornicating women be imprisoned in their homes: *If any of your women commit fornication, call in four witnesses among yourselves against them. If they testify to their guilt, confine them to their houses until death overtakes them or till Allah finds another way for them* (4:15). The "other way" is not specified. However, if the witnesses are lying, the Quran orders this: *Those who accuse chaste women, and produce not four witnesses, flog them with eighty stripes, and reject their testimony forever* (24:4). If the man swears his wife has committed adultery and the woman swears she has not (and there are no eye witnesses) the matter is considered undecided and punishment is left up to Allah.

The Quran does not prescribe stoning for adulterers, as the Bible does, but the Prophet once ordered it for a pair of Jewish adulterers.

They brought the Prophet a Jew and a Jewess who had committed fornication. He said to them, "What do you find in your book?" They said: "Our rabbis blacken the face of the guilty and expose them to public ridicule." Then Abdullah ibn Salam, who had been a Jew, said, "Messenger of Allah, tell the Jews to bring the Torah." They brought it, but a Jew put his hand over the verse which prescribes stoning and began to read what came before it and after it. Ibn Salam said to him, "Raise your hand," and there was the verse about stoning beneath his hand. The Messenger of Allah gave the order. They were stoned on the level ground and the man leaned over the woman to attempt to shield her from the stones.

Another stoning death ordered by Muhammad is also recorded. A man confessed to adultery. "Then the Prophet said to him, 'Are you insane?' The man responded in the negative. 'Are you married?' He answered that he was. The Prophet ordered him to be stoned at the mosque outside Mecca. When the stones struck him, he ran away, but he was caught and stoned until he was dead. Then the Prophet spoke well of him and prayed over him." On the basis of this, some Muslim countries punished adulterers with stoning, although this is not specifically commanded in the Quran.

A hadith, however, placed strict limits on capital punishment, at least for fellow Muslims. "The blood of a Muslim may not be legally spilt except in one of three instances: a married person who commits adultery; a life for a life; and one who forsakes his religion and abandons the community." However, it should be repeated that stoning to death for adultery is *not* enjoined by the Quran, which commands whipping instead. Still, 100 lashes with a whip can easily result in death. Presently, the penal code of Iran allows execution by stoning as the penalty for adultery as well as for murder. The law calls for stones large enough to cause pain, but not so large as to kill the condemned person immediately. The majority of the stoned victims are women.

Some scholars interpret Quranic punishments are mandatory—others see them as the maximum allowable; there is no agreement. Repentance is key: *But as for him who repents wrongdoing and makes amends, Allah will turn towards him, for Allah is forgiving, a dispenser of grace* (5:35).

SUICIDE

Suicide is considered a sin in Islam and is condemned (4:29). According to a reliable hadith, Muhammad did not bother offering prayers for a person who had killed himself. Muhammad also said, "Whoever strangles himself strangles himself into Fire and whoever stabs himself with a spear stabs himself into Fire." So-called suicide-bombers, a very modern phenomenon, are not behaving in accordance with Islamic principles. No suicide missions were ever undertaken during the time of Muhammad.

OTHER MAJOR SINS

Umar, the second caliph, listed what he considered to be the nine major sins: *shirk* (idolatry), murder, running away in battle, accusing an innocent woman falsely, usury, spending money rightfully belonging to orphans, talking heresy in the mosque, making light of religion, and causing one's parents to shed tears because of one's disobedience.

Drinking and Gambling

Muhammad said that wine (*khamr*) was the key to all evil, and alcohol is totally forbidden in Islam. *They will question thee concerning wine, and arrow shuffling* [gambling]. In the first revelations, neither gambling nor alcohol was expressly prohibited, only discouraged. (Gambling includes card games, betting, dice, raffles, and lotteries.)

The earliest stricture against alcohol was revealed about three years after Muhammad arrived in Medina. *Approach not prayer with a mind befuddled until you can understand all that they say* (4:43). Soon after another verse appeared: *Say: In both is heinous sin, and uses for men, but the sin in them is more heinous than the usefulness.* (2:219).

Other surahs plead strongly against it, stopping just short of forbidding it outright, and the last guidance appeared just before Muhammad's death: *Satan's plan is to incite enmity and hatred between you with intoxicants and gambling, and hinder you from the remembrance of Allah and from prayer. Will you not then abstain?* (5:93).

Today, in Pakistan, under sharia, drinking can be punished with eight lashes of a whip.

A minority of early scholars except liquors made from honey, wheat, barely, or millet as long as they were not drunk "in a wanton way." Because the prohibitions against alcohol were revealed piecemeal, many scholars derived a principle of "gradualism" in Quranic studies.

DEMOCRACY AND ISLAM

The relationship between democracy and Islam remains problematic. Standard rights such as freedom of the press, especially when it comes to religious matters, do not exist in many Islamic countries, as the Salmon Rushdie affair among others clearly shows. Only about a quarter of Muslim-majority countries have democratically elected leadership, and many that claim to be democratic have election results that look suspicious, with the majority party winning by more than 90 percent of the vote, something unlikely to happen in a true democracy.

However, a separation of church and state is not a requirement for a democratic government, although freedom of worship certainly is. England, for example, has a state church, and so do several European governments. A democratically elected government can also operate under sharia, and most Muslim see no inherent contradiction between religious and democratic values. Nor do most Christians. It appears that that most Muslims prefer a government that is neither completely secular nor wholly theocratic, but a balanced combination.

Islamic "Saints"

Officially, the cult of saints is condemned, although in practice it is frequently observed, especially in the Shia community. There is no Arabic word that correlates precisely to "saint" (sanctified one). The closest term is *wali*, which translates as "friend," or helper. There is certainly no formal saint-making process in Islam, such as that of the Catholic Church. Most Sunni Muslims oppose the concept. Several of the Islamic "saints" are honored by the mystical Sufi group, and their tombs are objects of pilgrimage.

Social Life and Citizenship

A cheerful greeting was ordered by Muhammad. Muslims greet each other *Assalamu Alaikum*, which means "Peace be upon you." "When you go into your family, give a salutation. It will be the first thing that brings about the well-being of the people." More elaborate forms of the greeting are "*Assalamu Alalikum Wa Rahmatullah*," which means "May the peace and the mercy of Allah be upon you," and "*Assalamu Alalikum Wa Rahmatullahi Wa Barakatuh*," which means "May the peace, mercy, and blessings of Allah be upon you." Even those whose claim to being Muslim was in doubt should be honored if they offer a greeting: *And say not to any one who offers you salutation, "You are not a believer"* (4:94).

Muslim men and women frequently greet each other with the title of "Brother" and "Sister" and are expected to behave as if they were family members. *And when you are greeted with a greeting, greet with one fairer than it, or return it* (4:86). When Muslims meet who have not seen each other in a while, they may try to "outdo" each other in courteous and complimentary greetings.

As mentioned, there is no concept of separate "church" (religion or *din*) and state. Indeed, no aspect of life is seen as being outside religion. Muslims do not compartmentalize their lives. In 1925, Ali Abd al-Raziq, a sheikh at the world-famous (and world's oldest) University of al-Azhar, published a book called *Islam and the Principles of Government*, arguing for such a separation. He was tried by a tribunal of other sheiks, found guilty of impiety, removed from his post, and forbidden to teach.

Sudanese theologian Mahmud Muhammad Taha founded an organization called the Republican Brethren, which advocated lessening the role of the Quran as a source of national law. In 1968 he was found guilty of apostasy, and his writings were burned. In 1985 he was publicly hanged in Khartoum. He was 76 years old.

Caring for One's Neighbor

Muhammad said,

If anyone removes one of the anxieties of his world from a believer, Allah will remove one of the anxieties from him on the Day of Resurrection; if one smoothes the way for one who is destitute, Allah will smooth the way for him in this world and the next; and if anyone conceals the faults of a Muslim, Allah will conceal his faults in this world and the next. Allah helps a man as long as he helps his brother.

According to a hadith, "None of you truly believes until he wishes for his brother what he wishes for himself." At another time, Muhammad reported, "Gabriel kept telling me how important it is to do good towards one's neighbors until I thought he was going to tell me that they have a share in one's inheritance!"

Clearly, charity is an important part of Islamic life. Muhammad said, "Each person's every joint must perform a charity every day: to act justly between two people is charity; to help a man with his mount, lifting him onto it or hoisting up his belongings onto it is charity; a good word is charity; every step you take to prayers is charity; and removing a harmful thing from the road is charity." And further: "Each one of you is a caretaker and is responsible for those under his care."

Family Life

Laws regulating the family are at the heart of sharia. A man asked the Prophet with whom it was most important to maintain good relations, and he replied, "Your parents, your siblings, and then your next of kin. This is an essential responsibility and a relationship that must be maintained." According to Islamic law, one owes support to one's family in the amount one can afford: beginning with oneself and followed by one's spouse, who takes precedence over other family members. Then come parents, grandparents, and children.

On another occasion, Muhammad said, "Kinship is a trial from Allah. Those who maintain its ties will have ties with Allah, but those who sever its ties will have their ties with Allah severed. On the Day of Judgment, the tongue of kinship will be loose and eloquent." Muhammad was clear about duty to support members of one's family and emphasized that even if one's efforts were not reciprocated, or if the recipients were "unjust," they should be maintained. When a convert asked Muhammad if all the good things he had done for his family in the past would be carried over to his credit in Islam, the Prophet gave an unequivocal answer: "Yes."

Honoring Parents

Muhammad is reported as saying, "The pleasure of the Lord is in the pleasure of a parent, and the wrath of the Lord is in the wrath of a parent." One is expected to support one's parents even if they are capable of earning their own living, because of the extreme respect in which they are held. One is not required to support one's adult children, however, if they are able to work but choose not to do so. Of the parents, primary honor was due to the mother. Muhammad said, "Paradise lies at the feet of the mother." A man asked Muhammad, "To whom should I be good?" The Prophet answered, "Your mother." He then asked, "Who after that?" "Your mother," replied the Prophet. And after that? "Your father, then the next closest relative, and then the next." The prophet was also heard to remark that even if one's parents were unjust, one should still act to please them.

Children are not permitted to speak roughly or carelessly to them. Yelling or swearing at them is forbidden, About parents, the Quran says, *If one or both of them attain old age, say not, "Fie!" unto them nor repulse them, but speak unto them a gracious word* (17:23).

Work

Industry is a valued trait in Islam, although some occupations are forbidden including pornography and prostitution; drug or alcohol dealing; handling pork. Prohibited activities also include earning a living by gambling, fortunetelling, or magic. (However, there is an authentic hadith in which Muhammad permitted the use of talismans under two circumstances only: in cases of jealousy and stings of venomous animals.) There is no dishonor whatever in menial work, so long as it is honest.

Wealth

It is acceptable to become rich in Islam, but material wealth is valueless compared to spiritual riches. The Quran says, *Alluring to people is the love of things they covet: women, sons, hoarded treasures of gold and silver, pedigreed horses, cattle, and land. This is the provision of this world's life. Yet with Allah is a better abode* (3:14). These words mean that the objects themselves are not evil, but the "allure" they cast can be dangerous. A hadith says that "whoever drinks from a gold or silver cup sips hellfire into his mouth," although this is understood to be metaphoric. One should keep one's mind on higher things. Muslims are of course required to spend 2.5 percent of their wealth to help the poor and needy. Muhammad said pragmatically, "Riches are sweet and a source of blessing to those who acquire them by the way, but those who seek them out of greed are like people who eat and are never full." Again the point is that wealth is not in itself evil but can be destructive when undue importance is attached to it. Wealthy people are expected to give generously to the poor.

Wealth is not considered a sign of God's favor, although it is not wrong. Muhammad said, "Allah loves the pious rich man who is inconspicuous," and further, "Allah does not look at your forms and possessions, but rather at your heart and your deeds."

Islam prohibits the charging of interest; those who practice usury (*riba*) are told that they will face *war from God and his prophet* (2:278–279). The origin of this idea is that in traditional societies, people asked for a loan only out of dire personal need—not to finance a new business.

However, because this policy proved somewhat impractical for carrying on business, the *ulama* developed a loophole. A lender could be justified in making a profit from his loan if and only if he himself was involved in the enterprise and took a risk. This made it comparatively easy to create polite legal fictions that enabled the lender to get his money (and then some) back. The Hanafi school, the most liberal of the four accepted schools, was particularly helpful in creating ways for Muslim merchants to work profitably. Because it is almost impossible to get along in contemporary life without taking loans, Muslims try to minimize their borrowing, taking out the smallest loan for the shortest possible period and only for necessities such as a first home.

Currently there are Muslim banks that operate according to Islamically permitted practices. These include having the bank a sharer in the business—if the business makes a profit, so does the bank. If it fails, the bank loses its loan.

Kindness to Animals

Muhammad had a great love for animals, with the exception of dogs, which he regarded as unclean (but which he nevertheless treated kindly).

Muhammad did not allow pack animals to stand loaded in the marketplace, for example, a practice he regarded as cruel. According to a beautiful hadith,

> The Messenger of Allah said, "While a man was walking down the road, his thirst grew strong and he found a well and descended into it and drank and was leaving when he saw a dog hanging its tongue and licking the ground from thirst, and the man said, 'This dog's thirst is like the thirst I had' and he went into the well again, filled his shoe with water, and held it between his teeth while he climbed out, and gave the dog the water to drink. And Allah approved the act and pardoned his sins." They said, "What, Messenger of Allah, shall we be rewarded for what we do to animals?" He replied. "Yes. There is a reward on every living creature."

He forbade the cutting of horses' manes or tails and prohibited the branding of animals in any tender spot. He also became distressed when he saw horses being kept saddled unnecessarily. He would not allow his men to gather the eggs of wild birds when he saw it disturbed the mother. "Fear Allah in your treatment of animals," he said. Animals are considered natural *muslims*, who do Allah's will (because they have not the gift of free choice).

Dress

In Muslim tradition, persons are not to appear unclothed before anyone except their spouse, and modesty is strongly encouraged. Women especially are expected to wear modest, nonsuggestive attire in public. At home, women can dress however they like to attract their husbands. They are also free to dress as casually as they wish in the family circle or when only other women are present. Relatives who are too closely related for marriage are called *mahram;* women need not wear head covering or cover-all clothing in their company. Men who are not *mahram* are expected to stay away from a house if women are there alone, even if they are a good friend of the family. There was a recent international scandal in which a 75-year-old Saudi woman was visited by two young men, friends of the family who were delivering bread to her home. All were sentenced to be lashed.

Dressing in public is different. The correct woman's dress for public wear is called *hijab* (from an Arabic word meaning "to cover") or *purdah,* and it differs from country to country. The parts of the body that are supposed to be covered in the presence of others are known as *auwrah.* Although the meaning of the word varies, it generally refers to a garment loosely covering the entire body except for the face, hands, and feet. In English the practice is sometimes called "veiling," although this is a word that does not occur in the Quran. Many muslim cultures demand that women wear plain or dark clothing, but there is no Quranic command about it, and Aishah loved brilliant colors, especially yellow and red. So do many other Muslim women. Tight clothing, however, is disapproved of.

As mentioned, the proper term for the Quranic command for modesty is *hijab,* and it includes both men and women. Men are expected to be covered from knee to navel at all times (including in front of other males). This area is allowed to be seen only by their wives. For women, the *auwrah* are generally considered to be the whole body except the hands, feet, and face. (One hadith suggests it is laudatory to cover the face and hands as well.) Women (other than the wives of the Prophet) are not absolutely required to cover their heads; this is cultural rather than strictly religious practice. Many Christians and Jews (Amish and Mennonite Christians and Orthodox Jews) also consider modesty and head covering for women as appropriate.

The piece of cloth covering the face in some traditions is called a *niqab.* In Muhammad's day, face-veiling was assumed by aristocratic women only, to protect their identities. It was also practiced by Greek Christians in Byzantium. The key to correct dress for Muslim women was not the veil itself, but modesty. The first "veil," however, probably referred to a curtain behind which the prophet's family could obtain a little much-needed privacy. There is no Islamic requirement for women to remain hidden in their homes, although in some traditional societies they may do so as a mark of piety. The idea of women veiling themselves behind clothing, however, was not unknown in pre-Islamic

Arabia and may have arisen as a protection against the hot desert winds and blowing sand, neither of which is good for the skin.

And tell the believing women to lower their gaze and guard their sexuality, and to display of their adornment only what is apparent and to draw head coverings over their bosoms and not to reveal their adornment exception to their husbands or father (24:31). "What is apparent" may be different in different lands. Today the hijab is becomingly increasingly popular among the Muslim diaspora (among both homemakers and career women) both as a rejection of Western fashion and as a statement of religious adhesion.

In another place the Quran states, *O Prophet, tell your wives and daughters and the believing women to draw their outer garments around them when they go out or are among men. That is better, in order that they may be understood to be Muslims and not annoyed* (33:59). In this latter case, dress is seen protecting a woman when less modest-seeming dress might call forth unwanted attention. Some exceptions are made for older women: *As to women past child-bearing, and have no hope of marriage, no blame shall attach them if they lay aside their outer garments, but not so as to show their ornaments. Yet if they abstain from this, it will be better for them* (24:60). The most famous and horrific incident of the demand for veiling occurred in March 2002, in ultra-conservative Saudi Arabia, when 15 schoolchildren died during a school fire. The religious police refused to allow them out of the burning building without their modest headgear, and they died trying to get it on.

The hadith of the Prophet, however, lays down further restrictions: "At the age a woman begins to menstruate," he said, "it is not right that anything should be seen except this and this," pointing to his face and hands. In strict Muslim culture, therefore, women often cover themselves except for the hands and face in a loose, opaque garment that is not overly attractive. Brightly colored, sheer, and tight-fitting garments are frowned on and in some countries forbidden. No jewelry except rings are to be worn in public, and women should not dress "like men." Men are also not supposed to wear silk or gold; these are reserved for women. Nor are men allowed to wear any jewelry other than a wedding ring, which must be of silver and not gold. Women may were any jewelry they like and can wear gold if they choose.

Both sexes frequently cover their heads—especially the back of the head. Some authorities believe this custom dates back to very ancient times when it was believed that "demons" could enter the body through a portal at the back of the head.

Muhammad himself was an extremely modest person, with his own wife Aishah claiming she had never seen him naked. One hadith reports of him, "He was shyer than a virgin in her green years. When he saw a thing he disliked, we knew it from his face."

EDUCATION

Knowledge, especially religious knowledge, is highly prized. In Islam knowledge is part of faith, and study of the Quran has always been considered the most essential element of a Muslim's education. Unlike study of the Talmud, which for many centuries was limited to men, both men and women are encouraged to study the Quran. *Allah will exalt those of you who believe by many degrees those of you who have attained the faith and who have been given knowledge* (58:11) The knowledge referred to here is usually interpreted to be that of Allah rather than that of biology or arithmetic, although both senses can apply. The earliest revealed verses of the Quran contain these words: *Recite in the name of your Lord who created: He created man from a clot of blood. Recite and your Lord is most honorable, who taught to write with pen, taught man what he knew not* (96:1–5). In other words, the Creator of the universe is equally honored for teaching humankind to read and write, which are important (although not the only) conduits of knowledge. In the Quran, we read, *And say, O my Lord! Increase me in knowledge!* (20:114). In some instances, "study" of the Quran has been limited to memorizing parts or the whole of it, but true Muslim scholars do not believe that is sufficient.

The Prophet said, "No gift among all gifts of a father to his child is better than an education." Muhammad maintained that the "seeking of knowledge was obligatory upon every Muslim," and learned people are the "heirs of the prophets—they leave knowledge as their inheritance; he who inherits it inherits a great fortune." Muhammad told his listeners to "impart knowledge to him who is absent" or to "go back to your people" and teach them. Even slaves should receive an education.

Muhammad himself gave the blessing to the search for knowledge: "He who goes out in search of knowledge is in Allah's path till he returns." He also prayed, "O Lord, do not let the sun set on any day when I did not increase my knowledge." Knowledge brings rewards: *And whoever is given knowledge is given indeed abundant wealth* (2:269), whether you interpret wealth in the material or spiritual sense.

Muslims are encouraged to seek knowledge, "even going to China" to find it. These journeys after knowledge were known as *rihlah* and may have been undertaken in imitation of the ancient *hanifs* who were said to roam the earth in search of knowledge of the one God. However, no one can ever have complete knowledge of Allah, and in any case, knowledge must be paired with obedience. Teachers are expected to be role models, not simply dispensers of knowledge.

Having the right kind of knowledge made one a better Muslim. Muhammad said, "The excellence of the learned over the devotee is like that of the full moon over the other stars." However, collection of knowledge for its own sake is not enough; in fact, it could be dangerous. Muhammad said, "The one who would have the worst position in Allah's sight on the Day of Resurrection would be a learned man who did not profit from his learning."

EDUCATION FOR GIRLS

Muhammad said, "If a daughter is born to a person and he brings her up, gives her a good education, and trains her in the arts of life, I shall myself stand between him and hellfire." He further announced, "How praiseworthy are the women of Ansar (the Medinans who helped the Meccans) that their modesty does not prevent them from attempts at learning and the acquisition of knowledge." Muhammad remarked that anyone who gave a slave girl the "best education" and then freed and married her would receive a double reward.

In Islamic countries, boys and girls are educated separately, usually beginning at the secondary level. It is at this point that girls begin to cover their heads if they are not doing so already. Girls are encouraged to attend college, and many do so with their friends to provide a support group. Countries in which the governments do not permit educating girls at all are acting in a distinctly un-Islamic fashion.

SPORTS

Sports are permitted in Islam, but modesty in dress must be maintained. Therefore, communal showers and locker rooms should not be used unless there are private cubicles available for changing. Many sports uniforms baring legs and arms are deemed unsuitable, especially for women.

Music

Although many Muslim scholars deem music acceptable, others would ban all Muslims from listening to it on the grounds that it weakens inhibitions and encourages loss of control. Some permit the use of *daff*, a tambourine-like drum, and Sufis allow lutes or flutes. Some groups allow unaccompanied singing. On the Indian subcontinent, certain songs in praise of Muhammad called *nasheed* are allowed. The Quran is silent on the subject.

WOMEN, SEX, AND MARRIAGE

The family is at the heart of Islam. For Muslims, the word *family* is not limited to the nuclear group, but extends to cousins, grandparents, uncles, in-laws, and distant relationships. And so when a couple marries, the families of each partner are part of the package.

The Quran assumes that men and women have distinctive parts to play in society, although it does not label what those roles must be. Muhammad himself was fond of housework and mending, for example. Because the Quran was addressed to a seventh-century Arabian audience, it deals with cultural practices that were common in that time. Most of what modern Westerners regard as strictures against women were actually improvements on their lot, giving them more rights than they had previously. These improvements include a restriction on the number of wives men could take, certain inheritance rights, the abolishment of female infanticide (16:58–59, 81:8–9), and more reasonable rules for divorce.

Although certain rights are guaranteed to them, in general women have an inferior place in Islamic culture. The Quran asserts that men and women were created from one source and are equal before Allah. *Men, have fear of your Lord, who created you from a single soul. From that soul he created its mate and through them he bestrewed the earth with countless men and women* (4:1). However, it reserved for men a higher status (4:34 and elsewhere) in society. Women are expected to defer to their husbands and once were even expected to get their husband's permission to leave their home. Even Hell, according to one reliable hadith, is populated mostly by women because Muhammad told them, "You curse frequently and are ungrateful to your husbands." It might be argued that he was speaking only to a small group of women in this instance, but it is debatable.

At one time, women in Islam fared better than their Christian counterparts. In early times, Muslim women were granted many more rights than their counterparts, including the right to keep their own property. However, in contemporary times, rights for Muslim women have not kept up with those of Western women. One of the more unsatisfactory passages in the Quran reads, *Your women are a tillage for you; so come unto your tillage as you wish* (2:223). This verse seems to equate women with a plow-field, whose sole purpose is to produce offspring. Muhammad is also reported as saying, "So come to your tillage as often as you like; come from the front and back and guard against the rectum and menstruation."

According to one dispiriting hadith, related by Aishah, women have no right to refuse sexual favors to their husbands. She was asked by if there was anything wrong with a woman refusing her husband when he wanted her, even if she was upset or not feeling well. Aishah responded, "Yes, his rights over you include your not preventing him from having you, even if you do not feel like it." The other woman responded, "What if a woman has her period and she and her husband have only one bed and one blanket? What are they to do?" Aishah replied, "Let her wrap herself in her garment and then go to sleep next to him. His is still entitled to the upper half." Another reliable hadith records Muhammad as saying, "If a man invites his wife to sleep with him, and she does not come to him, may the angels send their curses on her until morning." The Shafii school of law emphasizes that women have no right to refuse their husband's sexual attentions "at any time of the day or night." Muhammad was once asked how many nights a newly wed husband should spend with his bride. "Seven," he responded, "if a virgin, and three if she is a widow."

In a series of Gallup polls conducted between 2001 and 2007, it was found that only 67 percent of Muslims in 10 predominantly Muslim countries supported the right of women to drive a car, a *lower* percentage than those who favored women being permitted to assume positions of leadership (72 percent). About 78 percent of those polled said they believe men and women should have the same legal rights, and 82 percent believe women should be able to hold a job for which they are qualified.

COURTSHIP AND SEXUALITY

Although sexuality is recognized as a natural aspect of the human behavior, it is strictly regulated. "Natural" does not mean "free and unfettered" in the Islamic view. Muslims say that women are not to be treated as sexual objects, and sexual feelings are to be reserved for husband and wife. Because of this, not only schools but also hospitals, public conveyances, mosques, and other entities have separate entrances or sections for men and women. Physical contact between unrelated men and women is to be kept to a minimum or, if possible, avoided altogether. In Islamic countries, boys and girls are not permitted to date or establish friendships before marriage (*nikah*).

In itself, sexuality is pretty much neutral in Islamic thought, neither glorified nor demonized. When Muhammad was asked whether one would receive a reward for indulging one's sexual desire, he replied, "Do you not think that were he to act unlawfully he would be sinning? Likewise, if he has acted upon it lawfully, he will receive his reward." These comments may seem puzzling to those who believe that sexual activity is its own reward, but Muhammad had a longer view. However, indecency, fornication or "whoredom" are all grave sins, especially for women.

Such of your women as commit indecency; call four of you to witness against them; and if they witness, then detain them in their houses until death takes them or Allah appoints for them a way. And when two of you [men] commit indecency, punish them both; but if they repent and make amends, then suffer them to be; Allah turns, and is All-compassionate (4:15–16). From this it appears as if women bear the brunt of the punishment, even when the crimes are approximately the same.

In Surah 24:2, on the other hand, the punishment for adultery is the same for both sexes. *The fornicatress and the fornicator—scourge each one of them a hundred stripes. And in the matter of Allah's religion let no tenderness for them seize you if you believe in God and the Last Day; and let a party of believers witness their chastisement, except for such as repent, before you have power over them.*

Those who accuse others of sexual misbehavior falsely are also in deep trouble. *And those who cast it up on women in wedlock, and then bring not four witnesses, scourge them with eighty stripes, and do not accept any testimony of theirs ever; those—they are the ungodly, except such as repent thereafter and make amends* (24:4–5).

The situation is slightly more complicated if a husband accuses his wife: *And those who cast it up on their wives having no witness except themselves, the testimony of one of them shall be to testify by Allah four times that he is of the truthful. And a fifth time, that the curse of Allah shall be upon him, if he should be of the liars* (24:6–7). The accused wife, however, has recourse of her own. *I shall avert from her the chastisement if she testify by Allah four times that his is of the liars. And a fifth time, that the wrath of Allah shall be upon her, if he should be of the truthful* (24:8–9).

HOMOSEXUALITY

The Quran forbids homosexual activity (4:15–16; 7:80–84). And according to a hadith, "The Messenger of Allah cursed men who act like women and women who act like men, and said, 'Drive them from your houses.'" Muhammad expelled such people, and Umar did as well. Most Muslims see homosexuality as a selected rather than genetically imposed behavior.

MARRIAGE

Marriage is strongly recommended in Islam, and Muhammad actually forbade celibacy, at least for males, saying, "Those among you who can support a wife should marry, for it restrains eyes from casting evil glances and preserves one from immorality." He went to say that those who could not marry should fast because that would have a desirable "castrating" effect on them.

A perfect example was found in his own life, as one of the hadith reports. "The Messenger of Allah saw a woman, and so he came to his wife Zainab, as she was tanning leather and had sexual intercourse with her. He then went to his companions and told them, 'The woman advances and returns in the shape of a devil, so when one of you sees a woman, he should come to his wife, for that will repel what he feels in his heart.'"

Sunni Muslims men are permitted to marry Jews and Christians (who are free to continue to practice their own faith), but not a polytheist or Zoroastrian. A Muslim woman must marry a Muslim man.

Most Shia agree that both partners in a marriage must be Muslim, although some Ayatollahs will permit the marriage of a Muslim man to a Christian woman. For both Sunni and Shia, any children born of the marriage are considered Muslims.

Marriage between certain relatives is prohibited, as it is in most societies; however, marriage between first cousins is allowed, and Muhammad's daughter Fatimah was married to his cousin Ali. Women keep their own names in marriage and may make their own wills for the distribution of their property after their death. It is against Islamic rule to marry one's foster mother or foster sibling. Muslim men may not marry sisters.

Most Muslim marriages are arranged by the parents. It is usual for the parents to select or help select the marriage partners and extremely unusual for Muslims to marry against the wishes of their parents. However, women are not supposed to be married against their own wishes, and the Prophet ordered one such marriage annulled.

The Prophet said that a widow in particular could not be married off until she was consulted and that a virgin must assent to the marriage, even by remaining silent. The ancient authorities disagreed about whether an adult woman could establish a marriage relationship on her own, with some maintaining that a parent or guardian must agree. Most authorities did agree that an adult virgin could not be forced into marriage against her will. And a woman who has been previously married (*sayyib*) has even more right. According to some schools, a minor who is married off by anyone other than her father or grandfather can get the marriage dissolved when she reaches the age of majority.

Nowadays, because of changing demographics, many prospective couples meet through matrimonial agencies. In Islamic tradition the most preferred partner is not the richest or best looking, but the most devout. Muhammad said, "A man marries a woman for four things: her wealth, the nobility of her family, her beauty, and her religious character. You will attain success with the one possessing nobility of character."

Sometimes the bride and groom do not even meet before the big day, although this is a matter of custom rather than Quranic injunction. Love is expected to come after marriage, not before. Women have the right of refusal, however, if they do not like their parents' choice and are usually asked as to what they are looking for in a partner. Muslim law, with its emphasis on sexual purity, demands complete chastity of both marriage partners before the wedding.

Muslim men must bring a bride-price (*Mahr*) to the marriage. This dowry can consist of money, services, goods, or other valuables and becomes the property of the wife upon marriage, to dispose of as she sees fit. If the marriage is annulled before it is consummated, the bride may keep half the *mahr*. In case of a divorce, she gets it all. Women do not bring a dowry to their husbands, as is the custom in some countries.

Marriage is not a sacrament; it is a civil contract, and either partner may place conditions on it. However, the Quran is clear that the institution was created by Allah, just as kinship relationships were. *He has made for him blood-relationship and marriage relationship* (25:54). In the realm of religion, Muslim men and women have approximately equal rights and duties; both are responsible for the state of their souls, although women do not have to attend Friday mosque prayers.

The marriage contact is drawn up by the two parties and their families. A wife may stipulate that her husband is not to take another wife, and so on. Witnesses are critical. According to Islamic law, a proper marriage must have two male, or one male and two female, witnesses. Witnesses must be sane, free, of age, and Muslim. The Prophet declared, "Those women are adulteresses who marry themselves without the presence of witnesses." Nothing, apparently, was said about the groom.

The marriage ceremony itself is called the *nikah*; it might take place in a mosque but is equally valid if performed in a private home or rented hall. There is no requirement for a Muslim official to be present, although it is the usual practice. In fact, not even both partners have to be physically present, although both must consent, and two witnesses must be present. In countries such as the United States, where a marriage is a civil act, the signing of the papers will be done by a registered Muslim official. During the ceremony, the male give his consent first, and then the woman. The ceremony is accompanied by dancing and feasting. In traditional societies, the woman moves into her husband's home. Today the trend is for the couple to have their own home, although they often stay very near the husband's family.

Husbands are clearly "in charge" of their wives (4:34). They are considered to be the head of the household, which includes taking financial responsibility. Men are expected to foot the bills and maintain the household. If a woman chooses to work (and that is her decision), the money is hers to spend as she wishes. It should not have to be used for basic expenses; that is the husband's job. According to Muhammad, "A man is a shepherd for his family and he is responsible. A woman is a shepherd over the home, and she is responsible. Truly, all of you are shepherds and all of you are responsible for your flocks." While women have the right to work so long as they do not neglect their families, they are expected to choose a job in keeping with the modesty expectations for women.

Men are responsible for their wives. *Men are responsible for women because Allah had given one more than the other and because they spend of their property for the support of women. Virtuous women are therefore obedient, guarding in their husbands' absence that which Allah has guarded* (4:34). It appears from this passage that the expenditure of funds gives the male rights over his wife. If a woman remains single, her father and brother are responsible for her welfare.

Women are expected to "guard the honor" of their husbands, which usually means behaving in a seemly and modest way. Women are also expected to take care of the children. Although it is usual for women to be in charge of household chores, this is not a Quranic requirement. Muhammad himself was fond of housework, forever helping around the hut, and some Muslim men follow the example of the Prophet. Men are expected to remain sexually faithful to their wives, although the emphasis is on female chastity.

However, marriage is supposed to be of mutual benefit. *Wives are garments for their husbands, and husbands are garments for their wives* (2:187). Muslim men are expected to treat their wives with kindness. Muhammad said, "The best of you is he who is best to his wife." He also said, "No believer should be angry with his wife. If some of her qualities are displeasing, there will be many other qualities worth appreciation."

In his last sermon Muhammad addressed the issue of marital relationships, in a declaration that has caused acrimonious discussion: "You have certain rights over your wives, and they have rights over you. You have the right that they should not defile your bed and that they should not behave with open unseemliness. If they do, Allah allows you to put them in separate rooms and to beat them, but not with severity. If they refrain from these things they have a right to food and clothing, given with kindness." This is a direct quote from the Quran: *Good women are obedient. . . . As for those from whom you fear disobedience, admonish them, and send them to beds apart and beat them* (4:34). Some authorities insist that "beat" is an overstatement of what is meant, but most experts agree that some sort of physical chastisement is referred to. A few commentators suggest that the verse refers to successive stages in correcting disobedience: the husband should first admonish his wife, then banish her from the bedroom, and finally, if all else fails, strike her, although never on the face, breast, or other sensitive part of the body. Critics maintain, however, that the very idea of a husband being granted permission to strike his wife as punishment, no matter how lightly, betokens an inherently unjust situation.

At another time, Muhammad said, "Do not beat your wife as you would beat your slave girl." Although this saying is also reported by Abu Dawud and Ahmad, it is rejected by many Muslims on the grounds that it contradicts clearly established Quranic principles and that Muhammad never advocated the beating of women of any status, slave or free. However, another hadith states that Muhammad said, "If any of you ever beats a servant, avoid the face." Other hadith, however, declare that Muhammad ordered anyone who beat a slave for something he did not do to set him free (implying that it was all right to beat them if the slaves were guilty). The truth may never be known.

POLYGAMY

Men are permitted up to four wives in Islam, but wives may take only one husband. The pre-Islamic Arabians were polygamous; there is even evidence of polyandry, an unusual arrangement in which a woman takes more than one husband, although a man taking multiple wives is more common.

The Quran limits the number of wives a man can have to four, with strictures applied: *Marry of the women who seem good to you two or three or four* (4:3). However, the Quran throws doubt on the ability of a man to treat more than one wife equally: *You will not be able to deal equally between wives, however, much as you desire to do so. But if you have more than one wife, do not turn altogether away from one, leaving her as in suspense* (4:129). All this is generally interpreted to mean that each wife should have an equal share of the husband's wealth, time, and attention. It is not mandated that the husband *love* each wife equally, silently conceding the impossibility of doing so. Indeed, the Prophet is said to have implored Allah, "O Allah, I thus make equal partition as to that which is in my power; do not therefore bring me to account for that which is not in my power," by which he meant his affections, which he could not help. One time, Muhammad, after spending three nights with his wife Umm Salamah, was getting ready to leave when she caught hold of his garment and asked him to stay another night. He answered, "If you wish, I can stay a week, but then I shall have to stay a week with each of my other wives."

However, many Muslims maintain that because of the inherent impossibility of equal treatment for wives, the Quran effectively forbids polygamy, unlike the Hebrew Bible, which permits it. This unspoken prohibition has not resulted in the disappearance of the custom among some Muslims. In most Islamic societies, however, one wife is the custom.

Sterility or illness of the first wife was a common reason for taking on a second one, although the Quran itself does not list proper circumstances. It has been mentioned that a sterile wife who was simply divorced for this reason would have a hard time finding another husband, as most husbands would desire children from their wives. Polygyny (being married to more than one woman) was also a common practice where many women were widowed, and the chances for each of them to find a husband were bleak.

In ancient days, the Hanafi and Shafii schools stipulated that a Muslim who was a slave might have only two wives, not four as allowed to free men. The Maliki school allowed the same number to both classes. As mentioned, Muhammad himself was exempt from the four-wives-maximum ruling.

Temporary Marriage

Shia Islam has a provision for temporary marriage (*mutah*). In the early days of Islam, temporary marriage was apparently a common phenomenon, as was evident from this hadith, reported by a Companion of the Prophet: "We were on a expedition with Allah's Messenger and we had no women with us. We said, 'Should we not have ourselves castrated?' The Prophet forbade us to do so. He then granted us permission that we should contract temporary marriage for a stipulated period giving her a garment for a dowry." Another Companion reported that on a different occasion, the "dowry" consisted of a "handful of dates and flour." However, according to another hadith, reported by Ali, Muhammad forbade temporary marriage and at the same time forbade the eating of donkeys.

Today, Sunnis and Shia disagree about whether the prohibition should still be in force. Sunni say that the Prophet prohibited the practice, but Shia of the Jafari school point to the following Quranic passage: *To women whom you chose in temporary and conditional marriage, give their dowry [mahr] as a duty* (4:24). (This passage, however, can be translated in quite other ways, which do not seem to indicate anything like a temporary marriage.) Some early hadith state that the temporary marriage should last three nights, after which the pair may separate if they choose to do so. Opponents to the custom say that it is little different from prostitution and point out the easy availability of "temporary wives" around theological schools and other places where large numbers of unattached males are likely to gather. Other say that the custom allows a couple to get to know each other before an official marriage takes place or can be used by couples who cannot afford to marry. It is required that the date of the dissolution of the temporary marriage be fixed in advance and that it actually be ended at that time.

Menstruation

According to the Quran, women are unclean during their menstrual periods. The idea that menstruation equals ceremonial pollution is found in many ancient religions, including Orthodox Judaism. *They will question thee concerning the monthly course. Say, "They are a pollution; so go apart from women during the monthly course, and do not approach them until they are clean. When they have cleansed themselves, then come unto them as God has commanded you." Truly God loves those who repent, and he loves those who cleanse themselves* (2:222). Menstruating women are not permitted to pray, fast, or circumambulate the Kaaba because they are considered ritually unclean. Missed prayers as a result of menstruation do not have to be made up.

According to some jurists, menstruating women are not allowed to read the Quran or even touch it. The Quranic basis for this idea is: *This is a noble Quran, which originates in a hidden or well-protected book, and which no one but the pure may touch, and which is a revelation from the Lord of the universe* (56:77–80). Some hadith also forbid it. However, these hadith are not considered completely reliable. On the positive side, Malik and most contemporary scholars declared that a menstruating woman can recite whatever she likes from the Quran. The stricter Abu Hanifa forbade it. It should be mentioned, however, that ritual uncleanliness or pollution is not the same as sinfulness.

Muhammad made it clear that during a woman's menstrual periods, only sexual intercourse per se was off limits. "When a woman among the Jews had her menses (*hayz*), they would not eat with her and would not be in the same room; so the Companions of the Prophet asked him about this. Muhammad responded, 'Do everything except sexual intercourse.'" In this he was countermanding the Jewish concept of avoiding all physical contact with menstruating women. Aishah reported, "When anyone among us [the wives] menstruated, the Messenger of Allah asked her to tie a waist-wrapper over her and then embraced her." Aishah also mentioned that when she was menstruating, Muhammad would lie in her lap and recite the Quran. And perhaps to underscore the message that menstruating women were not really unclean, Aishah said: "I would drink when I was menstruating, and then hand over the vessel to the Prophet and he would put his mouth where mine had been and drink. And I would eat the flesh from a bone when I was menstruating, and give it to him and he would put his mouth where mine had been."

Sometimes he went further. One of the Prophet's wives, Maimuna, reports, "The Messenger of Allah used to lie with me when I menstruated, and there was a cloth between us." Another wife, Salama, said the same.

INHERITANCE

Women are allowed only half the inheritance of a man. *Allah commands you regarding your children. For the male a share equivalent to that of two females.* (4:11). And further: *If there are women (daughters) more than two, then for them two thirds of the inheritance; and if there is only one then it is half* (4:11). In the absence of any daughters, this rule is applicable to agnatic granddaughters (son's daughters). However, there is a bright side to this arrangement. Women are allowed to keep or save whatever they inherit; unlike men, they do not have to use it to support their families. That is the man's job.

COURT TESTIMONY

A woman's testimony is equal to only half a man's.

O you who believe! When you deal with each other in transactions involving future obligations in a fixed period of time, reduce them to writing. Let a scribe write down faithfully as between the parties: let not the scribe refuse to write: as Allah has taught him, so let him write. Let him who incurs the liability dictate, but let him fear his Lord, Allah, and not diminish aught of what he owes. If the party liable is mentally deficient, or weak, or unable himself to dictate, let his guardian dictate faithfully. And get two witnesses out of your own men, and if there are not two men, then a man and two women, such as you choose for witnesses so that if one of them errs, the other can remind her. (2:282)

However, many jurists say that this verse delineates an exception, and that in all other circumstances, a woman's testimony equals that of a man. The exception was made for circumstances in which the woman has little knowledge of business transactions and the law, and these scholars say these circumstance seldom apply today. This passage also emphasizes the importance of getting agreements in writing.

DIVORCE (*TALAQ*)

Although divorce is allowable (2:227–237), according to a well-known hadith, of all permitted things, nothing is more detestable than a divorce. One hadith notes that marriage is the completion or second half of one's Muslim faith. Surah 65, aptly called "The Divorce," or *al-Talaq*, deals with this issue. Literally *talaq* means "untying the knot."

If there is trouble in a marriage, the Quran (4:35) suggests immediate arbitration in an effort to solve the problem. Generally, an elder member of each family is appointed to help find a solution. If the attempt is unsuccessful, then divorce is permitted. One hadith reports, "The angel of Allah advised me so many times about women that I became convinced that it is not lawful for a man to divorce his wife, except when she commits adultery." (Muhammad once said that committing adultery with a neighbor's wife was as bad as committing it with 10 other women.) The Quran provides a procedure for divorce when adultery is involved. If a man accuses his spouse of being pregnant with another man's child, he must swear four times that she has committed adultery, followed by another oath that invokes the curse of Allah upon himself if he is lying. The woman can deny all these charges by the same procedure. In this case the divorce is final, but it is left up to Allah to decide who is lying, and no punishments for adultery are invoked.

A man usually has the option of initiating a divorce by repudiating his wife, a process known as *talaq*. He is not required to state his reasons, although he is encouraged to do so. If a wife wants the divorce, she must apply to a sharia court for permission. If it is granted, she may have to return part of the dowry she was given. To make things easier all round, some marriage contracts actually contain within them a provision for the wife to initiate a divorce if she chooses. Muhammad said, "If any woman asks her husband for a divorce without a strong reason, the fragrance of the Garden [Paradise] will be forbidden to her."

To be final, a divorce decree ("I have divorced you") must be pronounced three times. The husband is supposed to say it once, then wait a complete menstrual cycle, say it again, wait another menstrual cycle, and then say it for the third and final time. The waiting period (*iddah*), of course, is to make sure the woman is not pregnant. If she is, she is entitled to the support of her husband during the time the child is reared. Another three months must follow before the woman is free to marry again. She is even encouraged to do so. Some Islamic countries now have civil divorce proceedings and do not recognize the traditional *talaq*. Some authorities maintain that it is sufficient to say the divorce words on three separate occasions; a few maintain they can be said even at one sitting. One of Muhammad's grandson's, Hasan, had 90 wives over the course of his life. He changed partners so many times that people called him "The Divorcer."

If the divorced couple regret their decision and wish to marry again, they cannot do so, unless the wife marries someone else in the interim and is then divorced from the second man. A couple may divorce and reconcile twice (as long as she marries someone else between) but the third divorce is final.

WOMEN AND HELL

Despite often showing regard for women, the Prophet could be sharply critical too. According to one hadith, Muhammad said that he saw women "in bulk" among the inhabitants of Hell. When asked why this should be, he responded, "You curse too much and are ungrateful to your husbands." He also thought women lacked "common sense."

On the other hand, women will be accepted into Paradise, just like men: *Whoever does good, male or female, and is believer, all such will enter Paradise* (4:124).

ABORTION AND BIRTH CONTROL

Islam has various views about fetal life. A famous hadith reports the development of a human being in these words: "Verily the creation of each one of you is brought together in his mother's belly for forty days in the form of a seed, then he is clot of blood for a like period, then a morsel of flesh for a like period, then there is sent to him the angel who blows the breath of life into him." In most cases, Islamic teachings about birth control, sterilization, and abortion mirror that of most conservative Christians and Jews. Muslims believe the spirit or *ruh* is joined to the body sometimes between 40 and 120 days after conception. The term *ruh* is not the same word as is used for soul or self; that word is *nafs* and is the "personhood" of every individual, making up his real self that develops throughout his life. Birth control is usually accepted (if both husband and wife agree) to space out a family, usually after the birth of two children, a boy and girl. It is also permitted when conception may injure a woman's health. It is not permitted if the couple merely wishes never to have a child. In Muhammad's day, the only form of birth control known was coitus interruptus (*al-azl*). Muhammad permitted it but counseled that it was ineffective anyway because Allah controlled fertility.

During Muhammad's lifetime, some Muslims captured some women. The soldiers went to Muhammad and said they intended to have sexual relations with them—but did not wish to impregnate them (probably referring to the practice of *coitus interruptus*). They asked Muhammad if this was permissible. Muhammad responded, "It is better that you should not do it, for Allah has written whom he is going to create until the Day of Resurrection." This story is somewhat disturbing, not so much for the recommendation against birth control but for the fact that the Prophet apparently gave permission for intercourse (rape) against captive women.

Like the Bible, the Quran does not specifically mention abortion. Because the soul does not join the body immediately, some Muslims believe therefore that early abortion is permitted, although the later it occurs, the more objections there are. Other Muslims approve of later abortions if there are serious reasons. As more is understood about fetal development, however, Islam takes an increasingly negative view of abortion at any stage. No matter when it occurs, however, abortion is never considered as serious as murder in Islam.

External artificial insemination and surrogate mothering are likewise prohibited as they are considered an unlawful "mingling of blood."

Rape

Islamic law, or sharia, gives no clear definition of rape, and the rules of evidence disallow the testimony of the victim—proving the crime requires the eyewitness testimony of four males. It is not unusual for the *victim* of a rape to be prosecuted instead for committing adultery, as happened recently in Somalia to a teenager who was stoned for being raped. Her attackers were not prosecuted.

Some contemporary Muslim legal experts further say that forcible rape (*hiraba*) does not require four witnesses to prove the offense, opining that circumstantial evidence, medical data, and expert testimony are sufficient to prosecute it. And a hadith recounts the following: "A woman was raped. Later, when some people came by, she identified and accused the man of raping her. They seized him and brought him to Allah's messenger, who said to the woman, 'Go away, for Allah has forgiven you,' but of the man who had raped her, he said, 'Stone him to death.'" This event accords perhaps too much weight to the testimony of a single witness!

Islamic law allows for a rape victim to seek civil damages also, under the rubric of *jirah* (wounds). Islamic jurisprudence says that each person owns his or her body and all its parts and has a right to financial compensation for any harm done unlawfully to any of those parts.

CHILDREN

The birth of a new child is met with celebration. When a baby is born, washed, and clothed, the father or other senior male whispers the call to prayer (*adhan*) in the child's right ear and the call for the prayer to begin (*iqama*) in the left ear. Sometimes a little bit of pre-chewed date is placed in the baby's mouth. This stems from a story of the Prophet recounted by Abu Musa: "A son was born to me and I brought him to the Prophet. He named him Ibrihim, and he chewed a date and rubbed thereby his palate, and prayed for blessings for him and gave him back to me." The Prophet also recommended that two goats be sacrificed upon the birth of a boy and one upon the birth of a girl. The meat of the sacrifice is shared among friends and with the poor.

The child is generally named within the first 10 days after birth, with names drawn from the Beautiful Names of God being popular, as is Muhammad and various names of the prophets. Children may also carry the name of a parent, with *ibn* meaning "son of" and *bint* "daughter of." This addition is called the *nasab*. Parents may also add to their own names, taking *abu* for "father of" or *umm*, "mother of." This addition is called a *kunya*. Some people later acquire a name derived from the place of birth, profession, or special physical or character attribute. This is called the *laqab*.

Before Muhammad's time, infant girls were considered a burden, and unwanted ones were buried alive, a practice that Muhammad forbade and that is condemned in the Quran. Muhammad seemed fond of daughters in general. A hadith reports him as declaring, "Girls are models of affection and sympathy and a blessing to the family. If a person has one daughter, Allah will screen him from the fire of Hell owing to his daughter; if he has two daughters, Allah will admit him to Paradise; if he has three, Allah will exempt him from the obligation of charity and Jihad." Other hadith record the same sentiments. Most movingly, Muhammad said, "Shall I tell you what one of the greatest types of charity is? It is that you care for your daughter who has returned to you when she has no one else to support her but you."

Nursing of babies is encouraged, up to the time the child is two years old, if practical. In Muslim cultures it is not unusual for the children to sleep with the parents while they are young. They are also shown great affection. Parents are enjoined to love all their children equally.

Although adoption is common in Islam, in many ways the adopted child is considered a stranger who may not inherit anything. This seems curious, given that in pre-Islamic Arabia, an adopted child was considered a true member of the family with all the rights of a biological child. Even adopted children raised from birth with the family are considered technically allowed to marry one of their siblings, and thus, Islamic laws prohibit their mingling casually together.

CIRCUMCISION

Circumcision was an ancient rite that was rather widespread, although not universal in biblical and pre-Islamic times. The Egyptians and Canaanites practiced it, for example, but the Philistines and Babylonians did not. Circumcision is not mentioned at all in the Quran but does receive comment in the hadith. It is widely practiced among Muslims, following the example of Muhammad, but it is not mandatory, except for men going on hajj. Circumcision can be performed at any convenient time; no special rites or ceremonies accompany the event. In the West, it is usually performed soon after birth in the hospital by a physician; in traditional societies, it may occur years later.

Female circumcision (*khafd*) is a cultural practice annually inflicted on between 100 million and 140 million women, most of whom live in Egypt, Mali, Guinea, and Sudan. It is not practiced in Iran, Iraq, or Saudi Arabia. In December 2006, a conference of Muslim theologians declared the practice irreconcilable with Islam, although in some schools it is still either recommended or allowable. In cultures where female circumcision is the norm, it is practiced among Christians and people of traditional faiths as well as among Muslims. Muhammad said, "Do not cut severely, as that is better for a woman and more desirable to a husband."

SLAVERY

At the very bottom of early Islamic society were the slaves, who were always people captured in battle. Slavery is not specifically forbidden in Islam, and was a common feature of life in Muhammad's day. However, they were granted certain rights, including that of owning property. Slavery was based much less on skin color (although this could be a factor) than on religion. No Muslims, Jews, or Christians could be taken as slaves, only pagans. Muhammad urged that only those people who had engaged in warfare against Islam could be made slaves.

The Quran enjoined believers to treat slaves kindly and listed freeing a slave as a laudable action. Muhammad absolutely forbade the mutilation and castration of slaves, although this practice later became common. He also said, "Feed them with the food that you eat, clothe them from the clothes that you wear, and never torment those created by Allah," and also "Your slaves are your brothers, so do good to them." He also required that they not be given more work than they were capable of doing and that servants be allowed to sit and eat with their masters. At one time he said, "Any Muslim who frees an enslaved Muslim will have every part of his body freed from the Fire by every part of the body of the freed person."

Abu Masud reported, "I used to beat my servant. But once I heard a voice behind me say, 'O Abu Masud, it is far simpler for Allah to beat you than it is for you to beat that boy.' I turned and saw that it was the Prophet of Allah. Immediately, I said, 'O Prophet of Allah! The boy is free, for Allah's pleasure.' The Prophet replied, 'If you had not set him free, the Fire would have touched you.'" Muhammad was not fond of the word "slave" in general when referring to bound servants. He said we were all slaves only to Allah.

In his last sermon, Muhammad said, "As for your slaves, see that you feed them with such food as you eat yourselves, and clothe them with what you clothe yourselves; and if they commit a crime you cannot forgive, then part from them, for they are the servants of the Lord and are not to be harshly treated."

However, a very dark hadith (whose authenticity is disputed) tells that Aishah had promised to free a certain slave girl when she died. Soon after, Aishah grew very sick and called in a doctor from among the gypsy people. The doctor told her, "Why are you asking me to cure you? Don't you know a curse has been put upon you?" The slave girl confessed that she had done it to kill Aishah and thus obtain her freedom. Aishah then said, "Sell her to the Arab Bedouins who will treat her the worst." This does not put Aishah in a very good light, but perhaps it is understandable, considering the circumstances.

Muhammad also urged his followers to free their slaves, as the following hadith shows: A Bedouin once came to the Prophet and asked how he could obtain Paradise. The Prophet responded, "Manumit a human soul and free a slave." The Bedouin wondered, "Aren't those the same thing, really?" "No," the Prophet replied, "Manumission of a human soul is to manumit one enslaved. But to free a slave is to help the slave buy his own freedom, and to give the gifts truly desired, and to help support one's relatives. If you cannot do any of this, then enjoin the doing of good and prohibit the doing of wrong. If you are not in a position to do that, then prevent yourself from speaking of anything other than good." In other words, Muhammad placed a higher value on freeing slaves than on enjoining the "good" and prohibiting the doing of wrong. In instances where the freeing of slaves was not possible, Islamic law made attempts to regulate it in such a way as to preserve some dignity for the slave. Nowadays, slavery is officially banned in Islam, but it can still be found (in effect) in some Gulf Arabic states. It is also practiced in Sudan (where almost all slaves are Christians) and Mauritania (where almost all slaves are black).

DEATH

A dying person is positioned to face Mecca. The *shahada* is repeated in his ear, and passages from the Quran, especially Surah 36 ("Ya Sin") are read or recited. This surah deals with death and resurrection, and a hadith records Muhammad as saying that one who recited this surah with the right intention would be forgiven their sins.

BURIAL

Burial is the common way of disposing of dead bodies and the deceased is buried in the earth as soon as possible. If the death occurs in the morning, then the burial is performed later that day. If the person dies in the evening, the burial may wait until the next day. There is a general belief that the deceased person is "uneasy" until the burial is accomplished. Autopsies are frowned upon because the body is supposed to be "not interfered with."

The deceased body is washed an odd number of times, with water from a lote tree, followed by sprinkling camphor scent. No other decoration is permitted. The washers must be of the same sex as the deceased, and to preserve the dead person's dignity, the body is washed under a sheet. This is in accordance to instructions given by Muhammad when his own daughter died. He then gave his own waist wrapper to the women to wrap her in.

Males are wrapped in three white, clean cloths (not new) covering the entire body. These are often the same cloths used for their hajj. Women are dressed in a wraparound, head covering, shift, and two shrouds similar to those used for men. A coffin may be used, but it is not traditional or required. (A coffin is used only to carry the body to the place of burial; Muslims are buried in their shrouds only.) The funeral may be held at the deceased's home or at the mosque.

Respect is always to be shown to the bier (stand on which the body is placed), whether the deceased is Muslim or not, with Muhammad commanding people to stand up "until he leaves the bier behind or the bier leaves him behind." When he held a burial service, Muhammad would say, "O Allah! Forgive our living ones and our dead ones, and those of us who are present and those who are absent, and our young ones and our old ones, and our males and our females. O Allah! Keep those who are living in submission to you, and cause those who die to die in the faith. O Allah! Do not deprive us of our reward." A simple funeral prayer is performed while standing.

A burial service may be held even if there is no body. Women were encouraged not to follow the burial train, although they are not actually prohibited from doing so. All persons, even grave sinners and non-Muslims who have committed heinous acts, are entitled to a burial service. In fact, it is a requirement.

It is required (if possible) to place the deceased on his side facing the Kaaba. It is customary for the top of the grave to be gently mounded without building over it. The plastering of tombs or the erection of buildings upon the grave is heavily discouraged. A marker is left to denote the person's name; a verse from the Quran may be added. The funeral prayers (*salat al-janaza*) are generally spoken by an imam or the senior male from the family. These consist of sections from the Quran and special *dua* asking forgiveness for the sins of the deceased. If the person was a child before puberty, he is considered to be sinless; no forgiveness prayers are required.

After the service, it is customary to visit the bereaved family. The bereaved family should be consoled for three days after the burial. The bereaved may cry but should not scream, slap their faces, throw dust on their heads, or tear their clothes. Excessive mourning is considered un-Islamic because death is a part of life and decreed by Allah.

A stillborn fetus is washed and prayed over if it gave a cry or breathed. If the fetus is more than six months, it is treated exactly as an adult. The death of children should be spoken of as a blessing in disguise. When Muhammad's son Ibrahim died, Muhammad threw three handfuls of dust on the grave with both his hands, had water sprinkled on it, and placed pebbles on it.

Muslims who die fighting non-Muslims are not washed or prayed over because it is believed that they are already purified by their martyrdom. They are buried with the blood still on them. Dead bodies should be treated with respect. Muhammad said, "Do not abuse the dead, for they have gone on."

EATING, DRINKING, AND CELEBRATING

Muslims are expected to eat and drink moderately. Muhammad, an abstemious person himself, said that one-third of the stomach was for food, one-third for water, and one-third for air, underscoring the importance of not stuffing oneself. Before eating or drinking, Muslims pronounce the words *Bismillah al-rahman al-rahim*, "in the name of Allah the merciful and compassionate." This is a reminder as to the source of all food and drink. Food is never to be wasted, but rather stored or given to the poor or to animals who need it.

DIETARY LAWS

Muslims are not allowed to eat pork (or products that may contain pork fat), carrion, bloody meat, or meat sacrificed to another deity. *In all that has been revealed to me, I do not find anything forbidden to eat, if one wants to eat thereof, unless it be carrion, or blood poured forth, or the flesh of swine, for that, behold, is loathsome—or a sinful offering over which any name other than Allah's has been invoked* (6:145). Muslims also refrain from eating birds of prey, rodents, reptiles, anything with claws or fangs, and insects (with the exception of locusts, which were a well-known desert food).

Interestingly, Muslims rejected other Jewish dietary bans. Muslims believed that except for the three listed, food restrictions were visited upon the Jews as a punishment for their disobedience to Allah. *Due to their transgressions, we prohibited for the Jews good foods that used to be lawful for them; also for consistently straying from the path of Allah* (4:160).

Because water is considered pure, animals such as fish that live constantly in water are also pure and so are permissible food, although some Muslim schools follow Jewish rules and forbid shellfish as well as fish without scales or fins. No special laws about their capture or killing are in force, as long as they are alive when they leave the water. However, if one's life hangs in the balance, and there is nothing else to eat, it is lawful to eat forbidden foods, provided one takes no more than is necessary to sustain life. *If a person is forced because there is no other choice, neither craving nor transgressing, there is no sin committed* (2:173).

The meat of rats, snakes, crocodiles, dogs, cats, and other predators is also unsuitable for food, although it could be turned into "medicine" if the animal was properly slaughtered. According to some jurists, one should perform ritual ablutions after eating camel meat or mutton.

The slaughter of animals for food is carefully regulated. According to a hadith, Muhammad said, "Verily Allah has prescribed proficiency in all things. Thus, if you kill, kill well; and if you slaughter, slaughter well. Let each one of you sharpen his blade and let him spare suffering to the animal he slaughters." The slaughter is accomplished with an extremely sharp knife that slices the windpipe and jugular vein, cutting off oxygen to the brain and draining the blood quickly. This was believed to be the most painless way of killing. At the time of the slaughter, the words *Bismillah, Allahu Akbar,* recognizing the seriousness of the deed, are said. Animals must be properly cared for before slaughter and given sufficient food and water, and no animal is permitted to see another suffer or die.

The ritual slaughterer is the *dhabah*, whose job is to separate the "unclean blood" from the "clean flesh." The *dhabah* must be a Muslim, Christian, or Jew and can be a man or woman, circumcised or uncircumcised. Zoroastrians, however, are prohibited from being *dhabahs*, according to the express command of Muhammad. Proper slaughtering includes draining the animal of blood before eating it; this requirement is not necessary for game animals, however.

Holy Days

Islam goes by a lunar calendar and all the months are 29 or 30 days long. Important Islamic celebrations include two major feasts (*Eid*). The word *eid* is from the Arabic, meaning "returning at regular intervals," the object of which is to offer praise and thanks to Allah, as well as foster a sense of community. A special effort is made on each feat to include poor and lonely people so that no one will feel excluded.

The first one is the Eid of the Feast of Ramadan (*Eid Al-Fitr*) and the other the Feast of Sacrifice (*Eid Al-Adha*). It begins, as noted earlier, on the first sighting of the new crescent moon (*hilal*). The first feast is celebrated by Muslims after fasting during the month of Ramadan in thanks to Allah. It takes place on the first day of Shawwal, the 10th month of the lunar calendar, and is celebrated for three days (for this reason it is sometimes called the "little feast" because it is a day shorter than the Feast of Sacrifice). Many families decorate their homes for this feast—and some people even use Christmas tinsel! Eid cards are also sent out to family and friends.

The second is the Feast of Sacrifice. and it is celebrated in memory of prophet Ibrahim's trying to sacrifice his firstborn son Ismail (Ishmael). This Eid is celebrated for four days between the 10th and the 13th day of Zul-Hijjah, the 12th month of the lunar calendar (during the hajj). It is celebrated even by Muslims who are not at Mecca. The meat of the slaughtered animal is divided into three portions, one for the family, one part to be given away to friends and neighbors, and one part to be given to the poor. The meat given away is not cooked or prepared. These are important holidays for children, especially. In the Muslim community, it is customary to give them presents of money or clothing.

Another festivity is *walimah*, a dinner reception held after a marriage is consummated. It may be hosted by the parents, the married couple, or both. Another dinner is the *aqiqah*, held after a child is born. Relatives, friends, and neighbors are all invited. Some Muslims also celebrate the birthday of the prophet, although this is frowned upon in some circles.

CHAPTER 5

The Many Faces of Islam

The Quran says, *As for those who divide their way of life and break up into sects, you have no part of them at all. Their affair is with Allah. He will tell them the truth of what they did in the end* (6:159). Despite this warning, and like all other worldwide religions, Islam has broken up into various "denominations." Muhammad seemed to predict this, according to a reliable hadith, and told his followers that Islam would eventually divide into 73 sects. (He also announced that there were 71 sects in Judaism and 72 in Christianity.) Today, about 80 percent of the world's Muslims are Sunni, and about 20 percent (about 120 million) are Shia.

THE KHARIJITES: AN EARLY SEPARATIST GROUP

The Kharijites became the first splinter group in Islam. This extremist sect from Ali's caliphate became known as the Kharijites (from the Arabic word *kharaja*, meaning "to leave" or "secede") and became famous as hard-liners, rebels, and puritans. (In fact, they are sometimes called the "puritans of Islam.) They were the first "dissident sect" in Islam (appearing only about 25 years after the death of Muhammad), and they felt that anyone who disagreed with their interpretation of Islam was a heretic deserving of death or at least expulsion from their tightly bonded community. They also thought that anyone who committed a grave sin was excluded from their community, equating faith and works. They based their belief on a powerful doctrine of free will, saying that if we have free will, all our sins are entirely our own doing and therefore constitute an act of rebellion against Allah. As for themselves, they believed they were a veritable community of saints, rather like the early American Puritans, and with about the same degree of tolerance for others. Everyone else was considered a "person of Hell."

The Kharijites had their own version of the rightful succession of caliphs, maintaining that the first two caliphs, Abu Bakr and Umar, were legitimate, but Uthman, Ali, and all others following them were not. (At first they had supported Ali, but they then rejected him when he attempted to reach a compromise agreement with Muawiya, the other claimant for the Caliphate.)

They also disagreed with the doctrine that only Meccans could serve as caliphs—they wanted the position to be open to all Muslims, including black slaves, and so in that sense were true egalitarians. However, there was a caveat. Rulers could rule only so long as they remained sinless. Sunnis, on the other hand, thought that even a sinful caliph was able to keep order, and keeping order in society was more important than the personal character of the ruler.

It is the Kharijites who decided that jihad was the "sixth pillar" of Islam and that jihad was a duty enjoined upon all true believers. They considered themselves the only true followers of Allah, with everyone else being of the party of Hell. Unrepentant Sunnis (who are "sinners" of their own free will) are legitimate objects of jihad and were to be executed. The Kharijites were defeated in 658 at Nahrawan. However, they continued to wage guerilla warfare against both the Umayyads and Abbasids.

Although there is no true Kharijite sect still in existence (their inability to compromise produced inevitable split-offs), their descendant communities survive in parts of North Africa, Yemen, and Oman. In Oman, in fact, the Ibadi faith, which practitioners say is different from the old Kharijite tradition, but strongly resembles it, is the official state religion. This religion is distinct from both Sunni and Shia traditions. They differ from Sunni in maintaining that the faithful will not see Allah on the Day of Judgment and that the Quran was created at a particular point in time and is not "uncreated" as most Muslims believer.

Their puritan reformist spirit also lives on in the Wahhabi sect of Saudi Arabia, and their radical notions were inherited by contemporary Egyptian groups such as Takfir wal Hijra and Jamaat al-Jihad.

THE MUTAZILITES

Another early Islamic group was the Mutazilites. Mutazilite (literally, "one who stands aloof," a name given to them by their detractors) became a formal school during the Abbasid dynasty. The Mutazilites believed in a less literal interpretation of the Quran than was accepted by most Muslims and considered themselves rationalists.

They also believed that the Quran was a created book, not one that existed from forever, a view that put them at odds with most other Muslims. Their argument was that if the Quran was not created, it was coeternal with Allah, which to them was an impossibility because it would negate the idea of *tawhid*, of God's unique singularity. The Caliph al-Mutawakkil (821–861) decreed the death penalty to anyone who taught this "heretical" doctrine.

They also believed in free will—without it one could not accept responsibility for one's actions, and that would imperil the justice of Allah. The Mutazilites were fans of Greek philosophy and believed the study of it was an aid to understanding their own faith more rationally. They opposed any anthropomorphic understanding of Allah. This was another point of contention: Did Allah actually have ears and a voice and so forth as the Quran stated? The non-literalist Mutazilites claimed no. Those who believed otherwise, they claimed were guilty of idolatry. In this, they were opposed by a group called the Asharites (discussed later) who maintained that Allah did see and speak, but we humans could not understand the precise nature of this faculty.

Early Mutazilites appeared to place limits on the power of Allah by affirming that universal laws compelled Allah to reward the pure and punish the guilty. (Later Mutazilites returned to a more orthodox understanding of Allah's limitless power.)

Their rationalist stand, particularly in regard to the "createdness" of the Quran, was strongly opposed by the Hanbali school. In fact, during their period of greatest power, they had Ahmad ibn Hanbal, the founder of the Hanbali school, flogged and imprisoned because he disagreed with their elevation of Greek philosophy in Islamic study. Later, the Mutazilites became associated with the Shia movement.

In the 10th century, in reaction against the Mutazilites, the Sunni movement arose, representing the majority of Muslims. Its major figure was Abu al-Hasan al-Ashari (d. 945). Al-Ashari had started as a Mutazilite but eventually began to believe their ideas were not in accord with what Muhammad taught. His followers, the Asharites, tried to create middle ground between the literalists and the symbolists. They used rationality to defend what seemed to be beyond reason. The Asharites maintained that Allah had attributes, but that they were neither part of his essence nor mere "accidents" (qualities that were simply somehow "attached" to him). They believed that Allah was present always and everywhere, but that he often allowed events to unfold as they would without direct intervention. In the Asharite view, lying was evil because Allah had declared it to be so, and if he had declared it good, it would be so. Many Asharite ideas were accepted by all schools of Islamic jurisprudence except for the ultra-conservative Hanbali school.

One of the most important and celebrated of all Asharite philosophers was Abu Hamid Al-Ghazali (1058–1111). Al-Ghazali was a man difficult to characterize. At various times he was an Asharite, a scholar in the Shafii school of theology, and a wandering Sufi mystic. And more than al-Ashari himself, it was al-Ghazali who formed much Asharite thinking. Trained in Islamic jurisprudence in Baghdad, al-Ghazali suffered through a crisis of faith when he discovered the ancient Greek philosophers. He achieved spiritual enlightenment, however, not by abandoning his faith, but by turning to the writings of the great Sufi masters. Eventually, he left his teaching post at Baghdad and became a wandering pilgrim, spending 11 years in retirement and meditation. When he returned to his native Persia, he began his major work, *The Revival of the Religious Sciences.* In this book he opined that both Sharia and cultivation of the Sufi path were vital elements in salvation, and faith and reason were the twin wings to Heaven. He put a strong emphasis on direct religious experience.

He also wrote *The Incoherence of the Philosophers*, an ardent attempt to show that religion was superior to philosophy. "Nothing in logic is relevant to religion by way of denial or affirmation," he wrote. His work was answered by Ibn Rushd (Averroes), a Mutazalite, who penned *The Incoherence of the Incoherence.* Ibn Rushd wanted to prove that religion and philosophy were actually the same, and any differences between them were only apparent.

THE SUNNI

Sunnis depend on religious scholars or *ulama*, who worked out a system of laws and guidelines for implementing the teachings of the Quran and Hadith. The Sunni are the majority tradition in most Muslim nations and regard themselves as the only orthodox Muslims. Their name came from the Arabic word *Sunnah*, or "example" (although it literally means "beaten path"), for they believe they are following the example of Muhammad. The word appears in the Quran referring to an established practice of conduct. (The word *Sunnah* originally referred to accepted practices of the Bedouin tribes and later came to be understood as a tradition of the Prophet himself.) And according to a hadith: "I have left unto you two things—the Book of Allah and Sunnah of his Prophet; he who holds them strongly will never go astray." The Quran itself refers to Allah's ancient custom or Sunnah (48:23). Today's Sunni Muslims take their name from this term.

Throughout history the Sunnis have usually been dominant over the Shia and ruled over them politically. Sunni Muslims were originally organized under a caliph, whose title was *Amir al-mumaneen*, or "commander of the believers." Because Sunni is generally considered "mainstream Islam," most of this book has been devoted to their practice and history.

SHIA: THE PARTY OF ALI

Although they make up only 20 percent of Muslims worldwide, the Shia are the majority branch of Islam in Iran, Iraq, and Bahrain. The split from the Sunni began when certain Muslims maintained that the successorship had to come from the Prophet's family, the *Ahl al-Bayt*, indeed direct descendants of the Prophet himself. They base this understanding on a reading of the Quran 33:33, in which the family of the prophet is declared to be sinless and without spot. By family, the Shia specifically mean Muhammad's daughter Fatimah, his son-law Ali, and their two sons, Hasan (d. 669) and Husayn (d. 680). They believe that although Ali was the rightful heir to the leadership, he pretended allegiance to the first three caliphs in order to avoid civil war. This dissimulation (*taqiyah*) is accepted as a necessary tactic; it is still permitted, among Shia, to pretend to a different faith in order to escape persecution.

The Shia call their leaders Imams, which has a much stronger meaning than "prayer leader," as the term is used in Sunni Islam. In the Shia tradition, Imams are both political and religious rulers. It is they, not a scholarly community or *ulama*, who make pronouncements on laws. The Imams are also infallible and sinless, although they are not designated with the title of Prophet. Because Ali was regarded as the "soul" of the Prophet, it followed that his descendants shared in this special relationship with Muhammad. The Imams do not receive the same kind of direct revelation (*wahy*) from Allah granted to Muhammad, but they do receive *ilham*, divine inspiration.

According to their belief, succession to the Imamate depends on *nass* ("designation") with the "Imam of the Time," or spiritual predecessor, able to choose his successor from among any of his male descendants.

Because the Sunni never claimed that the caliph was infallible, the stipulation that the Imam *was* gave him, in the Shia mind at least, a higher status than the Sunni caliph.

While the Sunnis were enjoying political and military victories, the Shia were dealing with hardship, war, and oppression. This experience created for them a view of the world as a place of suffering and pain, to be ended only when the Mahdi should arrive to usher in a New Age of happiness and peace. This belief is aggravated by the fact that they believe that neither Muhammad nor any of their 12 Imams died a natural death—all but the 12th were murdered. (They believe that Muhammad was poisoned.) Only in the 20th century did the Shia become less passive and more ready to assert their rights.

PERSECUTION OF SHIA

The Shia are persecuted in some Sunni lands. Sunni Muslims in Saudi Arabia have been particularly hard on Shia Muslims, some going so far as to classify them as "infidels" because they are perceived not to follow the "traditions" of Islam. In Saudi Arabia, for example, the controlling Wahhabis limit the political participation of the Shia (who comprise about 10% of the population) to a few important members of the community. These men, in turn, are expected to keep the rest of their community under control. Even the Shia "elite" seldom or never hold positions of any real importance in the government. Many Saudis consider them "Iranians" and they are frequently accused of treason and other crimes.

SHIA SUCCESSORSHIP

Shia Muslims developed a view different from the Sunnis about the proper line of succession. Sunnis regarded their caliphs as political and religious leaders, not as men who had achieved a special spiritual status. The Shia, on the other hand, believed their Imam (successor to Muhammad) to be a spiritually gifted person who had the special blessing of Allah. Many Shia believe that their Imams were created from one preexisting Light and that all the blessings and knowledge of Allah come through them. Some say they were born already circumcised, a story that is occasionally bruited about in regard to Muhammad as well. Although Shia doctrine was fully developed by the 10th century, some principles blossomed anew in Iranian Ayatollah Khomeini's expounding of *velayat-e faqih*, the idea that the community of believers should be governed by scholars trained in religious law. These men are known as *mujtahids*. Although laypersons are expected to follow the dictates of the *mujtahids*, they may follow any *mujtahid* of their choice. The most prominent and important of them receive the title of Ayatollah, although this is a relatively new term, appearing only in the 20th century. The Shia reject the Sunni idea of the consensus of the community (*ijma*), which once arrived at is considered infallible. For the Shia, infallibility belongs only to the Imams, especially the Hidden Imam. Once in a while, a living Imam seems so full of divine knowledge that he is dubbed *naib al-Imam*, or a deputy of the Hidden Imam, and although he is not precisely infallible, his teachings have enormous clout. The Grand Ayatollah Ali al-Sistani (b. 1930) of southern Iraq is a *naib al-Imam*. (Shia clerics wear distinctive dress. In Iran, they wear a white turban and an *aba*, a loose, sleeveless brown cloak, open in front. A clergyman descended from Muhammad, or *sayyid*, wears a black turban and a black *aba*.)

Shia Muslims undertake pilgrimages to the shrines of the Twelve Imams and their descendants. Most Shia are less concerned with a pilgrimage to Mecca than they are to visit their own holy places. Many towns also contain smaller shrines, called *imamzadehs*, dedicated to saintly descendants of the Imam. Shia pilgrims believe that the Imams and their relatives can intercede with Allah on their behalf.

Unlike the Sunni majority, the Shia believe that Allah has foreknowledge of human actions, but he does not predestine them. They also have a somewhat different call to prayer and a different ablution ritual (*wudu*) from Sunnis. The most interesting social difference is that Shia Muslims permit the practice of *mutah*, or temporary marriage, which is denounced by Sunnis.

Shia Islam did not remain a stable faction; it split into further sects, such as the Twelvers, Seveners, and Fivers. The numbers refer to the number of perceived Imams since the death of Muhammad.

The most important event in Shia history is the Battle of Karbala in Iraq (680) in which Husayn was killed. In this battle the Shia were greatly outnumbered by the Umayyads and were brutally massacred. Husayn and his followers were killed and their bodies mutilated, making them martyrs. Husayn's son, Ali ibn Husayn, also known as Zayn ul-Abidin, was sick on the day of the battle and did not take part. He thus survived to become the Fourth Imam, after Ali, Hasan, and Husayn. *His* eldest son, Zayd ibn Ali, is held to be the true Fifth Imam by the small group of Shia known as Fivers.

Other Shia believe the true Fifth Imam was Muhammad al-Baqir, the grandson of Husayn. His successor was Jafar al-Sadiq (d. 765). Jafar lived and worked in Medina at a time when the split between Shia and Sunni Muslims had not yet hardened into warring camps. Both Abu Hanifa and Malik ibn Anas worked under him. When *he* died, a further split occurred, with some Shia recognizing his eldest son Ismail as the rightful Imam. However, Ismail died before his father, and so they recognized his son Muhammad ibn Ismail. They became the Seveners or the Ismailis. However, the biggest group of Shia accepted Musa al-Kazim, the younger son of Jafar, as the rightful Seventh Imam.

The Imams of Shia Islam

First Imam: Ali (d. 661)

Second Imam: Hasan (d. 669)

Third Imam: Husayn (d. 680)

Fourth Imam: Ali ibn Husayn (Zayn ul-Abidin) (d. 712 or 713)

Here the "Fivers," or Zadis, split off and accept Zayd ibn Ali as the next Imam

Fifth Imam: Muhammad al-Baqir (d. sometime between 732 and 743)

Sixth Imam: Jafar al Sadiq (d. 765)

Here the "Seveners," or Ismailis, split off and accept Muhammad ibn Ismail as the next Imam

Seventh Imam: Musa al-Kazim (d. 799)

Eighth Imam: Ali al-Rida (d. 818)

Ninth Imam: Muhammad al-Taqui (d. 835)

Tenth Imam: Ali al-Naqi (d. 868)

Eleventh Imam: Hasan al-Askari (d. 874)

Twelfth Imam: Muhammad al-Qaim

In minor occultation from 874 to 941

In major occultation from 941

The group recognizing the Twelfth Imam, the majority of Shia, are called the Twelvers.

The Fivers (Zaydis)

Of the Shia, the Zaydis are probably the closest to Arabic Sunni Islam and have a less established "identity" than other Shia groups.

The only real difference between them and Sunni Muslims is their refusal to recognize the legitimacy of any caliph after Ali. They have some differences from Sunnis in the matter of ablutions and the call to prayer but are otherwise very similar to them. Sometimes they are considered to form a "bridge" between Shia and Sunni groups. They are quite hostile to other Shia, and in Yemen, where they wield influence, they have banned Sufi orders. They will not eat meat unless the animal was slaughtered by a Muslim.

However, the Fivers are also in disagreement with the majority of the Shia community about the proper succession of the Imamate. The Zaydis recognized Husayn's surviving son Ali Zayn al-Abidin as the next Imam, followed by *his* son Zayd ibn Ali, Husayn's grandson, who was known as a fearless fighter for justice. Zayd was killed in 740 while fighting in an unsuccessful revolt in Kufa, Iraq, against the one-eyed Umayyad Caliph Hisham (724–743). Hisham ordered Zayd's body to be exhumed and hung on a palm tree, and the head sent to Damascus.

Most Shia recognize Muhammad al-Baqir and his son Jafar al-Sadiq (d. 675) as the rightful Imams. The followers of Zaydi do not believe that an Imam must be the son of another Imam, although they do believe that he should be a male descendant of Ali. He must also be an adult capable of leading the group in warfare. However, he could be *any* descendant of Ali, not just of Ali and Fatimah, as other Shia believe. The Zaydi also believe there can be more than one Imam at a time.

Nor do the Zaydis hold their Imams in quite the same reverent light as other Shia, in terms of belief in infallibility or that an Imam can act as an intermediary between human beings and Allah. For the Zaydi, the Imams are simply great scholars and leaders. This makes them much more like Sunni Muslims than like other Shia. Today Zaydis are mostly found in remote areas of Iran and Yemen. In the latter country they ruled for more than a millennium until a revolution in 1962, when the country became a republic. However, Yemen is still run on Islamic law, or sharia.

The Twelvers

The Twelvers are the largest group of Shia Muslims. They are also called the Imamiya, or Ithna Asharis, and are found mostly in Iran. Many of their beliefs are in line with those of the ancient Mutazilites, believing, for example that the Quran is created (not coeternal with Allah), that Allah is incapable of doing evil, and that human beings have free will. Although they accept many of the hadith as legitimate, they reject those reported by Aishah—Ali's old enemy.

They believe that the rightful line of Imams descended from Jafar al-Sadiq. However, Ismail died before Jafar, and Jafar did not designate another successor. Twelvers believe the line of Imams devolved upon Ismail's brother Musa al-Kazim. The Twelver Shia believe that the Twelve Imams who succeeded Muhammad the Prophet were sinless and inerrant, selected by God. They also believe that each Imam was persecuted by the reigning Sunni caliph and that all of them, except the Twelfth, was murdered.

Twelver Shia generally use the term "Imam" only for Ali and his 11 descendants; however, only Ali ever was the head of a government. Most were persecuted by Umayyad and Abbasid caliphs, who feared Imams would attempt to wrest control of the government from them. The Twelfth Imam was said to have been only five years old when the Imamate descended on him in 874 c.e., when his father died. The Twelfth Imam is generally known by his titles of Imam-e Asr (the Imam of the Age) and Sahib az Zaman (the Lord of Time). Because his followers were afraid he might be the Twelfth Imam, he was sequestered from public view. Only a very few associates were allowed to see him. He disappeared from view at Samarra in Iraq but according to Twelver doctrine did not die; he only remained hidden. All of this happened to prevent his being murdered by the Sunnis.

Twelver Shia say the Twelfth Imam remained hidden for 70 years, a time they call the "lesser occultation" (*gheybat-e sughra*). He never suffered death, but about 939 (or 941), he simply disappeared from earth. Since that time he has been in the "greater occultation" (*gheybat-e kubra*), a supernatural state where he remains. He will return on Judgment Day, when Allah will make him manifest as the Mahdi, the "Expected One" or Messiah. This is a role that many later Shia Imams have claimed for themselves, but those claims remain unsubstantiated.

The Twelver Shia believe that the Twelfth Imam remains spiritually or even materially present during this time, although the latter contention is unclear. While awaiting his return, the Twelver Shia are guided by the scholarly community, much as the Sunnis are.

The Twelfth Imam's name appears on Shia wedding invitations, and his birthday is a major celebration among Shia faithful. Sunni Muslims give the Twelfth Imam short shrift, contending that he either never existed or died in childhood.

Shah Ismail, the founder of the Safavid Dynasty (1501–1722) in Iran, established Twelver Shia Islam as the official religion of his country at the beginning of the 16th century. This brand of Shia Islam is also prevalent in Iraq and among Indian Muslims. Some Twelver scholars developed the concept that the Masumin ("Immaculate Ones"), namely Muhammad, his daughter Fatimah, and the Twelve Imams, had intercessory powers with Allah.

THE SEVENERS (ISMAILIS)

The Seveners emerged in the late ninth century; today they form communities in 25 countries around the world. The Ismailis trace their origins to the son of Ismail who predeceased his father, the Sixth Imam. Historically, they were called the "Assassins" in recognition of their penchant of murdering their opponents. The Mongols destroyed their center at Alamut in 1256. Afterward, their Imams went into hiding. In the 19th century, their leader came forth as the Agha Khan and fled to India, where he undertook to revitalize the sect. Once, the Ismailis were a vastly powerful group, and even today, after the Twelvers, they are the second largest branch of the Shia community.

The Seveners do not believe that Musa al-Kazim was the rightful heir of his brother Jafar al-Sadiq and hence differ from the Twelvers. Ismailis believe that the rightful line of Imams went from Jafar al-Sadiq, the Sixth Imam, through his eldest son Ismail, the last Imam directly in that line. They say that the Twelvers unfairly accused Ismail (the Seventh Imam) of being a drunk and recognized his younger brother in his place. Like the Seveners, they believe that their last Imam mysteriously disappeared.

The Seveners' mission was to vindicate Ismail. Otherwise, their doctrine closely resembles that of the Twelvers, although among the "initiated" there seems to be a strong Gnostic tendency.

The Seveners believe that the Quran has two meanings: first, a literal, clear meaning, but second, a secret inner message that was imparted to the Imams. Secrecy was also a part of their mode of survival to escape the Abbasid authorities, and Seveners frequently hid their true beliefs. They also believe that although truth is absolute, it is apprehended differently by different individuals. Many scholars see the influence of Hellenistic thought in Ismaili doctrine, particularly in the concept of Allah as the One without attributes and incomprehensible to the normal process of human thinking.

The Seveners who seized North Africa are sometimes called the Fatimids because they traced their Imam's lineage to Fatimah, the Prophet's daughter. They established a hereditary monarchy. In 909 they announced that their first caliph, Ubayd Allah, was the Mahdi; they founded the city of Cairo in Egypt.

The reign of the Fatimids marked the apex of Shia power. The Seveners even took over Mecca, Medina, and much of Syria, thus controlling profitable trade routes and growing rich. They even briefly held Baghdad.

In 930 a group associated with them, the Qarmathians, actually carried off the sacred Black Stone of the Kaaba during the pilgrimage season. It was returned in 952, after the Abbasids paid a huge sum for its ransom. During the same raid they also killed a great many Muslim pilgrims and stuffed their corpses in the well of Zamzam.

The Seveners always remained a minority, though an elite one. However, in 1094, when their leader died, his two sons fought each other for the title, and one, al-Mustali, killed the other, Nizar. Nizar's followers survived in mountainous strongholds in Syria, Yemen, India, and East Africa. The Mustalis controlled Egypt. Today the Nizari community is the majority of the Seveners. Their leader is Karim Aga Khan IV. He is the 49th Ismaili Imam and traces his descent to Ali and his wife Fatimah, daughter of Muhammad. He was also was educated at Harvard University and is the founder and chairman of the Aga Khan Development network.

The honorific title Aga Khan was bestowed on the Ismaili Imams in the 1830s. The other Aga Khans have been as follows:

Aga Khan I: Hasan Ali Shah Mehalatee Aga Khan I (1800–1881), 46th Imam (1817–1881)

Aga Khan II: Ali Shah Aga Khan II (about 1830–1885), 47th Imam (1881–1885)

Aga Khan III: Prince Sultan Mohammed, (1877–1957), 48th Imam (1885–1957)

Aga Khan IV: Prince Karim Al Husseini (b. 1936), 49th Imam since July 1957)

The Ismailis have yet another claim to history: the Assassins, or *hashishim*, who committed acts of ritual murder as political assassinations. At one time it was supposed that their name comes from the hashish, to which they were supposed to be addicted. However, these claims have proved completely unfounded, thus removing much of their romance, although they can legitimately claim to be some of the first Muslim terrorists. Certainly the Crusaders were scared to death of them.

THE ALAWIS

The term Alawi means "worshiper of Ali," and this sect goes much further in their veneration of him than deep respect. He is actually deified. They believe that Allah, though One, reveals himself periodically as a trinity. This has happened seven times in history, the final revelation being in Ali, Muhammad, and Salman al-Farisi, a Persian disciple and companion of Muhammad. They also believe that Ali taught Muhammad the Quran. Muhammad's role was to create and sustain the universe. Salman was another version of Gabriel. The rather confusing Alawi theology is expressed in their statement of faith: "I testify that there is no God but Ali ibn-Talib the one to be worshipped, no Veil but the Lord Muhammad worthy to be praised, and no Gate but the Lord Salman al-Farisi the object of love."

The Alawis also retain features of very old pagan practice, such as the veneration of groves of trees. They also have some rites apparently derived from Christianity and celebrate both Christmas and Easter. And in a Hindu twist, they believe in the transmigration of souls. Most of them live in Jebel Alawi, on the Syrian coast, and represent 10–12 percent of the Syrian population. Traditionally, Alawi regions contained no mosques, and prayer was not considered a religious obligation. Truth was contained in the teachings of the Alawi shaykhs; nothing else was required. Despised for centuries, they managed to wrest power in 1970 and are now considered part of the Damascus "elite."

The Syrian leader Hafiz al-Assad was the first Alawi, indeed the first non-Sunni Muslim, to hold the presidency of Syria. The Sunni resented the Alawis deeply and regarded them as not true Muslims, but disbelievers and idolaters. A great deal of pressure was put on the Alawi community to reform to Syrian Sunni standards. How long they will retain power before they are overthrown or completely assimilated is a matter of conjecture.

THE DRUZE

Many Muslims do not consider the Druze proper Muslims, a feeling shared by many Druze themselves. However, they are an interesting group who broke off from the Shia centuries ago. The Druze probably owe their name to the 11th-century Nashtakin ad-Darazi, who announced that the Fatimid Caliph Al-Hakim (r. 996–1021) was none other than the Hidden Imam, or even perhaps an incarnation of

Allah himself. Hakim was in total agreement with this idea, announcing it himself in 1009. He thought he was the "cosmic intelligence," whatever that might mean.

Most people considered him insane, and he certainly did some strange things. He made laws against dogs and outlawed chess. He persecuted Christians, Ismailis, Sunnis, and anyone else he did not like. In 1009, he ordered the Church of the Holy Sepulcher in Jersusalem razed. He apparently disliked the idea of women going out in public and so prohibited shoemakers from making shoes for them. Then he outright banned their going to the baths, and those who defied him were bricked up alive in them. Hakim simply vanished from the palace one night in 1021 but was more than likely murdered, perhaps with the aid of his own sister.

The followers of Darazi found a safe haven in the mountainous regions of southern Lebanon and later in Syria and Jordan. They were very secretive, even going so far as to deny their faith and pretend that they were Christians or Sunni. The Druze themselves, especially the clergy, prefer the name Muwahhidun (Unitarians) to Druze.

The Druze hold to seven principles:

- Love of truth
- Taking care of one another
- Renouncing all other religions
- Avoiding the devil and all wrongdoers
- Accepting divine unity in humanity
- Accepting all of al-Hakim's acts
- Acting in total accordance to al-Hakim's will

They also believe in reincarnation and apparently use the symbol of a calf to stand for all the evil in the world. Another symbol they use is a five-pointed star, each ray of which is a different color and stands for something different—green for the mind and life, red for the soul or love of humanity, yellow for the word and the sun, blue for faith and the mental power of the will, and white for purity, air, and the total realization of the will (blue) in the world.

They hold their weekly prayer meetings on Thursday nights rather than Friday. They do not follow sharia, but a modified version of Hanifa law. They do not fast during Ramadan. They promote equality between men and women. There is no obligation to perform the hajj.

They abjure the use of wine, tobacco, and other stimulants. They permit no one in *or* out of their faith. In other words, once a Druze always a Druze, and no one may convert to their religion. They are officially classified as Muslims, although there is plenty of doubt about such a designation. They themselves often pretend to be Sunni Muslims or even Christians, however, when they feel it is safer.

The initiates among them, the "sages" (*uqqul*) wear white turbans and are conversant with "secret knowledge" of their theology, or *hikma*. Although in theory any Druze can become a sage, this fact is that sagehood has long been monopolized by certain families. One out of every 50 or so of the *uqqual* are deemed to have reached perfection. They are called *ajawid* or "noble." The leader of the community is known as the *rais*.

The rest of the Druze, the "unenlightened" or "ignorant," are not permitted access to the six holy texts of the faith, the *Risail al-Hikma*, or Book of Wisdom. It is extremely difficult to find out exactly what the Druze believe, given that most of the Druze themselves seem to have no idea. They are not permitted to know the inner secrets of their faith.

There are about 680,000 Druze in the world today, most of them living in the Middle East as farmers and orchardists subsisting on a largely vegetarian diet, although they will eat meat, usually lamb, on special occasions.

THE SUFI

Sufism is the mystical face of Islam. Sufi Muslims aim to a have a direct and highly personal experience of Allah, following an "interior path" to Allah, wishing to return to what they felt was the lifestyle of the earliest Muslims. Sufis are found in both Sunni and Shia areas.

We do not know much about the early development of Sufism, except that it occurred during Umayyad times. Sufism grew out of an early ascetic movement and was established during the Umayyad Dynasty (661–749). Sufis regarded themselves as reformers against what they felt was an overemphasis on laws, although, interestingly some were highly qualified legalists.

The word Sufi may come from the Arabic word *suf*, or "wool," referring to the long, coarse woolen garments (rather than the more usual cotton) of the early ascetics. This robe is no longer in widespread use, although the name remains. (It was once suggested that the word Sufi was related to the Greek *sophia*, or "wisdom," but this appears not to have been the case.) Sufis are also sometimes called *fuqara*, "the poor," the plural of *faqir*. The Persian equivalent is *darvish*. These are the roots of the English terms *fakir* and *dervish*, used interchangeably for an Islamic mystic.

Sufism is heavily influenced by Christianity, Gnosticism, and even Buddhism. It is likely, in fact, that Sufi learned the used of prayer beads from Buddhist monks, among whom telling beads is a common practice. Many of them also have a decidedly pantheistic bent. The Sufi hold Jesus in very high regard, as the "last and greatest" of the saints. According to the mystic Muslim philosopher Ibn Arabi (1165–1240), Jesus is "unequaled," and Ibn Arabi calls him "the son of the spirit." Ibn Arabi, also called Muhyiddin (the "Reviver of Faith"), has been considered by some the greatest Sufi Master of all time. Born in Seville, he traveled the Muslim world and eventually settled in Damascus. He wrote more than 300 books, the most famous of which is the *Meccan Openings*, an extended commentary on a single passage in the Quran: *And we have given you seven verses of repetition and the Great Recitation* (15:87). (The seven verses referred to are probably the opening verses of the Quran.) Ibn Arabi believed that the path to truth consisted of three stages—sincerity, insight, and patience—and he laced his own work with examples. He experienced a Night Journey just like Muhammad, visiting Paradise with its four rivers and lote tree. During the journey Gabriel revealed more mysteries to him, especially about the mystical significance of the four rivers, the greatest of which is the Quran, and the lesser ones the Torah, the Psalms, and the Gospels. Although Sufism has been denounced by some "orthodox" Muslims as degrading true Islamic faith, others see the Sufi emphasis on spirit rather than on law as salutatory.

Sufis are hostile to the reigning religious establishment, both Sunni and Shia. Sufism developed as Islam spread to non-Arabic lands, and some members of the community were disturbed by what they regarded as the lack of equality granted to the non-Arab conquered peoples. Sufism arose in part as a protest against this sort of treatment. And they felt themselves at odds with the ruling class.

Unlike the Shia, however, they are not a separate sect and have no specific theology separate from mainstream Islam. However, their emphasis is always on Allah's mercy rather than on his judgment.

In a broader sense, Sufis believe the pathway to Allah begins with repentance for a previously sinful life, and steps along the path include abstinence, renunciation, poverty, patience, trust in Allah, and obedience to his will.

The Sufi were famous for spreading Islam far and wide and were adept at conforming their practices to local customs. Sufis helped bring Islam to non-Arab lands such as India, Africa, Anatolia, Central Asia, and Indonesia. This outreach policy made Sunnis and other traditionalists hostile to them, and they were accused of abrogating important Islamic customs and even principles in the name of assimilation.

Sufis seek "Sacred Knowledge" to help them perform the commands of Allah. To this end, Sufis keep close company with their sheikhs (leaders) and fellow disciples. The "rules" of the Sufi way of life include the following:

- God-consciousness, which is obtained by upright living
- Following the Sunnah (traditions) with caution
- Being indifferent to the acceptance or rejection of other humans and having patience and trust in Allah
- Being content with what one has and submitting to the will of Allah
- Being grateful to Allah in happiness and turning to him in affliction

Sufis are strict about keeping ritual purity and striving after "sacred knowledge."

For the Sufi this Life is of little value. One of the most famous of the early Sufis, Al-Hasan al Basri (d. 728), wrote, "Beware of this world with all wariness, for it is like unto a snake, smooth to the touch, but its venom is deadly."

BROTHERHOODS OR *TARIQA* (PATHS)

Sufis refer to *tariqas*, or "pathways," to Allah, pathways that they say are as many as the souls of men. However, the word now mainly refers to specific brotherhoods; these *tariqa* seem to have been first outlined during the 13th century. Sufi brotherhoods became highly organized, with "chains of transmission" that linked disciples to their masters, much as in Zen Buddhism. All the chains can be traced back to Ali and thus back to the Prophet himself.

Although there were many different brotherhoods, they can be classed into two types, the "urban" and "rustic," although this classification is somewhat inadequate. The so-called urban orders were closest to the Sunni understanding of Islam, whereas the "rustic" brotherhoods were less orthodox, but a good deal more popular.

One early *tariqa* was the Suhrawardi brotherhood, founded in Baghdad during the 1230s by Abu Hafs Umar al-Suhrawardi. Other famous brotherhoods included the Shadhili brotherhood in Alexandria, the Naqshbandi brotherhood in Central Asia, and the Kubrawi and Chishti brotherhoods in India.

Among the urban orders, the large Qadiriya brotherhood, founded about 1200 in Baghdad, was widespread across the Islamic empire. Others were confined to local areas or special ethnic groups. The Qadiriya was named after its founder, Abd al-Qadir al-Gilani. They are noted for their *dhikr*, or remembrance of Allah, which consists of repeating a number of phrases 100 times each: praising Allah, asking his pardon, followed by 500 repetitions of "There is no God but Allah."

Members of the urban Asian Naqshbandi order are charged with cleansing their hearts by drawing invisible pictures on them. The founder's nickname, Naqshband, literally means "the painter." This was a very important group in India and was known for being more dignified and restrained than some other groups.

The members of one urban brotherhood, the Mawlawi (Mevlevi), named after Mevlana, their mystical leader, were renowned as poets during the Ottoman Empire. These are the famous "whirling dervishes," and their dances are based on the teachings of the mystical poet Rumi (1207–1273; see discussion later in chapter). The dancers (*semazenes*) spin themselves around in a form of whirling meditation. As they dance, accompanied by flute and drum, one arm points to Heaven, and the other to earth. The dance lasts about 345 minutes, after which they sink to the floor in exhaustion. This sect was banned by Ataturk in 1925 as part of his secularizing policy, but dances are still performed for tourists. The dancers wear a camel hair hat (representing the tomb of the ego), a white cloak (representing the ego's shroud), and a lifted right hand showing the dancer is ready to receive Allah's grace.

The oldest of the rustic orders was the Rifaiya, supposedly founded by a nephew of al-Gilani, who himself had founded the Qadiya order. They were noted for dancing with their hands on each other's shoulders and "howling" their *dhikrs*, or remembrances of Allah. In fact, they soon became known as the "howlers." An offshoot of this group, the Egyptian Sadiya, was reported to perform a rite in which the participants allowed themselves to be walked over by a horse. They emerged from this ordeal without harm. Another Egyptian rustic group was the Ahmadiya, founded in the 13th century by Ahmad al-Badawi, to oppose the crusading French. This group practiced rites that were highly reminiscent of ancient Egyptian fertility cults as well as some Christian practices.

SUFI PRAYER AND CONTEMPLATION

Sufis pray continuously, asking Allah's forgiveness and praying both prescribed and non-obligatory prayers, usually in company of other Sufi. The Quran is to be recited with much "presence of heart" and thinking about its meaning. Mouthing the words is not sufficient. They also frequently invoke the blessings of Allah. In the ninth century, music and poetry were added to religious gatherings.

However, especially in the early days, Sufi disdained the ordinary forms of worship such as going to mosque and giving alms. Early Sufis were fond of meditating on and weeping over the so-called "Doomsday" or Day of Judgment passages in the Quran; later practitioners concentrated more on the passages that revealed Allah's love for his creation and his mercy. Their central purpose is called *tawakkul*, absolute trust in Allah. An important figure in this development was Rabiah al-Adawiyah (717–801), a woman from Basra in Iraq and one of the few major women founders in any religious tradition. She maintained that a truly devout person loved Allah for his sake alone, and without hope of reward in Paradise or torture in Hell.

Sufis make a continual effort to fight a jihad against the "lower self," commonly represented as a black dog. The also attempt to "cure the ego" by strictly limiting the amount they eat and drink. Most fast on Mondays and Thursdays as well as on the three full-moon or "white" days of each lunar month.

Like orthodox Muslims, Sufis maintain the absolute unity or *tawhid* of Allah. Some state that nature and God are two aspects of the same reality. The Sufis call their quest for God a *tariqa* or "path," which begins with becoming a disciple (*murid*) and submitting to a religious guide (sheikh or pir). The path usually includes sexual abstinence, fasting, and vows of poverty. The seeker's goal is *marifah* (inner knowledge) and *mahabbah* (love), a word that suggests a union of lover and beloved, but in reference to humans and God. Finally, the seeker hopes to reach *fana*, or annihilation of one's individual personal characteristics, accompanied by spiritual ecstasy. Some even aspire to what they call a "unity" with Allah. Sufis are careful to say, however, that this insight can never contradict the Quran.

Sufi mystics eat little, talk little, and sleep little in their quest for *dhawq*, or "tasting" of the divine, an illuminating experience that leads to eternal knowledge. Eventually Sufi fraternal orders developed, each of which was headed by a *pir* or *shaykh*. A shaykh must have the following qualifications:

- Sound knowledge of Islam
- Direct experience of the divine
- Exalted will and purpose
- Laudable character
- Deep insight

The Sufi movement was successful with both ordinary and learned people and has become very popular in the West.

The ritual prayer is called *dhikr*, a word that translates as "remembrance." This comes from the Quranic injunction to remember Allah often (Surah 62:10). *Dhikr* consists of a repetition of one or more of the names of God, or simply of the word Allah. The praying person may also repeat the Shahadah or another religious formula. The great Sufi philosopher al-Ghazali said this kind of repetitive prayer opened a window into the unseen world (*al-Ghayb*) in which angels and prophets and visions from other times would appear to him. During some periods alcohol was even used; at others times the mystics contented themselves with coffee. Each brotherhood would have its own specific *dhikr*.

SUFI SAINTS, MYSTICS, AND POETS

The Persian Bayazid Bastami (Abu Yazid) (804–874) was one of the greatest Sufi saints, who like many of his brethren was called "God-intoxicated." He was known to remark, "I am become Allah! There is no other God but Me!" When he came out of his trance and was told what he had declaimed, he told his fellow Sufis that if they ever heard him talking like that again, they should kill him at once. Sure enough, it happened again, but when the disciples struck at him with their swords, the points curved back into their own hands. Bayzid left records of his visions of Allah, saying he had ascended to Heaven and seen his shining face with his own eyes. It was Bayazid who introduced the important concept of *fana* (passing away of the self in Allah) to Sufism. When Bayazid died a the age of 70, he remarked, "I am four years old. For seventy years I was veiled. I got rid of my veils only four years ago."

Husayn ibn Mansur Al-Hallaj (the wool-carder) (d. 922) was a famous Persian mystic but ended up on the wrong side of the establishment and was charged with blasphemy. He became a wandering mystic, traveling through Persia, Iraq, Kashmir, and India, even to the borders of China. He went around saying, "I am the Truth," à la Jesus, which amounted to *shirk*, given that he was equating himself with Allah, who alone is Truth. (His real intention was more poetic than theological, however.) He was supposed to be able to materialize an apple from Paradise into the palm of his hand. It was ravaged by maggots, but that is because, Mansur claimed, it had descended into a corrupt world. He even made a model of the Kaaba and walked around it, rather than the real thing, and said that Mount Sinai was holier than Mecca. After being publicly whipped, Al-Hallaj's nose was smashed, his body tarred, and his hands and feet cut off. He was then crucified in Baghdad. His body was burned and the ashes scattered, his head exposed on a bridge. Following his death came a persecution of more Sufis.

Many Sufis, especially those from Iran, were also poets, writing in Persian rather than Arabic. Some of the most well-known among them were Abdallah al-Ansari or Pir-i-Ansar (d. 1088), who composed devotional poetry; Farid al-Din Attar, who wrote narrative and philosophical verse; Ibn al-Farid, who has been compared to both St. John of the Cross and John Keats; Jalal al-Din Rumi (d. 1273), a poetic theologian; and Jami, a biographer and scholar as well as a poet.

Jalal al-Din Rumi (1207–1273), who is possibly the most famous Muslim poet, has been called the author of the "Persian Quran." A renowned religious scholar in his early life, in his middle age he became a wandering Sufi who preferred poetry to prose. Rumi's encounter with the wandering Sufi master Shamsuddin Tabriz (known simply as Shams or "sun") changed his life. He wrote a vast amount of poetry dedicated to Shams and also dictated the *Mathnawi-e Manawi*, or "Persian Quran," a name he gave it himself. Rumi was literate, so the fact that he dictated it seemed to indicate that he felt the words were inspired from above. A friend of his once suggested that the poem was intended as a commentary on the Quran. Not so, Rumi averred ferociously. "You dog! Why is it not the Quran? You ass! Why is it not the Quran?"

This massive work (27,000 couplets) is the longest mystical poem ever written. He also founded the mystical Sufi order semi-officially known as the Whirling Dervishes. Wearing this hat, he is known simply as Mawlan, "Our Master."

Rabia al-Adawiya (d. 801), a non-Arab, was once a slave and a flute-player, but she became a well-known ascetic and contemplative poet. She was urged to marry, but the only man she would accept was the equally renowned Sufi mystic al-Hasan. She agreed to the union if he could answer four questions for her about the Afterlife. Al-Hasan responded that the answers to all four questions were "hidden." "That being so," she responded, "I must occupy myself with them, and have no need of a husband to bother about." Rabia also rejected ordinary morality, in which one behaves simply to gain a reward or out of fear of punishment. She said, "It is a bad servant who serves Allah from fear and terror or from the desire for a reward, although there are many people like that." They asked her, "Why do you worship Allah?" She replied, "The Neighbor first and then the House. Is it not enough for me that I am given leave to worship him? Even if Heaven and Hell were not, does it not behoove us to obey him? He is worthy of worship without motive." She was fond of going to her roof at night and praying, "Oh my Lord, the stars are shining and the eyes of me are closed, and kings have shut their doors, and every lover is alone with his beloved, and here I am alone with You."

AHMADIYYA

An Indian-Pakistani sect of Islam is known as Ahmadiyya Islam. It was founded in 1889 by Mirza Ghulam Ahmad (c. 1839–1908) in the Punjab region. Ahmad claimed to be the promised Messiah, the Prophet Muhammad, and/or an incarnation of the Hindu god Krishna. He taught that Jesus only pretended to be crucified and lived to be 120 years old in India. (The orthodox Muslim doctrine is that Jesus was taken into Heaven before his death.) He interpreted the word jihad to mean a completely nonviolent struggle against unbelievers, using the pen rather than the sword to gain converts. When Ahmad died, Mawlawi Nur-ad-Din was elected as successor (caliph). Following his death, Ahmadiyya Muslims split into two groups: Qadi-ani, who recognize Ahmad as a true prophet, and Lahore, who regard Ahmad only as a reformer of Islam. Today there are about 170 million Ahmadiyya Muslims. This branch of Islam is also associated with several Sufi orders, particularly the Al-Badawi order of Egypt, named for an Islamic saint who died in 1276. This sect is denounced as heretical by mainstream Muslims.

THE MUSLIM BROTHERHOOD

The Muslim Brotherhood (*Ikhwan al-Muslimin*) was founded in Egypt in 1918 by Hasan al-Banna (1906–1949). The original supporters were lower middle-class. The organization was banned in 1948 on the grounds that it was involved in the assassination of the prime minister, Nuqrashi Pasha. Soon after, Banna was also assassinated. The Brotherhood did not disappear, however, but dispersed to other parts of the Middle East, especially Syria and Yemen. In 1965 it was accused of engineering a plot to overthrow Nasser, and the leader of the Brotherhood, Sayyid Qutb, was later executed.

BLACK MUSLIMS

During the 1930s in the Detroit, a man named (or calling himself) Wallace D. Fard Muhammad announced the advent of "the Nation of Islam." His followers called him the Great Mahdi or Messiah, and he taught that blacks should separate themselves completely from the society of the "blue-eyed devils" (Caucasians) who dominated it. In 1934 he mysteriously disappeared, and his cult was taken over by Elijah Muhammad, formerly Elijah Poole (1897–1975). It was during this period that the Nation of Islam also became known as the Black Muslims. Although some of his ideas were drawn from standard Islam, a number of his announcements were distinct novelties. He taught, for example, that God was a black man and that he himself, Muhammad Elijah, was the last prophet—not Muhammad of Arabia. He did not teach the Five Pillars of Islam, the unity of all human beings, or the observance of Islamic rituals. In fact, it is rather hard to say in what respect he was a Muslim at all.

However, things changed when Malcolm Little, later known as Malcolm X, took over the movement, having converted in prison. Malcolm X was a brilliant, charismatic speaker, and he converted many people to Nation of Islam, including most famously the boxer Cassius Clay, who became Muhammad Ali. Malcolm X himself underwent a new conversion of sorts when he went on the hajj and saw the free and friendly mingling of thousands of believers on an equal footing. He became convinced that true brotherhood was possible among people. He renamed himself El Hajj (referring to one who has completed the Hajj) Malik El-Shabazz, an orthodox, rather than a Black Muslim. He was assassinated in 1965. Two members of the Nation of Islam were convicted of the murder.

During the same period, the Nation of Islam was changing as well. Wallace D. Muhammad and Akbar Muhammad, sons of Elijah Muhammad, were excommunicated by their father for challenging some of his teachings. Yet eventually even Elijah Muhammad made the pilgrimage to Mecca. When Wallace D. Muhammad (later renamed Warith Deen Muhammad) took over the organization, he made major changes in its teachings; these changes put the organization in conformance with orthodox Sunni Muslim teachings. Even the former "temples" were renamed mosques, and women, who had been shut out of positions of responsibility, saw their status improve. The organization was renamed the American Muslim Mission.

One man, Louis Farrakhan (b. 1933), objected to these reforms. Farrakhan left the Nation of Islam in 1977 to start his own organization but kept the name Nation of Islam and called himself "Chief Minister and National Representative." During his later years, however, he moved somewhat closer to mainstream Islam, although he remains a controversial figure. The connection between orthodox Islam and the Black Muslims remains problematic, and Farrakhan has been accused of being racist, anti-Semitic, and homophobic, all of which he denies.

ISLAM AND ISLAMISM

For some, the difference between "Islamism" and "Islam" is a useful distinction in which "Islamism" replaces the phrase "radical Islam." In any case, by the 1970s most Muslim societies came to have a group attempting to return Islam to what they regarded as a purer state. It occurred not only in Westernized states such as Iran in the late 1970s but also in strict fundamentalist countries such as Saudi Arabia in the 1990s. In Iran it came about in opposition to the shah's policies; many Muslims were influenced by the work of Ali Shariati (1933–1977). Their most enduring symbol, however, was the Ayatollah Khomeini.

REFORM IN ISLAM

Although Muslims believe that Islam is a perfect religion whose basis in the Quran is eternal, there is also a tradition in Islam that speaks of reform and renewal (*tajdid*) or rebirth. The source for this concept comes from the Prophet himself, who said, "Allah will send this Muslim community, every hundred years, those who will renew its religion." This renewal does not change the core of the faith but revives it and presents new perspectives in light of new economic, social, or cultural conditions. A related concept is *islah*, which means purifying or improving the faith. In another sense, principles are unchanging, immutable, and eternal, but history and circumstances may require them to be differently implemented. This notion can obviously be applied to dress codes but can apply also to social, economic, and political affairs.

Thus, it is perfectly in accordance with the basic tenets of Islam, as with every other faith, for it to be reinterpreted and renewed in the light of changing circumstances, without believers relinquishing their belief in Islam's ultimate and divine source.

Glossary

Abbasids (750–1258): Second dynasty of Sunni Islam.

Abd: Slave or servant. Commonly used in Muslim names.

Abdullah: Male name meaning servant of Allah.

Abqa: Eternal.

Abu Bakr: First Caliph.

Abu Dawud (817–888): A major collector of hadith.

Abu Hanifa (699–767): Founder of the Hanifi school of jurisprudence.

Adhan: Call to prayer.

Adl: Balance between two extremes; justice.

Ahl al-bayt: "People of the house." Muhammad's immediate family.

Ahl al-Kitab: People of the Book, especially Jews and Christians.

Ahmad ibn Hanbal (780–855): Founder of the Hanbali school of jurisprudence.

Ahmadiya: A rustic group of Sufis.

Ahwal: In Sufi traditions, a higher state of consciousness, granted by Allah.

Aisha: Second wife of Muhammad.

Akhirah: Life after death.

Alak: Something sticky or clinging; a clot of blood; a fetus.

Alim (plural ulama): Legal scholar; also knowledge.

Allah: God, a contraction of Arabic al-ilah, "the god."

Al-Lat: Pre-Islamic goddess honored at the Kaaba.

Alam al-Ghayb: The unseen, transcendent world.

Alam al-Shahadah: The material, witnessed world.

Al-Andalus: Arabic name for Islamic Spain.

Amir (Emir): A ruler.

Ansar: "Helpers" of the Muslims who lived in Medina.

Arkan al-Islami: The Five Pillars of Islam.

Ashraf: Descendants of the Prophet.

Asr: Mid-afternoon prayer.

Ataturk: Turkish secular leader.

Auwrah: Area of the body to be concealed by clothing.

Ayah (plural ayat): Literally "sign." A single verse of the Quran.

Ayatollah Literally, "sign of Allah." A top-ranking Shia religious leader in the Imami or Twelvers tradition.

Al-Badawi: Founder of the Ahmadiya, a Sufi brotherhood.

Bahira: Nestorian monk who recognized Muhammad's prophethood while Muhammad was still a child.

Baqa: Sufi term meaning "to abide with God."

Baraka: Blessing.

Barzakh: Period between death and resurrection.

Basmala: Invocation that begins most Quranic verses.

Basra: City in southern Iraq.

Batin: The inner, esoteric meaning of a text.

Bidah: An innovation or departure from traditional religious practice.

Bilal: A Companion of the Prophet.

Bukhari (810–870): Collector of hadith.

Bulugh: Puberty.

Buraq: Miraculous steed Muhammad rode into Paradise.

Burqua: Fully covering garment for women.

Caliph: In Sunni Islam, the successor to Muhammad.

Chador: Covering garment.

Dahr: Time or fate.

Dalil: Evidence brought from the Quran and Sunnah to prove a point.

Daraba: Strike.

Dar al-Harb: "Abode of war," territory not under Muslim rule.

Dar-al-Islam: "Abode of Islam," area under Muslim rule.

Daughters of Allah: Three pre-Islamic Arabian goddesses.

Dawah: Calling others to Islam, proselytizing, missionary outreach.

Dervish: A Sufi practitioner.

Dhabah: Ritual slaughterer.

Dhikr: Literally, "remembrance," referring to the Sufi practice of uttering the name of Allah as a means of gaining "God-conscious."

Dhimmi: Non-Muslims living in a protected status in Islamic countries. Usually refers to Jews and Christians living in an Islamic state.

Dhu al-Hijjah: The 12th month of the Islamic calendar, the month of the Hajj or pilgrimage to Mecca.

Din: Religion, especially religious practice.

Druze: Small, extremist Shia group located mostly in Lebanon, Jordan, and Syria.

Dua: Personal, petitionary prayer, as opposed to salat, or prescribed formal prayer.

Emir: Military commander or prince.

Fajr: Sunrise prayer.

Falah: Success, salvation.

Falsafa: Philosophy.

Fana: Literally, "passing away." A Sufi term referring to the annihilation of the self, occurring when the worshipper unites with Allah.

Faqih (plural fuqaha): A legal scholar or judge.

Faqir: Literally, a "poor person," an ascetic.

Far a-kifaya: Communally obligatory.

Fard: Obligatory.

Fasiq: A grave sinner.

Fatimah: Daughter of the Prophet.

Fatwa (plural fatawa): An authoritative legal opinion produced by a mufti.

Fiqh: Literally, "understanding." The science of Islamic jurisprudence.

Fitrah: The naturally good, original nature human beings have that leads us to Allah.

Ghaybah: The occultation of the 12th Imam in Shia Islam.

Ghazwah: Raiding, as of caravans.

Ghusl: Complete purifying bath, total ablution of the body.

Al-Gilani: Founder of the Qadiya sect of Sufism.

Hadath: Impurity.

Hadd (plural Hudud): The penalty specifically imposed by the Quran for adultery, theft, fornication, lying in court, and intoxication.

Hadith: A record of Muhammad's purported deeds or words, containing his exemplary practice. The hadith record the "Sunnah" or traditions of Islam. The correct plural of hadith is ahadith or simply hadith. This material is supplementary to the Quran.

Hadith qudsi: A "divine saying" in which the prophet reports a message from Allah, although not necessarily word for word, as in the Quran.

Hafiz: Literally, "guardian or keeper." A man who knows the Quran by heart. The female version is hafizah.

Hajj: Annual pilgrimage to Mecca, one of the Five Pillars of Islam.

Halal: Permitted activities or food. Opposite of haram, or thing forbidden.

Hanafi: School of law, generally considered the most liberal.

Hanbali: School of law, generally considered the most conservative.

Hanif (plural hunafa): A monotheist in pre-Islamic times, used to describe Abraham.

Haram: (1) Unlawful food or activity. (2) A sacred place.

Hayz: Menses.

Hijab: Literally "cover." Head covering or veil worn by Muslim women. Modest dress.

Hijra: Emigration of Muhammad and his followers from Mecca to Medina in 622.

Hikma: The theology of the Druze.

Houri: Companion in Paradise.

Husayn: Third Imam in Shia Islam.

Ibadat: Plural form of Ibadah. Acts of worship.

Iblis: The devil.

Ibn: "son of."

Ibn Ishaq (704–767): Wrote the earliest biography of Muhammad.

Ibrahim: Abraham.

Id: Festival (also Eid).

Id al-Adha: "Festival of the sacrifice," celebrated on the tenth day of the Hajj.

Id al-Fitra: Festival of the breaking of the fast, celebrated at the end of Ramadan.

Idda: Waiting period for a woman after the dissolution of her marriage before she can rewed.

Ihram: State of ritual purity; special clothes worn during the Hajj.

Ijma: Consensus or agreement of the community in regard to Islamic practice or belief.

Ikhwan al-Muslimin: Muslim Brotherhood, founded in Egypt in 1928.

Ilham: Divine inspiration.

Ilm: Knowledge, especially religious knowledge.

Imam: Literally "One who stands before." Religious leader. In Sunni Islam, a prayer leader. In Shia, one with religious authority, divinely appointed and infallible.

Imami: Twelver branch of Shia.

Imamzayah: Shia shrine to a saint.

Iman: Faith, belief.

Iman al Muffassil: The "beliefs in detail": faith in Allah, his Angels, his books, his messengers, and the Last Day.

Injil: The Gospel sent to Jesus.

Inshala Allah: "Allah willing."

Ijtihad: Independent opinion of analysis of the law, often used along with *qiyas*.

Isha: Night prayer.

Islah: Reform.

Islam: Literally, "surrender" or "submission." The faith taught by Muhammad.

Ismailis: The Seveners.

Isnad: Chain of transmitters of Hadith.

Isra: The Night Journey of Muhammad from Mecca to Jerusalem.

Istikhara: Prayer when facing a difficult decision requiring Allah's aid.

Ithna Ashari: The Twelvers, the majority Shia sect.

Jahannam: Literally, "the depths." Hell.

Jahiliyyah: "Age of ignorance," a Quranic term, usually referring to the period before the advent of Islam. Today, any non-Islamic state or society.

Al-Jannah: The Garden, or Paradise.

Jamrah: Pillar representing Satan, ceremonially stoned during the Hajj by pilgrims.

Jibril or Jizril: The angel Gabriel.

Jihad: Literally "striving." Effort or struggle, holy war in the service of Islam.

Jilbab: Long coat or cloak.

Jima: Sexual fluid.

Jinn (singular Jinni): Probably from a word meaning "darkness." Spirits made of fire inhabiting a parallel universe. They have some intelligence and limited free will.

Jizyah: (1) Poll-tax paid by dhimmis, the protected non-Muslims; (2) sword (verses).

Junub: Impure.

Juz: Part of the Quran (1/30th) read each night during Ramadan.

Kaaba: Located in Mecca, a cube-shaped sacred shrine of pre-Islamic origin, but now sacred in Islam.

Kafir: From kafara, "to hide or cover up." Unbeliever, infidel.

Kalam Allah: The eternal speech of Allah, preserved on a tablet in Heaven.

Karbala: Site where Husayn, the grandson of Muhammad was murdered.

Karim: Noble, brave.

Khadijah: Muhammad's first wife.

Khafd: Female circumcision.

Khamr: Intoxicant.

Kharijites: Early dissident Islamic sect, which maintained absolute free will.

Khatam: Seal.

Khitan: Male circumcision.

Khums: The twenty percent payment in Shia Islam.

Khutbah: Sermon.

Khirqah: Patched clothing worn by Sufis.

Kiraman katibin: Literally "noble writers." Angels on one's shoulders.

Kiswah: Embroidered black cloth over the Kaabah.

Koran: Alternate spelling for Quran.

Kufa: City in Iraq.

Laylat al-qadar: "Night of Power" when Muhammad received the Quran.

Madhhab: Literally, "road followed." School of law or ideology. Currently there are four recognized schools in Sunni Islam: Malaki, Shafii, Hanbali, and Hanafi.

Madrassah: Religious school often, but not always, attached to a mosque.

Maghrib: Nightfall prayer.

Mahdi: Literally "the Guided One." Divinely guided leader, Messiah. Also name of a Caliph, Muhammad son of al-Mansur.

Mahr: Dowry promised by the husband.

Mahram: A relative too close in consanguinity to marry.

Makrah: A reprehensible action.

Maliki: School of law, moderately liberal.

Mandub: A commendable or praiseworthy action.

Masjid: Mosque, "place of prostration."

Masun: A recommended act.

Matn: The content, subject matter, or substance of a hadith.

Mawali: Non-Arab converts to Islam.

Mawlawi (Mevlevi): Whirling Dervishes

Mawlid al-nabi: Celebration of the Prophet's birthday.

Mevlani: Founder of the Mevlevi Sufi order.

Mevlevi (Mawlawi): Whirling Dervishes.

Mihrab: Niche in the wall of a mosque indication the direction (*qibla*) to Mecca.

Minaret: Tower for call to prayer.

Minbar: Pulpit for sermon.

Miraj: Ascension of Muhammad into heaven.

Miswak: Toothbrush.

Mizan: Balance.

Mosque (from the Arabic *masjid*): Islamic place of prayer.

Muawiya: Rebellious Umayyad ruler of Syria.

Mubah: Permissible, neutral action, left to one's own conscience.

Muezzin: One who calls others to prayer.

Mufti: A specialist in Islamic law, a member of the ulema capable of issuing fatwa.

Muhajirun: Muslims who accompanied Muhammad in his emigration from Mecca to Medina.

Muhammad: Literally, "the praised one." The prophet who revealed Islam to the Arabs.

Mujahid (plural mujahidin): A Muslim holy warrior.

Mukallah: One of full legal responsibility.

Mullah: A member of the ulama or community of scholars.

Mumin: One who possesses faith.

Munafiq: A hypocrite.

Murid: A disciple in a Sufi brotherhood.

Muslim (plural muslimun): (1) One who submits to Allah's will; (2) Imam Muslim (821–875), a collector of hadith.

Mutah: Temporary marriage practiced in the Shia branch of Islam.

Mutazilalites: Rationalist school which maintained a non-literalist understanding of the Quran, a work they believed to be created rather than eternal.

Muwahhidun (Unitarians): The Druze.

Nabi: Prophet.

Nafs: Soul or spirit.

Najasa: Polluting matter that touches a worshipper.

Nakir and Munkir: Angels who question the soul of the deceased.

Al-Nar: Hellfire.

Nasheed: Song in praise of Muhammad.

Nass: Shia doctrine that each Imam designates his successor.

Nawruz: Persian New Year.

Nifas: Childbirth.

Nikah: Marriage ceremony.

Niqab: Face veil.

Niyyah: Intention.

Pir: Sufi master.

Purdah: Seclusion of women.

Qadar: Power.

Qadi: Judge.

Qadiya: Order of Sufis.

Qibla: Direction of the Kaabah, direction Muslims face at prayer.

Qital: Fighting.

Qiyamat: Day of Resurrection and Judgment.

Qiyas: Arriving at a judgment in Islamic law by using analogy.

Al-Quaeda: Literally "the base." Radical Islamic terrorist group.

Quari: Reciter of the Quran.

Qubbat al-Sakrah: Dome of the Rock in Jerusalem, built on the site of Solomon's Temple.

Quran: Literally, "recitation," the Islamic scripture.

Quraysh: Leading Meccan tribe, guardians of the Kaabah and opponents of Muhammad.

Qurban: Meat of the sacrificed animal at Id al-Adha, to be given to the poor.

Qutb: Literally, "pole" or "axis." In Sufism, the head of an invisible hierarchy of saints.

Rabb: Lord.

Rais: Leader of the Druze community.

Rakah: A prayer gesture or posture, such as bowing or bending.

Ramadan: The sacred month of fasting.

Rashdun: Rightly Guided Caliphs.

Rasul: Messenger.

Ray: Arriving at a judgment in Islamic law by using personal opinion or discretion.

Riba: Usury, charging interest on loans.

Ribat: Pious action connected with a war, a fort.

Ridda: Apostasy.

Ridwan: Allah's pleasure.

Rifaiya: Rustic order of Sufis.

Risail al-Hikma: Holy Scriptures of the Druze.

Sabr: Patience.

Sadaqa: Charity.

Sahahbah: Companion of the Prophet.

Sahih: Valid, authentic, genuine, or sound.

Sahn: Courtyard of a mosque.

Sakina: Allah's tranquility that descends on his servants.

Salat: Official prayer offered five times a day, one of the Five Pillars of Islam.

Salat Juma: Friday prayers.

Sawn: Fasting during Ramadan, one of the Five Pillars of Islam.

Say: The running ritual between two small hills, undertaken during the Hajj.

Sayyid: Descendant of Muhammad.

Semazenes: Whirling dervishes.

Al-Shafii (767–820): Founder of Shafii school of jurisprudence.

Shafii: One of the four orthodox schools of law, moderately conservative.

Shahadah: Literally "witness." Profession of Faith: "I bear witness that there is no God but Allah, and that Muhammad is his prophet," one of the five Pillars of Islam.

Shahid: Literally, "witness." Martyr.

Shariah: Literally "path" or "way." Islamic law drawn from the Quran and *Sunnah*.

Sharif (plural "shurafa"): Person claiming descent from the Prophet.

Shaykh: Literally "old man with gray hair." Also spelled "Sheikh." Honorific title for the head of tribe or a Sufi order. Also an Islamic scholar.

Shaytan: Satan.

Shia: Literally "party or faction." A major branch of Islam.

Shirk: Literally "association." Idolatry, the unforgivable sin.

Shura: Consultation or council.

Shurkh: Gratitude.

Sifat: Attributes of Allah.

Silsila: Literally "chain," referring to a spiritual lineage in the Sufi tradition.

Sipara: One thirtieth (1/30th) of the Quran. See Juz.

Sirah: Biography of Muhammad.

Subhah: Prayer beads, usually 11, 33, or 99.

Suf: Wool.

Sufi: One who follows the mystical path of Islam.

Suhuf: Sheaves given to earlier prophets like Abraham.

Suhur: Dawn meal before fasting.

Sultan: Leader who rules though force.

Sunnah: Tradition or usual procedure, drawn from the words and practice of Muhammad.

Sunni: Member of the Muslim majority branch.

Surah: Literally a "step up," or "fence." Chapter of the Quran.

Tabiun: Successors to the companions of the Prophet.

Al-Tabari (838–923): Historian and scholar.

Tafsir: Written commentary on the Quran.

Tafwid: Clause in a marriage contract stipulating that the wife can initiate a divorce.

Tahannuth: Solitary meditation exercises.

Taharah: Purity, purification.

Tajwid: The science of reciting the Quran.

Takfir: The act of declaring someone an unbeliever.

Talaq: Pronouncement of divorce.

Talbiyah: Prayer uttered upon entering Mecca.

Taqwa: Literally "to fear." God-consciousness.

Taraqah: The Sufi way or path.

Tasawwuf: Spiritual insight.

Tasbih: Prayer beads.

Tawaf: The rite of circling the Kaaba.

Tawbah: Repentance.

Tawhid: Unity and uniqueness of Allah.

Tawil: Allegorical interpretation of the Quran, practiced by Shia Muslims.

Tayammum: Dry ritual ablution with dust rather than water.

Tazaqqah: An early word for Islam, whose precise meaning is unclear.

Tilawah: Reciting the Quran.

Ulama: Religious scholars, plural of *alim*.

Umar: Second Caliph.

Ummah: Islamic community.

Ummayyads: First dynasty of Sunni Islam (661–750).

Umra: Lesser pilgrimage to Mecca, undertaken outside the pilgrimage season.

Uqqal: Druze sages.

Urf: Custom.

Urs: Marriage celebration.

Uthman: Third "rightly guided" caliph, after Abu Bakr and Umar.

Uzziah: Pre-Islamic goddess honored at the Kaabah.

Wahhabis: Puritanical school of Islam.

Wahy: Divine revelation, usually auditory.

Wajab: Obligatory action.

Wali: Literally, a "friend of Allah." Someone of great piety.

Wudu: Ritual washing of the face and limbs, prescribed before prayers.

Wuquf: Standing (in prayer).

Yathrib: Medina.

Yawn al-qiyamah: Day of Resurrection.

Yazid: Son of Muawiya.

Youm: Day.

Zabur: Book sent to Prophet David (Psalms).

Zahd: An ascetic.

Zahir: The outward, exterior meaning of a verse.
Zakat: Annual alms tax.
Zamzam: Well near the Kaabah in Mecca.
Zaydi: Branch of Shia Islam (Fivers), close to Sunnism in doctrine.
Zinah: Adultery or fornication.
Zuhd: Asceticism.
Zuhr: Mid-day prayer.

Selected Bibliography

Abdel Haleem, M.A.S., trans. *The Qur'an*. Oxford: Oxford University Press, 2008.

Ali, Maulana Muhammad. *The Holy Qur'an with English Translation and Commentary*. Lahore Pakistan: Ahmadiyya Anjuman Ishaat, 1991.

Ali, Maulana Muhammad. *A Manual of Hadith*. Lahore, Pakistan: The Ahmadiyya Association for the Propagation of Islam, 1941, new typeset 2001.

An-Nawawi. *Forty Hadith*. Translated by Ezzedin Ibrihim and Denys Johnson-Davies. New Delhi: Islamic Book Service, 2006.

Armstrong, Karen. *Islam: A Short History*. London: Phoenix Press, 2002.

Armstrong, Karen. *Muhammad: A Biography of the Prophet*. New York: Harper-Collins, 1992.

Bashier, Zakaria. *The Meccan Crucible*. London: Ithaca Press, 1978.

Bonner, Michael. *Jihad in Islamic History*. Princeton, NJ: Princeton University Press, 2006.

Bukari, Muhammad. *Imam Bukhari's Book of Muslim Morals and Manners*. Translated by Yusuf DeLorenzo. Alexandria, VA: Al-Saadawi Publications, 1997.

Christopher, John. *The Islamic Tradition*. New York: Harper and Row, 1972.

DeLong-Bas, Natana. *Wahhabi Islam: From Revival and Reform to Global Jihad*. Oxford: Oxford University Press, 2004.

Denny, Frederick Mathewson. *An Introduction to Islam*. Third Edition. Upper Saddle River: NJ: Pearson/Prentice Hall, 2005.

Egger, Vernon O. *A History of the Muslim World since 1260: The Making of a Global Community*. Upper Saddle River, NJ: Pearson Prentice Hall, 2008.

Esposito, John L. *Islam: The Straight Path*. 3rd edition. New York: Oxford University Press, 1998.

Esposito, John L. *What Everyone Needs to Know about Islam*. Oxford: Oxford University Press, 2002.

Esposito, John L. and Dalia Mogahed. *Who Speaks for Islam: What a Billion Muslims Really Think*. New York: Gallup Press, 2007.

Farid, Malik Ghulam, ed. *The Holy Quran: Arabic Text with English Translation and Short Commentary*. Tilford, UK: Islam International Publications, 2006.

Guillaume, A. *The Life of Muhammad: A Translation of Ibn Ishaq's Sirat Rasul Allah*. Oxford: Oxford University Press, 1955.

Haneef, Suzanne. *What Everyone Should Know about Islam and Muslims*. Chicago: Kazi Publications. 1996.

Harris, Lee. *The Suicide of Reason: Radical Islam's Threat to the West*. New York: Basic Books, 2007.

Hewer, C.T.R. *Understanding Islam: An Introduction*. Minneapolis: Fortress Press, 2006.

Ibn Warraq. *Leaving Islam: Apostates Speak Out*. Amherst NY: Prometheus Books, 2003.

Ibn Warraq. *Why I am Not a Muslim*. Amherst, NY: Prometheus Books, 1995.

Karsh, Efraim. *Islamic Imperialism: A History*. Princeton, NJ: Yale University Press, 2007.

Keller, Nuh Ha Mim, trans. *Al-Maqasid's Manual of Islam*. 2nd edition. Beltsville, MD: Amana Publications, 2002.

Küng, Hans. *Islam: Past, Present and Future*. Translated by John Bowden. Oxford: Oneworld Publications, 2007.

Lawrence, Bruce. *The Qur'an: A Biography*. New York: Atlantic Monthly Press, 2006.

Lewis, Bernard. *Islam: The Religion and the People*. Upper Saddle River, NJ: Wharton School Publishing, 2008.

Mernissi, Fatima. *The Veil and the Male Elite: A Feminist Interpretation of Women's Rights in Islam*. Reading, MA: Addison-Wesley Publishing, 1987.

Mir, Mustansir. *Understanding the Islamic Scripture: A Study of Selected Passages from the Quran*. New York: Pearson Education, 2008.

Muhammad, Maulana Ali. *A Manual of Hadith*. 2nd edition. Dublin, OH: Ahmadiyya Association for the Propagation of Islam, 2001. First edition 1941.

Nooruddin, Allamah, ed. *The Holy Quran*. 7th ed. n.p.: Noor Foundation International, 2005.

Payne, Robert. *The History of Islam*. New York: Dorset Press, 1959.

Ramadan, Tariq. *Radical Reform: Islamic Ethics and Liberation*. Oxford: Oxford University Press, 2009.

Robinson, Francis, ed. *Cambridge Illustrated History of the Islamic World*. Cambridge: Cambridge University Press, 1996.

Siddiqi, Abdul Hameed. *Jihad in Islam*. Lahore, Pakistan: Kazi Publications, 1979.

Siddiqi, Abdul Hameed. *Prophethood in Islam*. Revised edition. Lahore, Pakistan: Kazi Publications, 1974.

Spencer, Robert. *Islam Unveiled: Disturbing Questions about the World's Fastest Growing Faith*. New York: Encounter Books, 2002.

Swarup, Ram. *Understanding the Hadith: The Sacred Traditions of Islam*. Amherst, NY: Prometheus Book, 2002.

Unal, Ali. *The Qur'an with Annotated Interpretation in Modern English*. Somerset, NJ: The Light, 2008.

Von Grunebaum, Gustave E. *Medieval Islam*. Chicago: University of Chicago Press, 1954.

Wadud, Amina. *Qur'an and Woman: Reading the Sacred Text from a Woman's Perspective*. New York: Oxford University Press, 1999.

Waines, David. *An Introduction to Islam*. 2nd edition. Cambridge: Cambridge University Press, 2003.

Williams, John Alden, ed. *Islam*. New York: George Braziller, 1962.

Yusuf Ali, A. *An English Interpretation of the Holy Quran*. Bensenville, IL: Lushena Books, 2001.

Index

About the Author

DIANE MORGAN teaches courses in Islam, the Quran, and Eastern religions at Wilson College in Chambersburg, Pennsylvania. She has written over three dozen books on subjects as diverse as Buddhism, gems, mythology, magic, pet care, and gardening. Her Praeger titles include *Gemlore: Ancient Secrets and Modern Myth from the Stone Age to the Rock Age* and *Snakes in Myth, Magic and History: The Story of a Human Obsession*.